D0504800

# THE SOCIETY OF TIMID SOULS

## or, How To Be Brave

Polly Morland

PROFILE BOOKS

First published in Great Britain in 2013 by
PROFILE BOOKS LTD
3A Exmouth House
Pine Street
London EC1R 0JH
*www.profilebooks.com*

1 3 5 7 9 10 8 6 4 2

Typeset in Garamond by MacGuru Ltd
*info@macguru.org.uk*
Printed and bound in Great Britain by
Clays, Bungay, Suffolk

A CIP catalogue record for this book is available from the British Library.

Hardback ISBN 978 1 78125 190 4
Export ISBN 978 1 84668 513 2
eISBN 978 1 84765 940 8

The paper this book is printed on is certified by the © 1996 Forest
Stewardship Council A.C. (FSC). It is ancient-forest friendly. The printer
holds FSC chain of custody SGS-COC-2061

For my lovely father,
Edgar Williams
(1926–2010)

# Contents

A brave World, Sir, full of Religion, Knavery, and Change: we shall shortly see better days.

Aphra Behn, *The Roundheads*

# Introduction

The day is bitterly cold. I see steam blooming from a man's lips as he jumps down from the trolley car on the Upper West Side at Broadway and 73rd Street. His feet hit the icy sidewalk and the streetcar clangs away with all the acoustic precision that sound has on very cold days. He tugs the brim of his hat low over his eyes. The other passengers from downtown have been discussing the war, but he has not been thinking about the Japanese, or Hitler, or bombs. He has instead been thinking of his hands on the piano keyboard. The thought makes his mouth dry. Gripping the leather handle of his music satchel, he hesitates on the street corner for a moment. Then he sets off, crossing Broadway with a grey crowd of Sunday strollers. He skirts the upper edge of Verdi Square. Through the trees, the statue of the composer stands, his back turned as if to eschew the sorry kind of musician the man has become. He walks on past the Central Savings Bank, glancing up at the clock above the door that says it is a minute or two before four o'clock. Crossing Amsterdam Avenue onto West 73rd Street, he stops for a moment to check the advertisement torn from the newspaper and now folded – a little furtively – in his coat pocket. Number One

Hundred And Sixty. There it is – on the right. He passes beneath the portico and steps across the polished hallway into a wood-panelled elevator. With a clunk, he is lifted skyward and when the elevator boy yanks open the metal grille again, the man finds himself at the inaugural meeting of the Society of Timid Souls.

Only fragments remain about what really happened that January day. We know that the year was 1942. We also know that just four unsteady piano players responded to the first advertisement placed by Bernard Gabriel, a professional concert pianist, publicising a series of meetings to be held at his Manhattan apartment on the first and third Sunday afternoon of every month. In exchange for seventy-five cents apiece – to cover, so the notice in *The New York Times* read, 'refreshments' – fear-wracked musicians were invited to step in out of the cold and 'to play, to criticise and be criticised, in order to conquer the old bogey of stage fright'. They were to assemble at Sherman Square Studios, high above West 73rd Street, in a room bare but for two Steinway grand pianos and so extensively soundproofed that no one would hear what went on behind the closed door. Inside was Maestro Gabriel, with no formal qualification for this work other than a confidence beyond his thirty years. Gabriel was, it was said, 'non-timid' and duly he proceeded to deploy what he called 'strange and devious methods' to inoculate those in attendance against their fears.

By the early summer, the Society of Timid Souls numbered more than twenty and on 17 May, *The New Yorker* sent along a reporter, Charles Cooke, who happened to be a pianist himself. First Cooke encountered the silver-haired Mr William Hopkins, who told him, 'I'm old enough to know better and I'm scared to death', before plunging into a Respighi nocturne. Next came Mrs Moeller, who grew flustered if the audience was silent. Then Miss Simson, who panicked even when others played. Finally, the mysterious inoculation process was revealed, with the revival of a Timid Soul belonging to a Miss Flora Cantwell.

'This afternoon,' said Bernard Gabriel, 'I'm going to kill or cure her.'

Flora Cantwell sat down at one of the two pianos and began to play an étude. As she stumbled through – so Charles Cooke told his readers – Mr Gabriel moved among the Society members handing out props, a whistle here, a rattle there, occasionally pausing to whisper something into another Timid Soul's ear.

Miss Cantwell finished playing.

'Again,' said Gabriel and the moment the étude resumed – pandemonium.

Miss Simson blew Bronx cheers on a Bronx-cheer blower. Mr Carr spun a watchman's rattle. Mr Hopkins repeatedly slammed the door. Miss Cohen warbled *Daydreams Come True At Night* and Mrs Moeller flung the Manhattan Telephone Directory at the floor.

Flora Cantwell tucked her head down and kept playing.

Bernard Gabriel now crashed his hands upon the keyboard of the other Steinway, shouting, 'You're playing abominably, but don't stop!'

She did as he said and rising from the piano at the end, Miss Cantwell reported, 'I could play it in a boiler factory now.'

Bernard Gabriel's apparently comical methods proved to be remarkably effective. Many Timid Souls claimed to have been 'cured' by a dose of his 'anti-toxin' and, a year later, Society membership had doubled to include timid actors, timid singers, timid public speakers and timid parlour entertainers, each of them desperate to learn – or to remember – how to be brave.

The rudimentary exposure therapy techniques improvised those Sunday afternoons on West 73rd Street, while not unheard of, were certainly ahead of their time. In 1940s Manhattan, qualms like those of the Timid Souls would typically have been treated with rest and barbiturates; or if you were very modern, perhaps an evening of dream analysis at a 'Freuding' party. '*In vivo* flooding', as methods like Gabriel's later became known, would have to wait a further thirty years to gain much in the way of clinical credence. And yet this was how the Society of Timid Souls were healing themselves – and each other – every other weekend.

Copycat societies soon followed for nervous fashion models and others. Even Charles Cooke, the piano-playing reporter from *The New Yorker*, was whispered to have gone native and signed up as a Timid Soul himself. Said Bernard Gabriel triumphantly to the correspondent from *Reader's Digest* who visited in April 1943, 'I can see no reason why the shy and timid in any community couldn't get together and help each other.'

❧

It would be easy to dismiss the Society of Timid Souls as a period piece, quaint but scarcely important. I did at first, but then the timing of Bernard Gabriel's experiment in stress inoculation caught my eye.

For the first meeting of Timid Souls was called just four weeks after the Japanese bombed Pearl Harbor and the United States joined World War II. While Jewish refugees had been flooding into Gabriel's Upper West Side neighbourhood for many months, now America itself entered the fray. That very evening, 7 December 1941, a teacher at the Modern Piano School in New York City noted in her diary how Bernard Gabriel had been warming up to play a concert as news of the Japanese attack came over the wireless. And I imagined how pre-performance nerves must now have mingled with a deeper fear that ran through everyone gathered there that night and in the streets beyond.

My curiosity was piqued. Further scrutiny of what I still assumed to be little more than a historical coincidence revealed that this Society of Timid Souls had offered its whimsical response to big ideas and world events in other ways too. For the phrase 'timid souls' was not Mr Gabriel's own, nor did its origins share his affection, or at least his sympathy, for those cowed by life's little anxieties. 'Timid souls' comes instead from a famous speech given in 1910 by Theodore Roosevelt, in which the President invoked a muscular apparition of courage: 'the man in the arena, whose face is marred by dust and sweat and blood; who strives valiantly; ... who at the best knows in the end the triumph of high achievement, and who at the worst, if he fails, at least fails while daring greatly, so that his place shall never be with those cold and timid souls who neither know victory nor defeat.'

Roosevelt's rhetoric is thrilling, of course, but it was Bernard Gabriel's enterprise that I found myself admiring. I felt uplifted by how quietly radical its rehabilitation of the very idea of timidity was. For however stirring the ideal of 'the man in the arena', the substance of Roosevelt's argument seemed to have missed the point about timidity, a point that the Society of Timid Souls intuitively understood: that the world is not populated only by square-jawed heroes and snivelling cowards. Instead, whenever the times are troubled and fearful, then or now, the vast majority of us find ourselves somewhere in the middle, wishing to be brave and yet easily frightened by what is frightening. Either that, or we are capable of facing real danger one day, the next scared out of our wits by something comparatively trivial.

Consider, for example, this striking account of a Timid Soul redeemed on West 73rd Street, one of the last to have been printed about the Society. It concerns a young man, Sidney Lawson, who had grown up with a fine tenor voice and in 1941 had sung in Robert Shaw's Collegiate Chorale. Then came the war. Young Sidney joined the infantry and left New York before his twentieth birthday to fight overseas. A year later, he was shot and paralysed for six months. Along with his innocence, it seemed, gone too was Lawson's love of the stage. Technically, he could sing as well as ever, but performing now terrified him. Finally, in the late spring of 1945, Sidney Lawson joined the Society of Timid Souls. There, week after week, he forced himself to sing in a room full of people who 'stared glassily, milled about, rang bells, booed. When he bowed for applause, they shouted that he was a ham' – so reported *Time Magazine* in August 1945. Eventually, however, Lawson summoned the courage to take a party booking at the Hotel Pierre, one of New York's glossiest hot spots. With a gold army discharge stud pinned to his dinner jacket, Sidney Lawson took the stage once more and, singing songs from the shows, the young war veteran was reborn. He was signed the next day by a big Broadway agent.

As if to confirm what I now saw woven into the story of the Society of Timid Souls, the largest meetings at Sherman Square Studios – those with forty or more in attendance – and the swell of press coverage that accompanied them, turned out to coincide with the paroxysms of 1944 and '45. Most telling of all is that, by the end of 1946 – for no apparent reason other than that war was over and things were looking up – the Society of Timid Souls seems to have sunk without trace, its season passed. Bernard Gabriel moved on to other musical enterprises and the Timid Souls dispersed forever into the Manhattan crowds.

⋟

I began to wonder whether there was more to this Society of Timid Souls than met the eye. Gossamer threads of connection seemed to lead out from its trifling eccentricities across the twentieth century and into the twenty-first, suspended gauzily between war and politics, psychology and identity, courage and fear.

Certainly, in the years since 9/11, our understanding of these last two – courage and fear – has cleaved to a belief that there is now, more than ever, an awful lot to be frightened *of*. However cosseted and comfortable the age – or perhaps because of it – our collective nerve has faltered. We seem to have forgotten how to step up to the plate and our global media has surrendered to a taxonomy of terror: the planet warming, the bankers squandering, the terrorists bomb-making, the paedophile lying in wait. Whether justifiable or not, fear then becomes so infectious that once you are frightened about one thing, suddenly, you are frightened about another, and another, and another, however commonplace. Then your mother is frightened. And your kids. Soon your neighbours. Then the whole street. And on it goes. Before long, there is a Timid Soul quaking in his or her boots everywhere you turn.

In February 2003, in the run-up to the Iraq War, the international advertising agency, J. Walter Thompson, launched an Anxiety Index to track the market implications of this pandemic of dread across the globe. After surveying consumers about their levels of fear regarding issues such as war, terrorism, ill health, crime, job insecurity and economic instability, their findings were startling. According to the Anxiety Index in 2009, 78 per cent of Americans were nervous, compared to 22 per cent who were not. In Britain, that ratio was 73 per cent anxious to 27 per cent cool. The Russians were plagued by 84 per cent apprehension to only 16 per cent of people who lived relatively free of it. The most jittery of the lot? The Japanese, apparently, of whom 90 per cent were locked in a cycle of worry, and this was before the Tohoku earthquake and tsunami in 2011. The Chinese and the French were the only nations where fewer people admitted to being anxious than not. As the global economic crisis has eclipsed al-Qaeda as the fulcrum of our unease, the financial markets fix their gaze upon indices and metrics of fear too. There are scales of volatility that even offer opportunities to make money out of *how afraid we all are.*

Disquiet creeps everywhere. And, in the process, courage drifts into crisis. Everyday overcomings seem harder to achieve in a world where apprehension has become the norm and our ability to distinguish what is and what is not scary is skewed. Sensing and regretting our communal timidity, we then grow hungry for its opposite, this rare delicacy, bravery. Whereupon our media and politicians feed the appetite, dishing up an account of Courage and Heroes, so seasoned with drama and cliché that it is mouth-watering and easy to digest, but hardly nourishing. And so the cycle of timidity continues, a vicious (as opposed to a virtuous) circle.

All the same, What We Talk About When We Talk About Courage is not, thankfully, the same thing as courage itself. For what Michel de Montaigne called 'the strangest, most generous and proudest of all virtues' does exist and always has. It was there in the Torah, the Bible, the Qur'an, the Vedas, the scrolls of Confucius, the writings of Plato and Aristotle. Nor has it ever passed out of fashion, which cannot be said for all of the cardinal virtues. (Prudence, anyone? *Temperance*?) Yet today, in a secular culture that yearns for authenticity and belief, true courage remains pivotal to our morality and our aspirations, the best-loved of all the old virtues. Epic braveries or modest ones, ancient or modern, there is such optimism implicit in them all. They speak of the power of one small man or woman, or some group of men and women, and their refusal to be merely buffeted by fate. All courage involves some level of dynamic engagement with a world that, however cruel, it is possible to change in either great or subtle ways. This optimism *in extremis*, this silver lining to the cloud, is surely why courage stands unimpeachable and future-proof. And however out of touch with it we may be, it remains, as C. S. Lewis remarked to his old friend Cyril Connolly, 'not simply one of the virtues, but the form of every virtue at the testing point.'

The extraordinary staying power of courage is perhaps surprising if you consider how disconnected it is from the everyday. For these 'testing points' do not come often, and yet each of us hopes that when the hour of need arises an intention and a desire to act bravely will mean that we do. In an age of anxiety, where trouble is perceived to be around every corner, these 'testing points' feel closer and we worry about them because, of course, in a crisis, many people do not step up. Hoping to be brave but falling short is clearly of no use. And yet when someone, who seems apparently small and ordinary, *is* brave, it gives us all hope. It is this transformation, however momentary, from Timid to Brave Soul that sits at the heart of how we measure ourselves as human beings.

Which brings me back to the Society of Timid Souls. For what they discovered was that being brave can be as infectious as being afraid. Moreover, as a group, we can be taught to help ourselves. Together, we can learn to identify our enemy, or our fear. We can rehearse being brave, a kind of training that inoculates us against the most debilitating apprehensions. Indeed, put like that, it almost sounds like an invitation, does it not? I can all but hear that remark of Bernard Gabriel's, uttered with a bright, clipped delivery and a showbiz smile:

'I can see no reason why the shy and timid in *any* community couldn't get together and help each other.'

❧

These words and the story behind them had now well and truly worked their way under my skin. They seemed both timely, then and now, and strangely timeless too. And so I found myself increasingly identifying with the Timid Souls who met at Bernard Gabriel's studio, one of those diaphanous threads connecting to my own shoulder. The reason, of course, is that I too am burdened with a soul that is timid and, a little like my brethren on West 73rd Street nearly seventy years ago, I find myself yearning for a way to overcome it.

I have spent most of my working life making documentary films, often about apparently brave or at least daring people and so I have periodically found myself in hairy situations with guns, criminals or warring factions. Indeed, conscious of having an apprehensive nature, I got into the habit of egging myself on into these encounters, only to be so anxious once embroiled that feverish displacement activity seemed to be the only way to endure them.

Let me give you an example, one that combines the terrible aftermath of war and – God forgive me – unfeasibly large pants.

In the summer of 1999, I spent four weeks in Kosovo at the end of the war there. I was working on a programme about a British police team sent in on behalf of the International Criminal Tribunal for the former Yugoslavia to excavate a series of suspected mass graves on the edge of one small town. Our film crew had been told before the trip that we would be required to wear white paper forensic suits both at the graveside and in the makeshift mortuary, and that we would be changing alongside the police who were to undertake the exhumations and autopsies. Upon hearing this, a colleague had cracked a nervous joke about not getting caught in skimpy underwear and somehow the idea lodged. Hardly a seasoned war reporter, I spent the following week before we flew out haunted by febrile imaginings of what a mass grave might be like. And on the day of departure, I found myself in Marks & Spencer, procuring pants large enough that they might somehow protect me from the horror. Preternaturally vast though these smalls were, they did nothing to blunt the grim scenes we found upon arrival. What they did accomplish was to amuse everyone immensely, from bodyguard to pathologist, at a time when mirth was in short supply. My Martha Gellhorn moment it was not.

A decade on, I have three young sons, and I have found myself daily exhorting them to be brave – about a nightmare, or a grazed knee, brave about a spider high on a wall, or a first day at school. And they go right ahead and do it, inoculating their own Timid Souls against fear with astonishing efficiency. They are not striving to cut it as film-makers, nor to follow some blueprint of human virtue. They are just busy growing up and learning how to be happy. Consider then, how learning to be brave in adult life – and not just among soldiers or skydivers – could, should and does have the same liberating effect upon grown-ups too. As Anaïs Nin wrote in her diary in 1942, the same year that the Society of Timid Souls first came together, 'Life shrinks or expands in proportion to one's courage'. So am I crazy to imagine this one tiny transparent strand, threading all the way from the 1940s on West 73rd Street to me, sitting at my desk today?

That is why – a deep breath – I have decided, here in these pages, to call the Society of Timid Souls together once more.

Our strange times could do with such a fraternity, and so could I. If you would care to join me, then perhaps together we can work out how to be brave. I understand that you are probably not some havering, quavering piano player, nor am I any Bernard Gabriel. There will be no *in vivo* flooding, little music, perhaps only one or two Bronx cheers. Instead – and this shall be our new Society's undertaking – I intend that we discover what it means, *truly means*, to be brave and that we do it by seeking out some people who should really know.

And so it is that I have done, for me, a rather bold thing. I have quit my job, packed a voice recorder and a notebook. Welcome to the reconvened Society of Timid Souls. Now come with me. I am scared to go alone.

# 1

# Maŋ (I)

Stories can conquer fear, you know. They can make the
heart bigger.

*Songs of Enchantment*, Ben Okri

I had been planning to visit this street ever since watching
a young man on the TV news, waiting in a crowd for a line
of soldiers' coffins fresh back from war. His arm had been
hooked around the neck of another, his eyes bloodshot and
full of tears. I could not get his face out of my mind, nor what
he had said about the friend in one of the flag-draped boxes.

'He was a *lion heart*, he was!'

The young man had shouted it at the camera and I
remember thinking that his words could have been uttered,
in just such a pass, in any language, in any part of the world,
at any time in the last ten thousand years.

The idea is an ancient one: that courage is, above all, a
martial virtue, brought forth in conflict, man upon man.
Lately, the notion had found new life in this small English
market town's repatriation tributes to British soldiers killed

in the war in Afghanistan. Initially spontaneous – there was no other route the hearses could take – but soon highly ritualised, this bearing witness to the arrival home of their bodies had become a very English piece of theatre about Paying The Ultimate Price. And to me, the military courage implied seemed as good a place as any for a Timid Soul to start learning about bravery.

So that is why I was there, on a freezing afternoon in February 2011, on the High Street of Wootton Bassett in Wiltshire. I had parked and watched the military transport plane rumble in overhead, grey against a white winter sky. Now I stood amid a huddle of patriots and passers-by, shoppers and grieving families here to be reunited with their dead, all of us just waiting, like extras on a film set.

Several TV crews unfolded small metal platforms on the pavement from which their cameras could enjoy a better view of the action. Nearby a young woman with a large microphone interviewed a local man, nodding robotically at his answers and wearing a fixed considerate frown. Across the road, a group of bikers, long-haired in black leathers, stood smoking by the war memorial. They were the British Legion Riders Branch, ex-military motorcycle enthusiasts, and mingled among them were the more traditional British Legion members, with their ramrod backs and highly polished shoes. Unlikely as they looked together, it was these two cohorts who organised the repatriation tributes every week or two, whenever bodies arrived at the local airbase, RAF Lyneham, before the journey onwards by road to the military mortuary in Oxford.

I chatted to one six-foot-three, black-leathered veteran, silver skull in his earlobe. His role was to help the bereaved families find a parking place, the toilets, the right place to stand when the hearse came through, but he was nettled by my asking questions about courage.

'I'll tell you what annoys me,' he snapped, '*Afghan Heroes. Help for Heroes.* Heroes. Heroes. Heroes. A much misused word. Every guy that comes back through here is a hero to their family, I'm sure, and it's a tragedy that they've died, but what they were doing wasn't necessarily heroic. What they were doing wasn't necessarily brave. What they were doing was their job.'

Still, this was no ordinary day in Wootton Bassett. For months, I had been scanning the military obituaries from the Ministry of Defence, looking for particular mention of courage or bravery, valour or gallantry – terms which, I now realise, are not necessarily the norm – and that week, I had read this:

> Private Martin Bell died going to the assistance of a criti-
> cally injured friend in the most dangerous combat cir-
> cumstances imaginable. He knew the risks all too well;
> twice in the minutes before his death he had witnessed
> at first-hand the devastating human impact of IEDs. The
> term 'hero' is overused in contemporary commentary;
> take a moment to reflect on the image of Martin Bell,
> a twenty-four-year-old paratrooper who disobeyed a
> direct order in order to render life-saving first aid to his
> colleague. For that exceptional valour he paid the ulti-
> mate price.

And now the mortal remains of Martin Bell – the 318th to be saluted on this street in just over three and a half years – would be here any minute.

❧

At the end of the great Anglo-Saxon poem, *Beowulf*, there is a funeral, one of the finest in all of English literature. The warrior-king – he who dispatched the monstrous Grendel and his infernal mother – suffers, in his last heroic clash with a terrible but unnamed dragon, a fatal wound. Beowulf dies doing what Beowulf does best – fighting chaos and evil – and his people, the Geats, give him the send-off to end all send-offs. They build him a great pyre, hung with helmets and war-shields and gleaming armour. They set fire to it and, as the body is consumed, the flames roar so loudly it drowns out the mourners' weeping. Finally, as the blaze dies down, a lone woman begins to wail of fear and loss and nightmares.

Later, they bury what remains of Beowulf, speaking of how he has won the only thing worth having. And this is important: it is not entry to Heaven, for theirs is a world still strange to Christian ideas of virtue repaid with a harp and a cloud. Instead, Beowulf's goal and his eternal reward is his 'fame' – a nostalgic strain of pagan-epic celebrity, where the very act of recounting a man's bravery after his death is an end and a glory in itself. Then, as now, it seems that bravery exists in the telling as much as in the doing.

Our moral education, from Aesop to the Parables, Shakespeare to Harry Potter, has always relied upon stories. Nowhere is this more true – and more necessary – than in the military and with the cultivation of courage. And so there in Wootton Bassett, waiting for the body of Private Martin Bell, I was about to witness the end of a life usher in the beginning of a story.

❧

As the church bell begins to toll, the British Legion standard-bearers step forward in the salute and the street falls silent. An older, blonde woman, clearly distressed, has come to the front of the crowd. Unmistakably the dead man's mother, she is being held on her feet by a tall young man, whom I recognise from the press release photo as one of Martin Bell's brothers. He is talking to her, audibly and light-heartedly, in spite of the silence and what everyone knows is coming. At the bell, she lets fly a great volley of sobs and wails. For a moment, all you can hear is the sound of the bell, and the woman's wailing, and the click-click, click-click of camera shutters. Then the sound of an engine. Another loud gasp escapes the woman. A bus drives through. The saluting men remain motionless, but the dead man's brother laughs and says to his mother, a little too loudly, 'Oh it's the bus.' But then comes the hearse with its cargo neatly wrapped in a Union Jack and there are fresh cries and wails. They remind me of the wails of the Geat woman.

I am on the other side of the road, but through the glass of the hearse, which has stopped in front of the family, I can see the great crowd of mourners come forward, one by one, and touch their palms against the glass, before placing white and red roses on the roof of the car. There are sixty or more of them and it must take three or four minutes to do this, before the hearse drives on and out of sight. At the order, the standard-bearers and saluting soldiers stand at ease and people start chatting again. I overhear one bewhiskered British Legion veteran saying to another, 'Now, *that* was a good salute.'

As I drive away from Wootton Bassett, the tarmac is strewn with fallen flowers from the roof of the hearse and the petals blow around on the road, red and white.

❦

In the autumn of 2010, as Martin Bell and his platoon left for Afghanistan, commuters on the London Tube found themselves harried by an unnervingly personal question. Posters, billboards, illuminated hoardings began asking, 'HOW

BRAVE ARE YOU?' You turned a corner or changed trains and there it was again, in brightly coloured block letters. 'HOW BRAVE ARE YOU?' The posters were advertising the opening of a new gallery at the Imperial War Museum, which for the first time put on permanent and public display two hundred and forty one Victoria Cross and George Cross medals. These are the highest awards for bravery in British life, the first a strictly military decoration for valour 'in the face of the enemy', the second a civilian medal of equal rank, awarded chiefly in recent years also to the military for gallantry 'not in the face of the enemy'.

There were about fifteen or twenty of us at the gallery the morning I visited, including a pair of voluble Chelsea Pensioners, ancient and in full scarlet uniform, whose chatter was punctuated by 'Ooooooooo', as they leaned over medal after medal, like girls picking over engagement rings in a jewellery store. All the VCs looked the same, of course: the same plum-coloured ribbon with fine horizontal grooves; the same dark matt bronze of the cross, taken, so the story ran, from two cannon captured at Sevastopol; the same inscription, 'For Valour', 'For Valour', 'For Valour', 'For Valour'.

I had expected this repetition to be a little dull, but actually the recurrence was strangely compelling. It worked almost like a mantra to aid contemplation of how a man, in the hellish quagmire of war, might try to do the right thing. It also dawned on me how these medals were about death as much as about heroics. Black-and-white photos printed onto ceramic tablets sat next to each medal, young men staring out at you from across the last century and beyond, many of them killed by the action for which they won the VC, others killing to get it. And so heady was the spell that, for a moment at least, you found yourself quite certain that dire and mortal duress was the very thing (the only thing) that might lead a man to display the finest of human qualities.

Here, you doubters, you pacifists, you atheists and nihilists, *here* was redemption for the mess and the waste of war: that seemed to be the story.

Leaving the dark gallery felt, in fact, a little like coming out of a church, blinking into the sunshine and reacquainting yourself with a noisy, shallow world, where most people are timid, but where there are nice things to buy. Down in the gift shop they were selling replica VCs for £16.99. You could buy a badge saying BRAVE, or one saying BOLD, or FEARLESS, if you preferred; or a magnet for your fridge that would ask, 'ARE YOU BRAVE?' every time you went to get the milk. I bought some chocolate medals for my kids and I walked out into the street.

I should mention at this point that the medals in the gallery itself were no replicas. Indeed the provenance of this collection, and of the elegant, bespoke gallery that houses it, is even weirder than the souvenirs in the shop. The enterprise turns out to be the fruit of an expensive hobby, pursued by one of the most controversial tycoons in British life, and, with a fortune reported at the time to be around £1.1 billion, one of the richest: Michael Ashcroft, or to give him his full title, the Right Honourable Baron Ashcroft of Chichester, KCMG.

In 2010, Lord Ashcroft was at the centre of a protracted controversy over revelations relating to his offshore tax status and many millions of pounds' worth of donations made to the British Conservative Party. A political and media storm followed, but the most fantastical part of the pantomime was that it ran alongside the magnate's self-professed 'passion for gallantry' and habit of spending a portion of his riches, not on collecting Henry Moores or Bugatti cars, but on buying Victoria Crosses. Just eight weeks after his ensuing resignation as Deputy Chairman of the Conservative Party, the new Lord Ashcroft Gallery opened at the Imperial War Museum. And a couple of months after that, I was granted an audience with the billionaire peer in the gallery that bears his name.

In the United States, by the way, this costly pastime would be illegal. The buying and selling of military medals is outlawed there, but it remains perfectly respectable in Britain, with several major auction houses each running their own medals department. Moreover, they fetch serious money under the hammer. Michael Ashcroft's collection of Victoria Crosses is worth more than £30 million and the most valuable medal here, for which he reportedly paid £1.5 million in December 2009, is one of only three 'double VCs' ever awarded. It is the Victoria Cross and bronze bar (denoting the second, in this case posthumous, VC) that went to an army doctor who saved many lives in the Somme and at Ypres. It is an immaculate example of the double life led by the VC, whereby the more uplifting the story behind the award, the more folding money it seems to be worth, as though a little of the stardust, or should I say grit, might rub off on the new owner.

Of buying this double VC, Ashcroft said with a smile, 'It was the icing on the cake,' and when I asked about the price tag, he pointed out that 'it makes little difference to Roman Abramovich whether he pays £1 or £3 for his daily newspaper, whereas for the man with no money, it does.'

There was a little silence.

'There is a – ' he searched for the word – 'a *relativity* about it.'

Michael Ashcroft was born the year after World War II ended and as a schoolboy, he told me, the question, 'What did your dad do in the war?' was in every playground, with all the children looking for the kid whose dad 'did nothing'. So, aged ten or so, young Michael pushed his father for the story. There unfolded a bracing yarn about the D-Day landings and the mild-mannered Eric Ashcroft crashing through the waves at Sword Beach, not expecting to survive, but fighting on. This was not, the son pointed out, an unusual tale at the time.

'But what was unusual was that this was *my father*,' he said. 'I thought wow.'

Then he told how he rushed to the school library to learn all about Sword Beach – 'I was a bit of a geek about it' – and there began reading about Victoria Crosses and of a medal collector who had bought one. A childish fantasy ensued that if he, too, could buy a Victoria Cross, then he could be called Michael Ashcroft VC, which of course he soon discovered he could not. But the whole episode, as he told it, turned out to be one of those coming-of-age moments, one which, he said, cemented a lifelong closeness with his father, based on the fact that 'he had experienced something that I never had and never would'.

He paused for a moment and added, 'I would always measure myself against that.'

This reminded me of the posters around London advertising his exhibition by typographically yelling 'HOW BRAVE ARE YOU?' at commuters, so I asked him the question.

'In corporate life,' he replied, 'I've been known as someone who makes brave decisions, is not frightened and can be fairly ruthless. It's not the same, but I wonder if it might be transferred.'

'But you never thought of becoming a soldier yourself?' I asked.

'That was never what I wanted,' said Ashcroft. He went on to explain that it was not simply bravery, but conflict that fascinated him. He mentioned Thermopylae, as if it were a work of art, Genghis Khan, Attila the Hun, Alexander the Great, with hushed veneration. In adult life, the hobby turned into a form of battlefield tourism. Ashcroft said he had taken holidays to Rorke's Drift, to the Ukrainian valley where the Light Brigade had charged, to Gallipoli and Goose Green. But I was struck by how it seemed that the fascination lay at one remove. It was the stories, and often those that had acquired legendary qualities, that seemed to ignite his interest, stories that at length Ashcroft would look to *own* in his way.

'You see,' he said, 'the medal is the only tangible thing that is left of a moment of bravery and without it, the moment would be lost. Waterloo or Trafalgar would have been full of these moments, but we just don't know them.'

By 1986, Michael Ashcroft had made a lot of money and he treated himself to an auction at Sotheby's where he bought his first VC for around £30,000. At the hammer, he told me, 'A frisson went through my body.' He then described how the VC collection grew from there, in secret, via telephone bids, bids in the name of his long-serving head of corporate communications and ultimately through an ex-Sotheby's medal expert who had been the auction-eer at the purchase of that first VC and whom Ashcroft now employed to buy privately on his behalf. The secrecy sounded romantic and Gatsby-ish to me, but, I was assured, on the contrary, this was 'a mechanical process' about supply and demand.

'A pretty girl is always in demand,' he added, cryptically.

There were a hundred VCs in Ashcroft's private collec-tion before other major buyers and sellers within the medals business identified him. He said he never expected the col-lection to exceed twenty-five or so and that when he realised it might, he knew 'that it must be shared'. At the time we met, Ashcroft had bought a hundred and sixty-nine Victoria Crosses, more than 10 per cent of those ever awarded, as well as one George Cross.

'I am still amazed by it to this day,' he said, grinning, and we drew matters to a close.

I left the museum, puzzled as to quite what I had just witnessed, so I tried to map the chain of events in my mind. First comes the split second of extremity on a battlefield; then the witnesses who believe what they have seen to be courageous and they pass on the story. Next that story is distilled and evaluated by a committee, many miles away and many days later; they decide upon the award of a medal, the highest medal. So the story that goes with the medal is told again, and again, and again, and, in time, the medal itself becomes valuable. That is why a super-rich man wants to buy the medal and he duly does; it feels nice, so he buys another, and another, and another. These become a collection and the collection spawns a fine gallery, paid for in part by the super-rich man and bearing his name. All of which means that when I typed 'Lord Ashcroft' into Google, before I read anything relating to tax or business or scandal or politics, the search engine offered me, in an echo of the man's boyhood dream, 'Lord Ashcroft VC'. I know that this sequence of events is not of human design. It is not a lie or a conspiracy. It is simply what happens. And the fact that it does is testament to the sheer power of stories.

❧

The telling of a good yarn, of course – especially when it comes to courage – may make intuitive or narrative sense of why people do what they do, but it can also mask all sorts of holes in our understanding. And it has always been thus, even back to the time of Plato.

One afternoon in Athens, so he tells us, sometime in the fifth century BC, a pair of aging fathers found themselves in a quandary as to the importance of having their sons tutored in the latest technique for fighting in armour. According to Plato, they decided to consult two well-known generals, Laches and Nicias, and the generals suggested that the philosopher and war hero, Socrates, mediate the discussion.

Socrates soon steered, as was his wont, toward the ethical heart of the matter – the question of courage – insisting that in order to work out how a young man might best learn to be brave, the generals had better start by pinpointing what exactly courage was. Laches went first. To be brave is to hold your ground and not run away, said he. Too specific to the military, said Socrates. How about, offers Laches, 'a sort of endurance of the soul'? But what kind of endurance, replies Socrates, wise or foolish? Laches gets into a muddle and so Nicias helps out, suggesting that courage requires a knowledge of what to fear or not, but again Socrates shoots him down, saying that this boils down to a knowledge of good and evil, which clearly applies to more than courage alone.

At length, the discussion dwindles into *aporia*, or philosophical bewilderment, and everyone goes home.

❦

Having watched the salute and the coffins, having met the VC collector and his medals, I was growing impatient to talk to someone who had actually lived some of these things, who had actually *been brave*. And so I went to meet Colonel Tim Collins OBE.

Colonel Tim is the former Commanding Officer of the British Army 1st Battalion Royal Irish Regiment, and before that, he was a commander in the SAS, his reputation so tough that his men nicknamed him 'Nails'. In 2003, Collins became something of a celebrity, thanks to an inspiring eve-of-battle speech made as he and his battle group waited on the Kuwaiti border ahead of the Allied invasion of Iraq. The speech's power and its poetry were such that it drew comparisons with Henry V on the eve of St Crispin's Day or with William Wallace at Stirling. Collins exhorted his soldiers to be 'ferocious in battle', but 'magnanimous in victory' and to 'tread lightly' in Iraq. This, he told them, was 'the Garden of Eden'. The speech seemed to invoke a valiant rubric for just war and, transcribed by a journalist embedded with the soldiers, it was beamed around the world. A copy was even said to hang in the Oval Office.

Collins left the army a year later and now heads an intelligence-based security services company, which works 'in the most dangerous parts of the world' primarily for the US Department of Defense. He has also become an outspoken figure, with a reputation for calling a spade a spade. The day we met, Collins was wearing a jaunty, squireish outfit, a pale herringbone three-piece connected to two caramel-coloured brogues by an improbable pair of thick, canary-yellow socks, but everything else confirmed him as the flinty, battle-hardened man of reputation. He did not look me in the eye much and he talked fast, with a crisp Belfast accent, about dying more than anything else.

He told me that, for him, the worst fear had not been the 'instant fear' that gets you in the violent hurly-burly of conflict; rather, the anticipatory fear that comes along 'in the dark of night when you're waiting for the helicopter and you allow your mind to go over what could go wrong.' There had, he said, been two occasions in his life, one in Colombia, the other in Zaire, when Tim Collins thought that his 'number was up' and that he was taking his men off 'to do something that's most probably not going to be survivable'.

He cited these moments as an example of those times in a soldierly life where 'the discipline and team spirit and group pressure make it harder to go back than it is to go forward. There was never any mention of not doing it because it would have been much harder morally to opt out at that point, than to simply get on with it and hope for the best.'

Details of these Special Forces operations are restricted and, self-evidently, Collins did not perish, but his point was that resigning yourself to die does something to you.

'I certainly just closed off doors and it's like leaving a house,' he said, 'close off that room and say I'll never be going back in there. So there are certain things you just decide not to think about. If you've got small children, well you know you've done the best you can, made sure there's the odd thing you've left behind, because I want my son to have that one day and maybe he'll try and find out who I was, because he wouldn't know me. It's part of closing off those rooms of your house in your head. And in a funny way, when death doesn't come, and you do survive, you're in no hurry to reopen all that.' He paused and folded his glasses shut on the table. 'It takes a long time to come back to life. I think every time you prepare to die, you do die a bit and you never get that back.'

Some of the men who stood in the desert in 2003 and listened to Collins' famous speech later criticised him for making them fearful with all his talk of mortality. Yet Collins told me that many circumstances call for a commander to tutor very young, often teenage, soldiers in the truth of how very deadly war can be, via a kind of fatalism tempered by comradeship, which he paraphrased like this: 'This is history. You can't change it. What will happen will happen. But be as good as you can be and try to be true to yourself and more importantly to those around you, because the people around you are very important.'

I asked him at the end what a civilian like me, and a Timid Soul at that, might learn from the military about how to be brave.

'What is extraordinary about the British Army,' he said, 'the courage in it and the lesson for us all, is that those first two weeks of the hard twenty weeks of training we put soldiers through are all about the very un-modern and old-fashioned notion of being a good neighbour. That is what you are trying to teach.'

And this was the first hint I got that bravery could, in part, be learned.

❧

For some years, I have lived near the garrison town of Chepstow on the Welsh–English border. Here the British Army 1st Battalion the Rifles are barracked on a spoon-shaped peninsula called Beachley, where the River Wye flows into the River Severn. In April 2011, 1 Rifles were set to deploy more than five hundred troops for six months to Helmand in southern Afghanistan. I had grown accustomed to their Chinooks thundering over the treeline here and convoys of army lorries on the roads. I had also grown familiar with their faces, the ones I passed in the supermarket or at the school gates. I became aware that the people who fought these wars in our name looked and sounded just like the rest of us, and I got to thinking how very extraordinary it was that they were expected to show courage as part of their job, just as others might be required to type sixty words per minute, or to display good interpersonal skills. And so before they left for Helmand, I spent a few days with 1 Rifles to try to understand how you might train an army to be brave.

By way of introduction, one of the senior men ran me through the fundamentals of basic military training, those early weeks that were all about physical and mental drilling: rendering reflexive the best actions under fire, by repeating them over and over and over, and shifting the civilian mindset of the individual, also by repetition, to that of the group. Next comes the training specific to the Afghan theatre of war and to the brutal intensity of the Green Zone that flanks the Helmand river. This relies upon enactments of ever more complex, ever more realistic scenarios, narratives that begin the process of what the Commanding Officer called 'battle inoculation'. These reduce the shock and the fear of the real war zone in a way that is strangely not a million miles from Bernard Gabriel's antics with the petrified piano players. Finally, the soldiers take part in a set-piece exercise in Norfolk or on Salisbury Plain, where 'Afghan villages' have been set up, complete with markets, livestock, real villagers, and genuine double amputees waiting in the wings with sachets of stage blood to play out the aftermath of an IED (Improvised Explosive Device) attack. The battalion live the fiction day and night for two weeks and, provided there are no major blunders, they are then deemed ready for war.

1 Rifles had passed this test a few weeks before my first day with them. This was an unexpectedly upbeat pre-deployment press junket at an army training area not far from their base. What I had been invited to see, along with the local press and a handful of town councillors, was part of Continuation Training, where the cycle of repetition goes on, ensuring that not a memory flags until the moment of deployment.

A minibus collected us from the car park and drove for a few minutes across scrubby grassland until we arrived at the mocked-up patrol base with its stage-set command post, a large tent bristling with the high-tech kit of the electronic battlefield, the details of which they made us promise not to report, in case the Taliban should pick up a copy of *The Society for Timid Souls* or the *South Wales Argus*.

Next, we were treated to a dress rehearsal of a 'hard knock' on a Taliban compound. 'That means loud and violent,' offered a nearby officer cheerfully, 'with shots fired and grenades.'

We all braced ourselves for something noisy and fast and compelling. Instead, we watched three groups of four men advance at a glacial pace and in complete silence on a long, low building at the end of a scraggy piece of ground. At the front was the Vallon man, as he is called, because of his metal detector, manufactured by a company called Vallon. He inched forward clearing a safe lane free of IEDS. At one point, as the scene unfolded, I spotted one of the reporters from the local paper checking his text messages. After many minutes, the soldiers reached the 'compound', firing a few shots that broke the silence, made the spectators jump and 'killed' some dusky-looking men dressed up as insurgents, who then lay dead, most convincingly, as we all filed away to get a polystyrene cup of tea back by the 'command post.'

This slow-motion routine, they told us, was the key change in drill since 1 Rifles were last in Helmand through the winter of 2008/2009. The IED threat had gone through the roof since then, as these makeshift bombs rose to replace the ambush as the primary weapon of the insurgency, and with grim results for casualties among the NATO-led force. OK, so this new kind of war did not look particularly adrenaline-fuelled, but I was assured that, day after day, week after week, and month after month, this creeping around proved a sustained test of the infantryman's nerve. How you learned to wear that pressure was by rehearsing (and rehearsing and rehearsing), until you knew each movement, like a reflex, as instinctive as blinking.

Their departure for Afghanistan was still about three weeks away at this point and, as they took over from the previous battle group, it would be one man in, one man out, 'high fives on the tarmac', as one captain put it.

'The thing is,' he said, eagerly, 'it's *exciting*. Most people just do their jobs. All year round. We spend only six months every two years doing ours.'

A few days later, at the barracks, in a classroom with acid-yellow walls and a large map of Helmand on one of them, the mood was different. Everyone who filed in to talk to me, one by one, seemed serious, tense.

Three of the eleven soldiers I met were about to get their very first taste of war, their eyes wide with what lay ahead. The others had cut their teeth in Northern Ireland, the Balkans, Iraq, but had only learned what war really meant in Afghanistan in the autumn of 2008. For them, Helmand changed everything. None had ever experienced conflict at this pitch; none had ever needed to be brave *like this*. Adrian Farmer was the regimental serjeant major, the highest non-commissioned rank in the battalion, and had served twenty-four years in the army. He described it as a situation where senior and junior ranks alike were under what he called 'the courage cosh' for the first time in their careers.

Corporal Julian Heal, whom everyone called 'Clarence', was thirty-nine and had spent twenty years in the army. He described his first weeks on the ground in Nad-e Ali, in the heart of the Green Zone, as being like medieval total war. I must have looked at him blankly at this point, because he explained, 'Medieval: Total War. The computer game.' It was terrifying, he said, but it made him feel 'alive'.

Much younger, Lance Corporal Jon List cut a gaunt figure, hollow about the eyes and lean within his uniform. He described getting off the helicopter in Marjah in Helmand in December 2008 and getting shot at within hours. 'You suddenly realise,' he said, 'that, "hold on, these people are actually trying to kill me"'. And they were. Three months later, and just three days before he was due to fly back to Camp Bastion on his way home, Jon and his multiple were ambushed and in the very first volley, Jon was shot in the face.

'When it actually hit me,' he said, 'I remember it felt like having a train run over my face. I was knocked out by it a couple of seconds later and then the next thing I know I was on the floor on my back but I couldn't feel anything at all. Everything was numb. I could see. I could hear. I could move. But I couldn't feel a thing. At the time I wasn't unhappy or really frightened that I was going to die' – Jon shifted in his chair a little – 'I just got used to that idea pretty quickly.'

He lay there in the field, drifting in and out of consciousness in the middle of a firefight that lasted for another forty-five minutes. With him was a medic called Kate Nesbit, who had sprinted across open ground under fire to treat him and who without doubt saved his life. Jon told me that was why his baby daughter's middle name was Kate.

The round had entered Jon's head through his upper lip. It had travelled through his teeth, through his tongue, shattered his jaw and come out of his neck on the other side, but miraculously, it had missed his windpipe, his oesophagus, his jugular, his carotid artery, his spine. It was three months before Jon could chew again, nine before he could return to work, a year before he could speak without a heavy lisp.

I asked him why, knowing what he did, he wanted to go out to Afghanistan again. This, I said, was surely courage or something like it. But Jon replied, 'I want to prove to myself that I can still do my job. I think the only way to describe it is if you tried to do something and you failed then you would go back to prove that you can do it.'

'But you didn't fail, did you?' I asked.

'It's not that I see it as a failing,' Jon said, 'but that's the only thing I can really compare it to. If I turned into a nervous wreck and all of a sudden I was like *I'm not going I'm not going*, then younger blokes would see it. Fear is infectious so if they see me being scared because of what happened last time then they'd get scared because they don't want what happened to me to happen to them, so in a way, I think my going could instil a bit of bravery in other people.'

Jon List's is not the only tale of life-and-death luck. Near misses are routine in the theatre of war and I hear several stories – the soldiers seem to enjoy telling them – of men kneeling down in the dust and realising that their patella was half an inch from an IED pressure plate, or leaning forward to pick something up or light a cigarette and a round whistling through the space where their head had just been. Of course, the military at war do not run a monopoly on good and bad luck. It is simply that the scale is so entirely different especially in an IED war like this one, where often you are not fighting to the death, but simply happening upon it.

Which is why each soldier's nerve seemed to rely upon the construction of his, or her, own story about the bargain that they have struck with risk. A senior officer from the previous battalion deployed that winter in Helmand told me that he had begun to see lucky charms and crucifixes all over the camps, checkpoints and patrol bases. And 1 Rifles seemed to be no different. I heard about photos of 'the wife' inside helmets, and lucky stones or charms. One soldier believed in guardian angels, another two prayed when the chips were down. Lance Corporal Hayley Ridgeway, a twenty-three-year-old medic, told me she had just got a St Christopher for this, her first Afghan tour, a lucky teddy knitted by her mum and, tucked in her daypack, a sweet wrapper from when her younger brother was little. 'I think these little things do keep you safe,' she said, 'Definitely.'

Of the eleven men and women I met over those few days, more than half, right through the ranks, came from broken homes or had a parent die in childhood. That is more than fifty times the national average for such misfortunes and each of them had, to a greater or lesser extent, found a new family in the army – one that would not let you down, one where you looked out for each other, within a clan purpose-built to withstand death and destruction. When I started asking questions about courage or actions that the outside world might deem courageous, everyone, *every single soldier*, invoked that sense of belonging, of loyalty and collective identity, rather than any notional obedience or individual ambition.

'You just want to look after your blokes,' said Clarence, 'and this is going to sound pretty politically incorrect – I don't care about the Afghans or their terror of the Taliban or hearts and minds, all I know is I want my boys to survive.'

This is where the young medic, Hayley Ridgeway, said that her worst dread resided. 'The fact is that not everyone will come back,' she said. 'And I'm scared a lot of that is down to me. My job could actually kill someone or save them. I've lost mates before, but I wasn't treating them and this time, I am. It's your family, at the end of the day.'

This powerful fealty, and the collective bravery that goes with it, is no emotional fortuity. It is a story these soldiers have been told again and again, since day one of basic training and it runs right up through the Battalion 'family'. The Commanding Officer of 1 Rifles was Lieutenant Colonel James de Labillière, scion of an eminent military clan, and he explained that this was the great strength of the regimental system. 'It creates that framework,' he said, 'and it's not necessarily brotherly love either. There might be a commander who feels he has a responsibility to one of his blokes – he might not like him particularly – but he nevertheless has that responsibility.'

Then, within this system of loyalty and responsibility, he said that the key was to train people at all ranks to make quick decisions in nightmare-ish circumstances.

'That means that the time it takes them to have recovered from the initial shock of a scenario, like an IED where one of their muckers was walking along on foot in front of them and then is suddenly lying on the floor with two bleeding stumps. From the shock of that moment to making a decision as to what to do about it: it's that gap which, through the training process, I'm trying to reduce.'

I remarked that this sounded like courage to me.

'No,' he said quickly, 'funnily enough, I'm not sure it is and I think, actually, what training does is it almost tries to obviate the requirement for courage. It tries to make things so normal that actually what you've just done might be extraordinary, but you don't realise it, because that's what you've been trained to do. I'd draw the difference between confidence and courage. I think what the training gives you is the confidence.'

It was exactly this distinction between confidence and courage that de Labillière and his commanders would have to make in the coming months in Helmand. It may seem surreal to anticipate and then rank acts of gallantry before they have even taken place, not least because of the extremity in which they are born, but this was exactly what the command team had to do before deployment. The Commanding Officer had, he told me, just talked them through the Honours and Awards procedure, a complex process, riddled with politics and protocol. He would, he said, 'personally' write every award citation to come from the tour. 'It's extremely important,' he added, 'you know, I've seen this plenty of times before and they're very, very contentious, Honours Awards, they can go very badly wrong, if they're badly managed.' And this, I realised, was where, in the life cycle of any brave deed, Action would hand over to Story again.

But first they had a war to fight. Three weeks later, by 24 April 2011, James de Labillière, Adrian Farmer, Hayley Ridgeway, Clarence Heal, Jon List and the other soldiers of 1st Battalion Rifles were in Helmand, with all their luck and their training and their friends. They were posted to Nahr-e Saraj South, the same place where Martin Bell, whose coffin

I had watched pass through Wootton Bassett, had died three months and a day before. 'I'll see you in November', I said, but we all knew that not everyone would come back.

🌿

It was the first explosion at half past five that morning that woke them. It shook the tent where nine officers of the 2nd Battalion Parachute Regiment Battle Group were sleeping. A few of them said, 'God!' involuntarily, and then they waited, as the tent filled with dust, listening for the sound of feet running on the plastic matting that ran between the sleeping quarters and the Operations Room at Patrol Base 2.

Explosions were not, in themselves, unusual, animals can tread on things, other things can go off prematurely. This was, after all, Nahr-e Saraj, the second hottest spot, after Sangin, in the Helmand Valley and even though this was supposed to be the winter lull, the whole place was studded with IEDs.

Thirty seconds went by and everyone began to relax; then came the running footsteps and within a minute everyone was up and in the Ops Room.

Lieutenant Colonel Andy Harrison, the Commanding Officer of 2 Para, is telling me this, six months after I have watched the hearse bearing the coffin of one of his soldiers, Private Martin Bell, through Wootton Bassett. We are sitting in the small, dark dining room at Harrison's home at the Colchester Barracks. His kids are on school holidays and, as they clatter around cheerfully in the room next door, their father tells me about what happened to Martin Bell on 25 January 2011. I have wanted to hear the tale behind Bell's extraordinary obituary and repatriation, and now I will.

The explosion that woke Harrison and his team happened just a quarter of a mile to the north of the patrol base. That night, C Company had been setting up an ambush in an area not visible to the base surveillance. It was a rough patch of ground between fields, covered with elephant grass that stretched more than ten feet high, and there had been insurgent activity up there, including the movement of weapons and intimidation of the locals.

Two squads of ten men had gone out at around 4 a.m. Even with night-vision goggles, clearing an IED safe lane in complete darkness and in thick vegetation was difficult. The Vallon man, Private Liam King, could not make the usual sweeping arc with his metal detector and after ninety minutes they were still edging forward through an impossibly narrow lane in pitch blackness. Then Liam King's foot touched a pressure plate.

It was an instant traumatic amputation. Both legs.

Maybe two years ago King's patrol mates could have run to help him, but during 2010 the threat of multiple IED clusters had grown exponentially and wherever there was one IED, there was almost always another, and often another, and maybe another. That made this patch of elephant grass potentially lethal. And so it was that the rest of the patrol crept, metal detector in front, slowly, through the darkness, up to the wounded man, dragging him, oh-so-carefully, out of the reeds and into a field. That is when they realised that the explosion had ripped King's own metal detector and assault rifle from him. And these could not, it was decided, be left lying around in the enemy area. At first light, someone would have to go back in and look for them.

The blast had not only woken Battle Group Headquarters. It also woke Private Martin Bell and his Platoon Sergeant Marc Thompson, in a checkpoint about a mile to the south. As King was being helicoptered out, Thompson's squad was called in to recover the missing kit.

They got there around seven o'clock and, as the sun rose, they began searching the fields of low wheat that encircled the elephant grass. First, Thomo, as everyone calls him, spotted one of Liam King's legs. He wrapped it in plastic and put it in his rucksack. Next, someone spied the grenade launcher from the bottom of King's rifle and soon after, the rifle itself, badly damaged; after that, some ammunition and grenades, scattered like seeds by the breath of the explosion.

The only thing now missing was the Vallon, the metal detector itself, the only place left to look, the most dangerous area, the long elephant grass.

A conversation took place over the radio.

'Do you still want us to go in for the Vallon?'

A decision came back.

'Yes.'

'Right,' said Thomo, 'seven of you, stay there in the field. I'm going to go in and I'm just going to take the two Vallon men, Scott and Martin.'

Martin Bell had joined 2 Para from 1 Para the summer before, not long before his twenty-fourth birthday, and once in Helmand, he became the lead man on his patrol, the one with the metal detector. It was a role that had previously been rotated among junior soldiers, due to the pressure that came with the job, but, as the IED threat had intensified, the expertise was deemed to be more important than the psychological burden. Once you had a good Vallon man, you kept him there. In return, Vallon men like Martin won a level of respect from colleagues and senior ranks alike rarely afforded the most junior soldiers. All the Riflemen I met at Beachley, for instance, had mentioned courage and the Vallon man in the same breath.

So that morning, it was Martin who first stepped into the elephant grass, not long after 8 a. m. The three men inched forward, Martin at the front, Scott Meenagh some metres behind and off to one side and at the back, Thomo, who scanned the ground for the missing metal detector.

A few minutes passed.

'Look, I'm not comfortable with this.'

Thomo was talking into the radio.

'I've got a bad feeling about this.'

Seconds later, a huge explosion.

The blast threw Thompson backwards and he yelled out, 'Who's been hit? Are you alright? Who's out there?'

There was silence and then Martin Bell stood up some fourteen or fifteen metres away, mildly concussed. The elephant grass was not at full height in this patch and Thompson could see Martin from the waist up. He held up his hands, empty, his Vallon gone.

'I'm here,' he said. 'I'm OK.'

Nothing from Scott Meenagh.

'Stand still,' shouted Thomo to Martin, 'Just stand fucking still. Don't move anywhere. This place is riddled with IEDs.'

'OK,' said Martin, 'yes, OK.'

Thompson set off back the way they had come. In theory at least, this was safer than any other option. If he could get to the other seven men waiting in the field, he knew that they had one metal detector between them and then they could come around the other way and try to clear another route in through the elephant grass to find Scott Meenagh.

This was to take Thompson and the squad six minutes, six minutes during which Martin Bell did something quite extraordinary.

No one knows why, no one even knows exactly how, but as the figure of Thompson retreated and disappeared into the grass, Martin ignored the order he had just received. He knew that this was one of the most dangerous bits of ground in the world, but something made him move. With no metal detector, no electronic counter-measures, with nothing but luck, Martin Bell ignored the order to stand still and began to look for the section mate with whom he had spent twenty-four hours a day, for three months, sleeping six-abreast in sleeping bags in the mud hut at the checkpoint.

Meenagh had been blown by the explosion into a ditch. He had lost both legs, high up, arms injured too. When Martin found him, Meenagh was struggling to put a tourniquet on one of his own stumps. Martin ran down to him and using his own tourniquets, as well as Meenagh's – each infantryman carries a pair – he tightened two onto each stump, saying over and over that it was going to be OK. He unfolded a plastic field stretcher from his pack, rolled Scott onto it and began clipping the webbing straps, so that when the others arrived they could get Scott out quickly.

Knowing nothing of any of this, Thompson and the other seven men were approaching from the new angle, when suddenly Martin's voice came over the radio.

'It's Scott Meenagh,' he said. 'He's lost both his legs. I've applied two tourniquets.'

*What? Martin? How... ?* But there was no time for that. When Thomo and the others arrived, Martin was so clearly in control of the situation that it was he, the private, who organised how to get Scott out. Doctors later confirmed that in the six minutes that it had taken the other men to get there, Scott Meenagh would have bled to death, but for the tourniquets applied by his friend.

'Right,' Martin said, 'you get on that part of the stretcher. You, on that corner. I'll take the front and I'll pull it out.'

These were Martin Bell's last words. He bent down and forward, to lift the stretcher out of the ditch and as he did, his foot touched a pressure plate, his torso taking the full blast of a third explosion.

Martin Bell's Commanding Officer, Andy Harrison tells me that, in a long career of soldiering, Bell's is the bravest act of what he calls 'cold courage' to which he has ever been party. His point is that the action was not a reflex, nor fuelled by rage or pain. It was considered. And this was not the kind of courage for which you could train, either. In fact, it was the very opposite: a solitary defiance of a sensible risk assessment reinforced by a chain of command. Martin Bell did the wrong thing, but it was the right thing to do. And it speaks volumes about the pervasive loyalty system of the army.

'He gambled with his own life to save a mate,' Harrison says. 'And in the end, he won the first part of the gamble – he saved Scott Meenagh's life – but there was a third device there and he trod on it and that gamble, he lost.'

As though to prove the power of a story like this one, Martin Bell's Commanding Officer says that he believes this young man to be defined less by his twenty-five years of life, than by the outstanding moments that led to his death. That, he concludes, 'must inculcate future soldiers with a spirit of which you can't quantify the value. Sad though his death is, the nature of it is such that it will continue to resonate long after he's gone, and far beyond the narrow island of his family and friends.'

It sounds almost like something that you might find in the pages of *Beowulf*, but maybe that is the point: for, in this single story of that poor boy whose mother wept so loudly and bitterly for him, comes an ageless collision of danger and friendship, of good luck and bad luck. Two months after Harrison and I meet, this account sees Private Martin Bell posthumously awarded with a George Medal, the highest British gallantry decoration of that year of war in Afghanistan.

a few steps, then wrinkle her snout and wag her curly tail, while emitting a shrill, staccato oinking sound. And, until you switched Amanda off, she would continue repeating the sequence over and over, bearing down on you. At first, whenever the beast within Amanda was awakened, my son would recoil violently and start wailing. Yet, as the days passed, he taught himself to stand his ground and eventually, the only sign of the old dread as Amanda stirred was one great flinch of his podgy shoulders. After some weeks, and when the pig was at repose, Sam finally found the switch, identified what it did, and Amanda's reign of terror was broken.

I was reminded of Amanda last spring at the *Plaza de Toros de la Maestranza* in Seville, as I perched a couple of rows behind the *callejón* on a red-and-yellow-striped cushion bought from an old crone by the bullring gates. It was the last afternoon of the *Feria de Abril* and I had come to watch the famously short, famously valorous matador, Rafaelillo (meaning Little Rafael) fight two deadly Miura bulls.

I had been in Seville for three days, building up to this moment – the *corrida* – and I had done little but think about bulls, read about bulls and talk about bulls for seventy-two hours. I had passed a long afternoon with an aficionado in his *caseta* at the *feria*, the great riot of party tents by the River Guadalquivir, as he talked me through the key acts of the bullfight over a jug of *rebujito*. I had spent hours mooning around the bar at the Colón, the city's venerable bullfighting hotel, waiting for Rafaelillo's manager, the former torero and son of the bull-breeding Miura clan, Eduardo Dávila Miura. Eduardo was a busy man. It was the *feria* after all and this was southern Spain. So meeting him to discuss Rafaelillo or the forthcoming fight had turned out to be as much about hanging around at hours of the night foreign to a nice English girl like me, as it was about Senor Dávila sharing a handful of gnomic, Andalucían wisdoms about the sadness and beauty of the *corrida*, while he twiddled with the buttons on his two mobile phones.

Above all, as I waited for him, I had watched endless re-runs of the afternoon's bullfights on a bank of TV screens in the hotel bar. They were showing Canal+Toros. Bull after bull after bull came galloping out of the 'Gates of Death' and into the ring. I had watched, repeatedly and in slow motion, the yellow and pink swirl of the *capote* as the *cuadrilla* goad the bull to vent his rage; the demonic high camp of the *banderilleros* as they stab him in the back of his huge neck; the point of a horn millimetres away from the brocaded thigh of a *traje de luces* ('suit of lights'); the matador's gesture to the crowd, as if to say, 'You see? You see what I can do?' as he turns a glittery back on the colossus and struts away; his fatal sword lunge, on ballet-pump-point, into the bull's bloodied shoulders; the lurch of the beast in its submission on to the sand. Even when I finally got to bed, these images fed nightmares of English farmyards turned labyrinthine and with the horns of so many Minotaurs waiting in the darkness for a soft human belly to puncture.

At any rate, by five o'clock on Sunday, packed in with the bullring crowd, I felt I had mentally prepared. I had reckoned upon some equity between knowing what this *looked* like and what it actually *felt* like when you were sitting there. And yet, when Dador, well over half a ton of prime Miura bull and Rafaelillo's first adversary that afternoon, appeared on the yellow sand of the *Maestranza*, not a dozen strides away from my seat, I silently jumped a foot in the air, just as my son had done with Amanda, the battery-operated pig.

It is remarkable how terrifying a dumb animal can be.

❧

In her seminal essay, 'Virtues and Vices', the English moral philosopher Philippa Foot revived the old Aristotelian view that the virtues exist in some state of balance with their attendant vices. Virtues are, she said, essentially 'corrective', that is to say that their origin lies in the resisting of a transgression, or the amelioration of a deficiency. 'One might say,' she wrote, 'that it is only because fear and the desire for pleasure often operate as temptations that courage and temperance exist as virtues at all.' In other words – and this is good news for Timid Souls – the uniquely nuanced and variegated experience of fear that is exclusive to the human animal is also entirely inseparable from our potential to be brave. As Mark Twain puts it in *Pudd'nhead Wilson*'s Calendar, 'Courage is resistance to fear, mastery of fear – not absence of fear ... Consider the flea! – incomparably the bravest of all the creatures of God, if ignorance of fear were courage.'

There is, in fact, a corner of the human brain that Fear can call its own, a place where it can put its horrid feet up and feel at home. Buried deep within the anterior medial section of each temporal lobe, it is called the amygdala, an almond-shaped structure present in all complex vertebrates, including humans. Brain scientists have long known that the amygdala plays a vital role in fear-related behaviours and memories, stimulating the hypothalamus to activate the sympathetic nervous system and prompting the production of epinephrine (adrenaline), cortisol, dopamine and the other hormones that support fight or flight. Furthermore, ever since an 1888 experiment on rhesus monkeys with bilateral lesions of the amygdala, it has also been known that if this part of the brain is damaged then fear reactions are undermined. Yet it is only recently that a greater understanding has come about of how this plays out in human terms. This is thanks to advances in MRI brain scanning and to the presentation and subsequent study of a rare case: a woman with bilateral lesions of the amygdala and, yes you guessed it, with No Fear. On the face of it, this absence of fear might look like courage, it might sound like courage, but was it courage?

The paper, 'The Human Amygdala and the Induction and Experience of Fear', appeared in *Current Biology* in January 2011. It detailed the extraordinary story of the patient SM, a forty-four-year-old woman who suffers from a rare congenital disease known as Urbach-Wiethe disease that causes calcium deposits to appear on the amygdala. An earlier study of SM had already established that she had little intuition of fear, demonstrating few physical signs of the emotion as well as an inability to recognise fear in others' facial expressions. The latest researchers, Justin Feinstein and Daniel Tranel of the University of Iowa, Ralph Adolphs of Caltech and Antonio Damasio of the University of Southern California, now designed a set of experiments to shed light on SM's actual experience of fear, or lack of it.

First, SM was taken to an exotic pet store where she cheerfully handled various snakes and had to be deterred, *fifteen times*, from trying to pick up one of the larger, more dangerous snakes. When it came to the tarantula – I just shivered, typing the word – SM had to be stopped as she put her hand down into its box. Throughout, SM's anxiety was measured via a commonly used psychological questionnaire. She felt no detectable alarm, just, in her own words, 'curiosity'.

The next scenario sounds less like serious science and more like *Scooby Doo*. It involved taking SM, on Halloween, to one of the most (allegedly) haunted places in the United States – Waverly Hills Sanatorium in Kentucky. Waverly Hills, an early twentieth-century tuberculosis hospital where hundreds died, has enjoyed a lively afterlife on the paranormal TV circuit, featured on *The Scariest Places on Earth*, *Ghost Adventures*, and many more. The building's enterprising owners run an annual spook-fest, where visitors pay to be freaked out by eerie music and a cast of ghoulishly clad resting actors. And yet, insofar as fear, or even fright, was concerned, SM remained unmoved by Waverly Hills. In fact, she even unnerved one of the monsters by trying to poke him back.

Finally, the team showed SM clips of scary movies from *Arachnophobia*, to *The Shining* to *The Blair Witch Project*, interspersed with clips aimed at inducing other forms of emotion in her, like surprise or sadness, happiness or disgust. While she duly laughed at the clips of babies giggling, grew sad watching the faces of starving people in Africa, yelped with revulsion when a large transvestite apparently ate dog excrement, SM was merely interested or at best 'entertained' by the scenes of Buffalo Bill in *The Silence of the Lambs* or of the mutilated man who awakens from the dead in *Seven*.

Before the onset of her symptoms, SM recalls feeling fear as a child. In the paper, the researchers recount a contrasting anecdote from SM's adult life, once the lesions on her amygdala were established. One night she had been walking home around ten o'clock. It was dark and she had been beckoned into a park by an apparently 'drugged-out' man. She went and he proceeded to grab her and threaten her with a knife.

'I'm going to cut you, bitch,' he said.

SM replied calmly, 'If you're going to kill me, you're going to have to go through my God's angels first.'

He let go and she walked on, happy to take the same route the following evening. So here again is the question: was it bravery that SM was demonstrating? Is fearlessness tantamount to courage?

A few years previously, a pair of clinical psychologists with no knowledge of SM's brain condition had interviewed her about the knife incident. They had noted that she came across as a 'survivor', 'resilient' and even 'heroic' in the way that she had dealt with this and other misfortunes. Feinstein and Tranel's new study, however, elected to read SM's attack in the park in the light of her dysfunctioning amygdala and their conclusions instead warned of the heightened dangers of living 'without the evolutionary value of fear'.

This is just one of hundreds of neuroscientific studies exploring what happens in our brains when we are scared (or not). So it is perhaps no surprise that neuroscientists have not only discovered where fear lives, but have located courage in our brains too.

In the summer of 2010, neurobiologists at the Weizmann Institute of Science in Israel published findings that claimed to have identified the nook within our grey matter where fear is overcome. At pains to emphasise that it was not fearlessness that interested them so much as the moment when courage triumphed over fear, Uri Nili, Hagar Goldberg, Abraham Weizman and Yadin Dudai designed an experiment that placed either a nasty snake, or a nice teddy bear, on a conveyor belt leading towards the head of a patient lying in an MRI scanner. The group of patients to be studied divided into two types, either fearful or fearless, Timid Souls like you and me or seasoned snake handlers. Each was asked to get as close to the snake as possible, by controlling with a button the motion of the conveyor belt, either to advance or retreat, bringing the snake either nearer or further from their heads.

Is it not revealing that an encounter between man and dangerous animal – that which did for Adam in Eden no less – is deemed to be the prevailing shortcut to fear? Paradise was not lost on account of an AK-47 or a car, after all. Indeed, Arne Öhman (2009), the Swedish neuro-psychologist, puts this discrepancy down to evolutionary fear conditioning, namely that natural selection favoured an ancestral amygdala that reacted particularly strongly to snakes, our foremost predator back then.

At any rate, the Israeli researchers went on to map what happened in the subjects' brains. They discovered that six seconds after each exposure to the nasty snake (as opposed to the nice teddy) – and this is among the fearful folk (as opposed to the snake handlers) – came the moment of bravery. This is when they chose, voluntarily and against their better judgement, to advance the snake towards their own heads. This plucky choice could be observed on the MRI by a marked drop in activity in the amygdala and a flurry of activity in two other parts of the brain, the subgenual anterior cingulate cortex (sgACC) and the right temporal pole (rTP). This, the researchers concluded, was 'courage'. Indeed, perhaps a day might come when a therapeutic intervention could be designed to manipulate the sgACC and so help the most acutely frightened people to overcome their fears.

So that is where to find courage: the subgenual anterior cingulate cortex and the right temporal pole.

Much the wiser, Timid Souls?

No, nor me.

As Raymond Tallis, the philosopher and distinguished medical doctor, wrote in an essay called 'What Neuroscience Cannot Tell Us About Ourselves' (2010): 'While to live a human life requires having a brain in some kind of working order, it does not follow from this fact that to live a human life is to *be* a brain in some kind of working order. ... If we are just our brains, and our brains are just evolved organs designed to optimise our odds of survival ..., then we are merely beasts like any other, beholden as apes and centipedes to biological drives.'

In one sense, we are at our most 'animal' when in the grip of fear. Fear forces us to capitulate to a set of chemical and physical reactions controlled by the brain. At the same time, *how* we fear, with all our imagination, cognisance of time and mortality – all that hope – seems to distinguish the human animal from all others. It is both our blessing and our curse. And it adds a petrifying *je ne sais quoi* to any adversarial encounter between man and beast. An animal's gripe at that moment of confrontation is not personal – he is not that clever – but if you look with a Darwinian eye, then you realise, in a heartbeat, that this is also *intensely* personal, you or him. And he is not the one bringing a lifetime's emotional baggage to the fight.

⁂

As evening fell on Christmas Day in 2008, Sally-Ann Sutton went for a walk in the English village of Wigmore in Kent. Earlier that afternoon, a friend of Sally-Ann's daughter brought her baby son over and Sally-Ann had thought, 'Oh, that'll be lovely, that'll lighten the situation a bit'. This had been one lousy year and the Christmas spirit was scarce. Sally-Ann's elderly mother had died in the summer; then the two family dogs expired in a single week; next the beauty salon Sally-Ann ran with her husband folded and now the strain of it all had brought their marriage to the brink of collapse.

'You know when you get one of those years when everything goes wrong?' Sally-Ann says to me and laughs. She is sitting neatly on a pristine leather sofa at her flat, a bird-like woman in her fifties, pretty and well turned out, with a light girlish voice. She smiles a lot, but has a pair of those huge, sad, blue-green eyes that you find in a certain sort of 1950s wall print of wide-eyed children.

The last straw had come just days before Christmas, when an old friend had fallen down the stairs and died. The dead woman's husband, so Sally-Ann tells me, had gone 'completely to pieces' and had asked her if she might look after their dog, a small Shih Tzu, for Christmas. 'As we're doggy people,' she adds.

So there they were, five of them and the dog, celebrating, or rather surviving, Christmas together.

As darkness fell outside, the baby, Bobby, was getting fractious and as Sally-Ann had to take the Shih Tzu around the block, she suggested Bobby and his mum, Hannah, come for a walk too.

'We'll go and look at the lights,' said Sally-Ann.

They walked around the corner to Grain Road. This was 'a very posh road,' as Sally-Ann says, of well-to-do modern villas and bungalows. Every Christmas there was something of an unspoken contest here, in which the residents would try to out-twinkle one another with the opulence of their decorations.

Sally-Ann, the Shih Tzu, Hannah and baby Bobby were strolling, admiring the scene, when they heard a commotion further up the road. At first, it sounded like a domestic argument. A woman was screaming and there were other raised voices too. It was Christmas night, after all, and in many British households the sherry bottle had been out for some time. A moment later, a woman ran past, holding a spaniel in her arms and shrieking at Sally-Ann to pick up the dog. She did and looked up. In the distance, she could make out a slender woman, obviously drunk, with a huge Rottweiler on a flimsy extendable lead. The woman was struggling with the lead and then she let go. The next bit, Sally-Ann tells me, seemed to happen in slow motion.

'The Rottweiler just absolutely made for us,' says Sally-Ann, 'I've always had dogs and I had no fear of this dog when it was running towards me because I thought I'm so good with dogs it would behave itself.' She laughs. 'But it ripped the Shih Tzu out of my arms and I thought, "Oh God, if John loses his dog as well as his wife", you know, it's going to be ...'

Sally-Ann pauses, lost for words. Then she tells me how the Rottweiler dropped the small dog, which ran under a car, where the larger animal could not follow. The Rottweiler was, in Sally-Ann's words, 'going absolutely berserk' and now baby Bobby was screaming too. The dog turned, looked at him and lunged straight for the pushchair.

This was the moment when Sally-Ann, or rather *her* animal instinct, moved her to do something astonishing, which, according to the police who later attended the scene, undoubtedly saved Bobby's life. She simply jumped forward, putting herself between the Rottweiler and pushchair. The Rottweiler took Sally-Ann instead.

Weighing more than she did, it grabbed her by the arm and yanked her off her feet.

'I remember saying to Hannah, "Run!" which she did, in the opposite direction with Bobby. I could hear her screaming. He would have killed Bobby, this dog. He was shaking me all the time. Bobby was just one and he was in an open buggy, the ones that fold up, so it's easy to get in and out of the car. One shake, I would have thought,' – you can see in those big eyes of hers that Sally-Ann is picturing this – 'or two shakes and that would have been it.'

The dog then dragged Sally-Ann, on her side and back, up the street to his home four or five detached houses away.

'The strength of these animals is unbelievable when they're in full flow,' she says. 'All I remember – because your adrenaline takes over, you don't feel any pain – I could feel the entry when it bit me and I remember thinking, "just stay on my arm and don't go anywhere near my throat". Because I knew it was going to kill me. They say when you die you get flashes of your life. I didn't get any of that. I just thought, "I'm going to die". But it all happens so quickly you don't really get time to *think* anything. You just feel. It's an old feeling that comes up. Of absolute terror, you know.'

A minute or so passed on the cold, damp, dark grass of the suburban front lawn, illuminated only by Christmas lights, Sally-Ann still being shaken violently in the vice of the dog's jaws. Eventually, the owners came out and got the creature off. They took Sally-Ann into the kitchen and stood around, drunk and quarrelling about who had let the dog out in the first place. Meanwhile, Sally-Ann, who is asthmatic, just tried to catch her breath and bled copiously onto their white kitchen floor.

'This chap kept wiping all the blood up,' says Sally-Ann, 'and I kept apologising. Nobody rang an ambulance. And I knew ... I could feel my arm hanging in my coat'. In the end, Sally-Ann's husband arrived, having been fetched by Hannah. He bound the arm with strips of wet tea towel and called 999.

Her injuries were so severe that Sally-Ann was lucky not to lose her arm altogether and, a number of operations and skin grafts later, she shows me the scars. Three years on from the attack, these scars resemble a cartoon version of how your arm might look if some large, jagged-toothed beast were to bite a chunk out of it.

The police who dealt with Sally-Ann's case demanded the destruction of the Rottweiler. They were so impressed by what this diminutive woman-of-a-certain-age had done that they publicised her story, and Mrs Sutton was showered with bravery awards. She makes an unlikely hero.

Around the time we met, I had recently interviewed a veteran Zambian safari guide who had been attacked by a crocodile in the lower Zambezi and who had fought the beast off. This man had been a difficult interviewee. He lived out in the bush and was hard to track down. When we did speak, by crackly telephone line, he was so laconic about the drama with the croc as to leave one somewhat hungry at the end of the interview; all of which, of course, added to the mystique. I remember thinking that Hemingway himself might have fashioned a taciturn courage like this.

---

In contrast, the bravery of Sally-Ann Sutton, sitting there in a tidy, cream and black outfit that matches the three-piece suite and colour-coordinated pictures on her living room wall, comes quite without poetic precedent. She picks me up from the train station in her clean, warm car and, chatting all the while, offers to make me a sandwich when we get back to her flat. She is very nice and very warm and very ordinary. But when the moment came to step up to an utterly feral danger, step up Sally-Ann did. And when you talk to her about it, she is confident, adamant even, that this is simply the way she is wired to behave.

'You either run away, or you react. And so you do whatever your brain tells you to do – I believe this sincerely. I mean, Hannah froze. It's her baby and she didn't do anything. And I'm not being rude about her. That is how she reacted, she was so terrified. So I just think you've got no power over what you do. It's just inherent.'

Sally-Ann tells me about various lesser occasions when she has intervened between quarrelling couples, or queue-bargers, or a man beating his dog with a stick. This inability to stand by is clearly an important part of her identity. 'In an ideal world, I want everyone to be nice to each other, to do the right thing,' she says.

I ask whether a Timid Soul might not, somehow, teach him or herself to be brave?

'No.'

It's the only moment when Sally-Ann sounds stern.

'Really?' I ask.

'I think it's either in you, or it's not. I don't consider myself brave anyway. I am just not terribly fearful of things.'

Yet when we begin to talk about the psychological aftermath of the Rottweiler attack, toward the end of our afternoon together, it becomes clear that it has made its mark. 'I'm constantly aware of dogs,' Sally-Ann tells me. 'I'm always aware when I'm out, if a dog could be running. I would never walk past a dog off the lead. Ever.' Then she tells me about the nightmares. By day, she says, 'I can see the good in everything, but at night I just can't and ever since then, I have horrendous dreams. I'm always running, always running away. Running on the Underground, running up stairs, running, running, running, running. All the time. Always being chased. And the terror ... I wake up absolutely shaking and too frightened to go back to sleep.' Finally, Sally-Ann says that whenever she comes across an account of someone else's fear, an ugly news story or feature on *Crimewatch*, she is profoundly affected by it. 'I really overreact. I can't get it out of my mind and I will really feel terror for that person. I can feel the terror that I felt'.

'So in a way,' I ask, at the end, 'above all, you've learned something about fear?'

'Fear? Probably, yes.' And she smiles, apologetically.

Strange, is it not, how a moment of courage can so illuminate a whole hinterland of dread?

❧

An attacking Rottweiler may certainly be seen to be vicious, but few would take that to mean that these creatures are furnished with actual *vices* as such. Yet, how ready we are to assign virtue to the animals we humans love. Not two years after Mrs Sutton was attacked, another Rottweiler was given a bravery medallion by the RSPCA in recognition of the afternoon in 2009 when it went to the rescue of a woman during a sexual assault in a Coventry park.

So can an animal really be brave? Lord Byron certainly thought so. He buried his Newfoundland dog, *Boatswain*, who died of rabies in November 1808, with an epitaph that would equally well have served a saint. 'Near this Spot,' the inscription runs, 'are deposited the Remains of one who possessed Beauty without Vanity, Strength without Insolence, Courage without Ferosity [sic] and all the virtues of Man without his Vices.' I found myself wondering whether an animal's less nuanced experience of fear might be the key to a certain form of instinctive bravery. So I ventured into the moist-eyed world of the Dickin Medal, internationally recognised as the VC for our brutish cousins and awarded for 'conspicuous gallantry' in a military conflict. For the record, that is thirty-two brave pigeons, twenty-six brave dogs, three brave horses and one brave ship's cat.

To get in the mood, I visited the monument to Animals In War, on a traffic island halfway down Park Lane in London. The memorial is a vast and somewhat mawkish affair unveiled in 2004, in which life-size bronze sculptures of two put-upon-looking mules struggle toward a symbolic gap in a tall, curved stone wall, beyond which ('On The Other Side', if you get my drift) are two more life-size bronzes, one of a horse, another of dog, both looking chipper and as if they are enjoying either the Elysian Fields or peacetime or whatever the tatty patch of grass on which they stand is supposed to represent. The stone wall bears a dedicatory inscription and, set apart as a final, baleful thought, one floating and strangely unpunctuated sentence:

THEY HAD NO CHOICE

This non-sentence has been bothering me ever since. I hate to split hairs, but it strikes me that if one is to go beyond simply paying tribute to animals deployed in war and to invoke 'animal gallantry' as such, then that must surely rely upon some level of choice on the part of the beast. *Choice* is the point, is it not, courage meaningless as a virtue if not propped up by at least some degree of free will? And most philosophers, from Plato to Schopenhauer, Descartes to Dennett, would agree that free will is inextricably linked to moral responsibility (that fount of courage). My point is simply that, in order to assign and admire courage, I, for one, wish to sense that either the human or the animal involved had *chosen* to do the right thing in a moment of fear or crisis. That ability to choose and then act is, to my mind, the only thing that might yet save us Timid Souls from ourselves.

The Dickin Medal was instituted in 1943 by Maria Dickin, the animal welfare campaigner behind the British veterinary charity, the People's Dispensary for Sick Animals, now known simply as PDSA. The aim of the medal was to honour the 'gallant' and 'devoted' work of animals during World War II. It was awarded fifty-four times between 1943 and 1949, when it fell from use. The Dickin Medal was revived in 2000 and came into its own with 9/11. Duly, PDSA stepped forward to anoint the search and rescue dogs who worked in the aftermath of the World Trade Center attacks with a collective Dickin Medal, as well as two guide dogs who had shepherded their blind owners down seventy floors of the burning Twin Towers. The reception and the press coverage that followed was so ecstatic that it was soon decided that this so-called animals' VC should have a 'civilian' equivalent, a 'George Cross', if you like, and so began the PDSA Gold Medal. A lesser award, the PDSA Certificate for Animal Bravery was created too.

So I wrote to PDSA, asking if I might be permitted to sit in on an Awards Committee meeting to witness the adjudication of animal courage at work. I might as well have asked to watch the Director General of the charity take a bath. A shocked silence was followed by the retort that I was very unlikely indeed to be allowed *anywhere near* what the press officer called 'The Inner Sanctum'. In the end, I was permitted access to what appeared to be a small store room at PDSA headquarters, on an industrial park outside Telford, in the West Midlands. There I was given an hour with two very congenial PDSA employees, Gill Hubbard, Events and Heritage Manager, and Ian McKenzie, Internal Communications Manager, who were part of the team that researches and refers animal bravery cases up to the charity's trustees.

It soon became clear that we were not going to get far discussing the knottier questions of animal free will or morality. Instead, we sat hemmed in by a ceiling-high wall of generic cardboard storage boxes, with Gill finishing Ian's sentences and Ian finishing Gill's. We talked about how *Simon*, the ship's cat, caught rats and kept the sailors' spirits up, or how *Treo*, the mine-detection Labrador, discovered a daisy-chain IED in Helmand. I heard how a Staffordshire bull terrier called *Oi* sustained a terrible head injury defending his owners from machete-wielding burglars, or how funds had recently been raised to renovate the consecrated pet cemetery at Ilford where Dickin Medal winners were once buried with full military honours. When Gill told me about *Toonie*, a beagle that had returned to a burning log cabin in Canada to wake six men sleeping there, I noticed her eyes prickle with tears. It happened again later when she mentioned *GI Joe*, the messenger pigeon who had braved an aerial hell over wartime Germany.

The protocol for deciding upon PDSA animal bravery awards is intricate and relies upon citations, just like any military medal, witness accounts, and independent verification from PDSA's veterinary experts, all of which finally goes before the aforementioned Inner Sanctum of charity trustees for the ultimate decision. The criteria, Gill and Ian told me, focus on saving either a human or an animal life, via either courage or devotion to duty. When I asked about what the grey areas might be, Ian offered this example:

---

'We got [a nomination] recently,' he said, 'where someone was walking across waste ground and his dog went off and found a small bundle and barked at it. And it turned out it was actually an abandoned baby, which was as a result then saved. It went to hospital and recovered.'

Now, this was my kind of redemption.

'But we didn't consider it to be an act of bravery,' added Ian.

'Oh,' I said. 'Why not?'

'Well, it could have been a box of chocolates,' said Ian, as though that settled the matter. I must have looked disappointed, because he explained.

'It just so *happened* to be a bundle which the dog was barking at. It's not gone out of its way to do anything that you'd consider to be something it wouldn't normally do, so although it saved a life, we consider that it wasn't an act of courage, bravery, devotion to duty.'

'So it saved a life almost by accident?' I asked.

'Yeah,' said Gill and Ian in unison, nodding.

I tried later to clarify this question of how one decided what was within or outside of the behavioural norms for an animal when we discussed *GI Joe*, the World War II messenger pigeon.

'The pigeons,' I suggested, 'in a way aren't behaving out of character; they are just doing what homing pigeons do, aren't they?'

'Yeah,' said Gill, 'That's it.'

'Yeah,' added Ian.

'So those medals are just acknowledging the part they played?'

'Yeah,' said Ian again.

'That's it,' said Gill.

'Rather than saying,' I asked, a little desperately now, '*Wow, you really stuck your neck out there?*'

'Yeah,' they replied again as one and Gill fiddled for a moment with the ID tag strung on a lace around her neck.

I changed tack. Discussing the most recent award in the spring of 2011 to Dotty the donkey who defended her friend Stanley the sheep from a vicious pit bull attack, I wondered out loud whether Dotty had some rudimentary moral sense, a notion of right or wrong?

'It's a difficult one,' said Gill.

'I'd be guessing to be honest,' said Ian, 'I can only give you my opinion, but that's not really worth the paper it's on.'

A little later, he added, 'Personally, I can't see that you can prove that an animal is actually *being brave*. I can't see how you can actually prove it. It's all about interpreting a story, isn't it?'

The interview ground slowly and amiably to a halt. *Aporia* you might call it. They referred me to the PDSA senior veterinary expert, Elaine Pendlebury, with whom I talked on the phone some weeks later. Pendlebury was very clear that one must think of the animal bravery awards in terms of devotion to duty, rather than anything too complicated involving morality, and that it must be an exceptional devotion to duty, where the animal is seen to have gone beyond its immediate comfort or 'convenience' (her word, not mine) to help someone or something else. She spent much time, she assured me, seeking specialist expertise on where the bounds of usual behavioural traits may lie, but she warned against getting too mired in the philosophical 'concepts', as she called them.

'If you go down the philosophical route,' she said, 'you begin to wish you hadn't. It all becomes very difficult.' Rather than getting into some ontological tangle, one might, she suggested, instead look at the animal's selfless actions and simply say to oneself, as Pendlebury puts it, 'I should do that, really.'

❧

Maria Dickin's charity, so they told me repeatedly, is about raising the status of animals in our society, but it is not always so betwixt us and our beastly cousins. As Charles Darwin observed in his 1837 notebook, 'Animals, whom we have made our slaves, we do not like to consider our equal' and one place where his observation is laid bare, in an exuberantly savage and dangerous piece of theatre, is the Spanish bullring.

I arrived in Seville one hot night in May. Eduardo Dávila Miura, manager to Rafaelillo, the renowned bullfighter you will recall I had come to meet, had agreed to give me a preliminary interview the following morning. But upon switching on my mobile in Seville Airport, I received a message asking me instead to meet him at 11.30 p.m. that night at the bullfighters' hotel in the old town.

An espresso and a taxi later, there I was. Presently, Senor Dávila arrived, aloof, tanned and beautiful in an unsmiling, patrician sort of way. I followed him, meekly, into a room off the main hotel lobby. There he removed and neatly folded a silk tie and began, with little preamble, to go through the motions, telling me about fear and how central it is to the life of a bullfighter; how the fear of failure is always the worst; how a good bull is brave too, although they do not comprehend their own end, and how the perfect bullfight relied on a communion between man and bull, in which the man succeeds in dominating the animal. This, said Maestro Dávila, half watching a muted television set in the corner of the room and occasionally checking texts on his mobile phone, was where the beauty lay, the art, the passion. Then he said that he was tired and could I come back tomorrow night at ten? I did and, after a long wait, enjoyed another half-hour audience, during which we talked about his family's breed of dangerous bulls, the Miuras; Rafaelillo's fight the coming day; how it was 'almost impossible' to be a decent bullfighter as a woman – 'the only time I don't like women is when they are wearing the torero costume' – and how, even though a matador might be brave in the ring, many of them feared other things, like, he said, 'sleeping alone'.

We did not discuss the ethics of the *corrida de toros*. I had been told that Eduardo did not want to, but that will not stop many being appalled by what happens at a bullfight. It is gory, cruel and, some might say, pointlessly dangerous. And yet the *corrida* relies so profoundly upon a theatre of courage – that of the bullfighter, that of the animal – a courage further magnified by the process of performance, that to overlook it on ethical grounds alone would seem to me to ill-serve the Society of Timid Souls. Just as you might acknowledge bravery in the actions of a soldier fighting a war that you believe to be morally tainted, so, whatever you make of the ethics, it is difficult to accuse a bullfighter of timidity. The question of how one 'spends' or 'squanders' one's courage – and whether one can have too much – remain good ones and we shall return to them, but not before Rafaelillo, all five foot and five inches of him, in a brand new *traje de luces*, has stepped into the ring of the *Maestranza*, on Sunday 8 May.

The band trilled their nasal *pasodoble* and so 'the little bullfighter with the giant heart', as his fans among the Spanish press call him, took on his first adversary of the afternoon: Dador, meaning 'Giver', five hundred and seventy eight kilos of black Miura bull.

Miuras are the most infamously dangerous breed of bulls in bullfighting. Hemingway wrote about them in *Death in the Afternoon*, Lamborghini named a range of cars after them and one of the most famous matadors of all time, Manolete, was killed by one in 1947 in front of his adoring public. The *corrida* originated as an extempore display of pure *cojones*, but developed over the centuries into a highly rarefied art form in which great store is set by an ability to be still and to create long, elegant shapes with your body, *estatuario* as it is called, while the bull thunders by. That is why many fighting bulls have been bred to run straight and with horns that curve inwards, to allow the closest possible passage of the beast past the taut silhouette of the torero. Not so the Miura bulls. The line of their charge remains unpredictable and the horns point wide. They are larger and heavier than most fighting bulls, with a penetrating gaze that un-nerves, and, above all, they are clever. Every *corrida* is predicated upon the fact that the bull has never before this moment seen a man on foot, only on horseback. That is why he does not know that it is the man holding the cape who is his adversary, and not the cape itself. This is the trick at the heart of the torero's art, how one small man can dominate such a beast. Yet each time the bull's horn touches the cloth of the cape, the animal learns a little. This learning is called *sentido* (or sense) and the whole structure and timing of the bullfight is built around it. A bull who knows too much is a dangerous beast indeed. And if there is one thing that has earned the Miura their formidable reputation, it is that they are inclined to acquire *sentido* more swiftly than any other breed of fighting bull.

As a prelude to the first act of the fight, every bull is put through its paces with the large yellow and pink *capote* by both the matador (or killer) and by his *cuadrilla* (or team), giving the bullfighter the chance to assess him. It is also the matador's first opportunity to impress the audience and, that May afternoon in Seville, as I watched, Rafaelillo promptly extracted a cheer from the steeply banked seats by dropping to his knees in front of the bull and swirling the *capote* across his body and above his head in a flashy set move known as *la larga cambiada*. It looked suicidal to me, but Rafaelillo leapt to his feet afterwards and, smiling fixedly, gestured to the audience with outstretched arm. There was a ripple of approval. Meanwhile, the sheer size and aggression of the bull was palpable. You could smell the animal, a strong manure tang that wafted in waves, blending with all the other smells from the tightly packed crowd: cigar smoke, sweat, a discreet garlicky burp, expensive perfume. You could hear every grunt, the scuffing of the animal's hooves as it turned on the sand, almost feeling the air move as it passed. Then the trumpet sounded a tinny warble and a plump *picador*, dressed from head to toe in baby blue and gold, like some infernal cherub, rode in on a horse swagged in padded costume and blindfold. The bull charged at the horse and, as it did, the picador drove and twisted a long spear with a crossbar into the *morrillo*, the large muscle at the back of the bull's neck. This is to drop the head of the animal so that the matador can later kill it from in front and over the creature's horns, as the long-established choreography requires.

Next came the 'placing' of the *banderillas*, six long, colourfully decorated wooden sticks with metal barbs at the end, although it does not look like 'placing' to me. Here, Rafaelillo's *banderilleros* ran in on tiptoe towards the bull, arms aloft with limp wrists and barbs dangling, before jabbing them sharply into the animal's shoulders. Then they sprinted off, chased by a furious Dador. This is a kind of pantomime of peril, all men in tight, fancy costumes, mincing about at high speed, glancing theatrically over their shoulders, but it serves to enrage and invigorate the bull, ready for the final act, *tercio de muerte* (the third of death) in which the matador will show his mettle.

Rafaelillo sipped something from a small tin cup offered from the *callejon* and stepped forward, hatless, as a mark of respect to the bull, and with his smaller, red cape suspended from a slim wooden cane, the *muleta*. He began to work the bull and the crowd, with another pass on his knees, eliciting a long low 'Ooooooo' from the spectators.

Another pass. And another. This time, the bull jerked the *muleta* clean out of Rafaelillo's hand and he stood there, as though defrocked, while one of his *cuadrilla* stepped forward to distract the bull and the *muleta* could be retrieved. Another pass. Then another, in which the *muleta* went flying again. Again it was recovered. The atmosphere grew tense, everyone knowing that, especially with a Miura, this meant that *sentido* was growing and the kill must come soon. Rafaelillo executed one last pass, again on his knees, clearly his signature move, and he retired to the *barrera* to exchange the fine wooden cane for the killing sword.

Once a matador has the killing sword, then he must drive it down behind the neck of the animal, while standing in front, severing the spinal column between its great shoulder blades. It is the most dangerous moment for any bullfighter, the *faena* (the labour). As it involves leaning with one's body over the horns much has been made of the poetic potential to kill and be killed at this exquisite instant. Earlier on, the matador is part of a team, the display of courage a group effort, but now the man is on his own. An elegant, swift kill is the holy grail of all bullfighters. More to the point, although the bull must die come what may, it is a clean, skilful end that above all makes the audience go wild. But, more often than not, the death turns out something of a hash, drawn-out, all carnage and no grace. This is when, although the risk to the bullfighter remains as vivid as ever, he will hear the crowd shift and sigh, fiddle with their programmes, light a cigarette or mutter among themselves about another botched *faena*.

So Rafaelillo stepped forward with the sword and *muleta*. And let us not forget his height. For the pocket-size matador, this killing move is more difficult to execute with any elegance, not to mention more dangerous. One foot flat on the sand, the other on tip toe, shoulders at an angle and tilted sharply forward, brow furrowed, chin lowered and lips thrust out in a grimace that might look a trifle silly if the whole situation were less mortal for both man and beast, Rafaelillo then jerked the *muleta* towards the bull and lunged up and over with his sword. As the sword hit bone and as Rafaelillo turned out of the lunge, Dador tossed his great head upwards catching Rafaelillo with a massive horn on the back of one shoulder. First pushing him forward and then yanking him backwards and up, the bull hooked under the ornate shoulder piece of the bullfighter's *chaquetilla* and jolted the red cape out of the man's hand for the third time that afternoon. For a split second, you saw not the face of Rafaelillo, *torero muy valiente*, but that of Rafael Rubio, a small, scared, thirty-one-year-old man, with sandy hair, a square jaw and a big nose, his close-set eyes wide and his mouth stretched open, baring his teeth in anticipation of an agony that never arrived. By the time he was back on his feet an instant later, he was Rafaelillo again, the only signs of what had just happened a thick dangling spiral of the white wadding from inside the shoulder of his costume and the sword sticking half a meter out of Dador's back, handle swaying. As one of his *cuadrilla* skipped in, lifting the sword out and returning it to the matador, Rafaelillo exhaled sharply and barked some collision of vowels at Dador.

Eventually the bull was despatched with a clean sword thrust, to which the crowd shouted 'Ole!' The animal ran around for a few seconds, then tilted sideways and dropped, with Rafaelillo triumphantly steering the dying descent with his arm. It was not a perfect death, but it was not bad. There was applause and a shimmer of white handkerchiefs and Rafaelillo enjoyed a couple of laps of the ring with outstretched hat as disbursement for his, and for Dador's, courage.

Rafaelillo's second bull came a little over half an hour later. Heavier than Dador, he was called Navegante, or Navigator – a good name, for this was a clever bull, the very epitome of Miura so-called 'difficulty'. Navegante clearly had some suspicion about the man-cape con from the outset. Gone was any beauty or poignant struggle and watching what followed was a bit like watching a car crash (at an abattoir). Within minutes, during the preliminary passes with the *capote*, this bull simply ignored the cape and rammed Rafaelillo with his head, then, on the recoil from the blow, filleted the man's *traje de luces* with his right horn, from waist to knee, this undressing accomplished as Rafaelillo fell backwards, his hat flying, and hit the sand below the bull's head. I have seen slow-motion footage of what Rafael Rubio did next, rolling on his back, below the bull's flailing horns, and back up on to his feet the other side, leaping on to the wooden *barrera* and over it, like a circus tumbler. I was sitting near this section of barrier and so as it happened I saw Rafaelillo disappear behind the red painted wood, followed by the enormous head of the bull; I heard a thud and then the small man scrambled over to the audience side, with a torn costume and wearing that fearful expression for another second or two. More white fluffy wadding and, this time, white underpants too. As the *picador*, then the *banderilleros* gave it to Navegante with what looked like more than usual rancour, Rafaelillo stood in the *callejon* and someone bound his *traje de luces* back together with wide, off-white bandages around his waist and right leg, while a clearly rattled Eduardo paced next to him, talking rapidly. He returned to the ring, looking more wounded soldier than torero. The *faena* was short – this was simply too dangerous – a pass or two and Rafaelillo went straight in for the kill. The sword entered the bull's back up to its hilt but Navegante seemed impervious. The *verduguillo*, the stabbing sword with crossbar, was fetched and seven ugly thrusts later, the huge bull died, just as the trumpets piped up with a few clanging bars to signal that time was up. The audience did not bother to clap this time and all but ignored Rafaelillo as he left the ring. The bull was dragged out by the horses, and men in blue uniforms appeared with red-handled brooms to rake and sweep the yellow sand.

I was due to spend the following morning with Rafaelillo, but got a text from Eduardo before breakfast to say that the matador was shaken by what had happened and had left Seville before dawn to go and see his doctor back in Murcia. If I wanted to talk to him, then I would have to fly back to Seville a few weeks later.

※

It is early June when we meet again at the suburban bullring in Espartinas, an affluent suburb of Seville. Rafaelillo is here with Eduardo having a bull-less rehearsal called *toreo de salon*. I spend a morning with them in the ring, perched on the sandy step of the *barrera* with Antonio, my translator. Antonio grew up in Seville and he can barely contain his excitement to be standing on this hallowed ground even at a minor bullring like Espartinas. He whispers to me, grinning, that every Sevilliano plays the bullfighter with his bath towel when no one is looking.

Both Rafaelillo and Eduardo are in shorts and trainers and on each man's thighs you can see the silvery tracks of long, thick scars, a reminder of long-dead bulls. One of Rafaelillo's *cuadrilla*, a tall man called José Mora, is holding a pair of bull's horns, glued onto a length of wood, like the inverted handlebars of a bicycle, and he mimics in slow motion the line of a charging bull. Rafaelillo stands in front with a dirty *muleta*, enacting the moves, every grimace just as it had looked in Seville, every chivvying 'ah-ha-ah-hey-ha,' every 'Toro!' The whole effect is comic, but the aim is clear: to replicate everything, but the danger, and the fear, of a real bullfight.

Eduardo, whom everyone calls 'Maestro', is sitting on a *capote* spread out on the sand, which has R-A-F-A-E-L-I-L-L-O stencilled on it, and occasionally he jumps up to demonstrate. José soon swaps his handheld horns for a kind of metal trolley, with a plastic bull's head on the front and with a bale of hay behind for the body. Rafaelillo begins to practise the kill, over and over and over again.

'If you find the right place, Rafa,' Eduardo calls over, 'it is like butter.'

I watch him repeat it thirty or forty times over the next hour. It reminds me of the soldiers practising their battle drills for Afghanistan.

The session ends with a surreal and strangely private moment. The ring is empty now but for Rafael, and Eduardo, who is holding the first set of fake horns on the stick. For a few minutes, they practise passes wordlessly. As Eduardo shuffles in slow motion with the horns held out in front of him, you can see that he is now really acting how terrifying a bull can be. His head is down, knees bent, shoulders hunched, his handsome face gurning so grotesquely that veins stand out on his temples. With eyes that bulge, and jaw that juts, Eduardo Dávila Miura emits ferocious, bestial snorts, like one of the animals his family has bred for generations. And Rafael Rubio rehearses, in equally theatrical manner, what the courage to face him might look like too.

After the session, Rafaelillo takes me to a café nearby, which has bulls' heads mounted on the walls and where the waiter recognises him, offering much admiration along with our drinks. We sit outside and sip cold Coke and Fanta through straws as I ask him about that second bull I saw him fight in Seville, Navegante.

'A real son of a bitch,' he says. 'That was one of the most frightening bulls I have killed in my entire career. He was really clever. He was like a human being in the way he was analysing the *faena*. He predicted all my ideas.'

What I had not known at the time of the fight was that Rafaelillo's wife was heavily pregnant and a week or so later a baby daughter was born. Within hours of her birth, Rafaelillo was at the *Las Ventas* bullring in Madrid to fight his biggest booking of the year as part of the *Feria de San Isidro*. But what had happened with Dador and Navegante in Seville conspired with new fatherhood to make Rafaelillo more risk-averse than usual. Notorious as the toughest bullfighting audience in the world, the ten-thousand strong crowd had not come there to watch anything that smacked of timidity, and they booed and cat-called from the rafters of *Las Ventas*.

Rafael disappears into a bitter digression about the 'ungrateful' Madrid audience, and how they did not appreciate the risks he was taking and were asking him to do something 'kamikaze' – like 'diving into an empty swimming pool', he spits in his high-pitched, quick-fire voice. Still, Rafaelillo has a tried and tested method for coming back from the brink of failure.

He tells me about his working-class childhood in Murcia, the youngest of six children. His father was an ardent fan of the bullfight and so little Rafael faced his first *vaquilla* (young cow) at eight years' old. 'She was Bambi!' he hoots and yet he had peed his pants in terror.

'However, today,' he adds, lest this irony be lost on me, 'my reputation is that of a very brave matador.'

This transformation from timid soul is one he describes in detail. It began with some lessons at a bullfighting school, where his peers laughed at Rafael for being small and his lack of nerve in facing a real animal. 'I was a coward,' he tells me, but eventually the opportunity came to cape another *vaquilla* and, out of the blue, Rafael performed *a larga cambiada*, that highly risky move on the knees I had seen in Seville.

'From that moment, my career rocketed,' he says, 'I managed to break that fear barrier.'

This pattern has characterised Rafaelillo's career, every impasse breeched, every obstacle overcome apparently by virtue of a flamboyant leap of courage. '*Valor*' of the sort that is entwined with fear, it would seem, has long been Rafaelillo's trademark.

Rafaelillo's *alternativa*, in which a junior bullfighter is presented to the crowd as a matador for the first time, came just two months after his seventeenth birthday in 1996. For several years, he enjoyed moderate success, but, through his mid-twenties, the bookings began to dwindle and by 2007, Rafaelillo's career was on the skids. A last chance came in the form of an option to fight Miuras at the *feria* at Alicante. This was the first major festival booking for many months and Rafaelillo had little choice but to take it. It turned out to be a surprising and *valiente* performance and he was awarded the ear of the bull. Rafaelillo's career reignited. Soon came another Miura booking at Pamplona. And another, and another. 'From that moment,' says Rafaelillo, 'my name and these difficult bulls were linked. Big animals, the toughest ones. These are not the most suitable for the *toreo* that I would love to do, fine and pure *toreo*, but I am a brave bullfighter and am able to dominate these scary, big bulls. Managers and fans now associate the name Rafaelillo with these particular bulls.'

I ask Rafaelillo about injuries, specifically *cornadas* or goring, and he proudly leaps to his feet. 'I can show you several, look,' he says, 'I have four or five' and he tugs up the hem of his shorts to point out each upper thigh scar. 'This one is twenty centimetres. The horn went through my thigh here. That time, I broke my collarbone, my wrists. This one is twenty-five centimetres. I lost a litre of blood.' The fact that I am a little embarrassed by this display brings home what I already intuitively know from watching all that groin-first posturing in tight trousers that strikes anyone who sees their first bullfight as an adult. It is clearly no mere turn of phrase that this sport, or art, tests a man's *cojones*.

'This,' says Rafael having shown me the scar from his worst *cornada*, some eighteen months earlier in Quito, Ecuador, 'is the price we who risk our lives have to pay, but afterwards, as the days go by, you feel better. I felt proud of myself. It began to feel like a triumph. You feel,' he searches for the word, '*torero*, more in tune with yourself and your profession. You are more authentic, because you know that what you do has truth. Until you get wounded for the first time, you are hesitant, because you don't know how you'll react. An injury is a medal.' I think for a moment of Lord Ashcroft's VCs as Rafael goes on, 'so believe me, every torero is waiting for his first *cornada*. From that moment on, you are more respected. You know that you are able to do things that most people would never do.'

Listing the perils faced by the torero, in his boyish voice, Rafael says, 'Not just *cornadas*, but failure, indifference.' He takes a sip of Fanta. 'Disappointment,' he adds. Just before emerging into the ring, Rafaelillo goes, he tells me, to the small bullring chapel to pray. His eldest brother, Joaquín, died of cancer five years ago and Rafael says he knows that Joaquín and other relatives are there. 'I entrust myself to them.'

'Fear is always there,' says Rafaelillo. 'You never know if you are going to come home from the ring.' He repeats this sentence twice more. 'This is the greatness of our profession,' he tells me. In those moments when 'you can feel your heart racing', he says, 'you have to dominate yourself. You have to say to yourself, this is not going to ruin the day. You must be friends with fear.'

'So what *does* frighten you?' I ask, just before we part company.

'Death,' says Rafael Rubio. 'Like everyone else. Who is not afraid of it? And being ill, of course. Having a serious illness frightens me most of all.'

It is impossible, I suppose, to rehearse the mortality of the human animal inside that glittering costume. There is no audience to impress.

# 3

# The Enemy Within

It's no fun to appreciate to the full the truth of the materialist proposition that I don't *have* a body, I *am* a body.

Christopher Hitchens, December 2010

Before we go on, a brief thought experiment: suppose, if you will, that angels exist; could one such angel be capable of bravery? Think about it. Your answer, I hazard, would be 'no'. OK, now how about ghosts? Could there be such an entity as a courageous spectre? Again, I suspect, most people would say no. And so, as far as the Society of Timid Souls is concerned, the important question is *why not?*

The answer lies in the way that we intuitively believe bravery originates and is experienced in the very organs and tissues of our bodies. It has long been so. Hippocrates, or rather the followers who wrote down many of his ideas, outlined in antiquity how the heart was the literal, physical locus of a range of sentiments from lust to boldness. A Hippocratic tract on epilepsy from the fifth century BC declares that 'veins from all parts of the body run to [the heart], and it has valves, so as to perceive if any pain or pleasurable emotion befall the man.' Aristotle developed the idea, as, later, did Galen of Pergamon. Nor was this notion exclusively a western one. In the Imperial East, a century earlier than Hippocrates, the *Tao Te Ching* connected the ability to love, via the heart, with the ability to show audacity. Even the etymology of the word 'courage' is all about heart – it comes from the Norman French, '*corage*', which is derived from the Latin '*cor*', meaning 'heart'. In other words, courage emerges as an ideal bound fast with our physicality and its inevitable frailty. It resides in the heart or nerves, guts or balls, and in turn, we attach subtly distinct moral values to each bodily location, almost like medieval humours.

And that is why neither my imaginary angel nor that putative ghost could ever quite be brave – without bodies, and mortal ones at that, what could they possibly have to lose?

❦

One Sunday morning late last year, I found myself wearing a certain quantity of comical spandex clothing and clutching a curious drinking bottle with a hole in the middle, as I limbered up among the crowd to run a provincial half marathon. I am still not entirely sure what I was doing there, other than pursuing some sort of fantasy of the lissom youth I had never actually gone in for first time around.

For this race, the fifteen thousand entrants were lined up, according to the runners' expected finishing times, along a wide thoroughfare in the town centre, at the far end of which was the starting line. I was a long way off from the elite athletes, wedged in instead at the rear of the crowd with the fat people and the runners dressed up as bananas, gorillas

and, on this occasion, a duo of large, white Styrofoam lava-
tories. Before the gun, the atmosphere was skittish, nervous,
with much unnecessary stretching and jogging on the spot,
people saying things like 'Well, this is it,' or 'There's no going
back now.' All of which might sound a bit silly were it not for
the fact that then the starting gun fired, the race began and
everyone did their utmost to run the allotted thirteen miles,
whether nature or training had equipped them adequately
to do so or not. Risking pain or humiliation or both, here
were people puce in the face, silvery-haired pensioners, a pair
of soldiers in full combats lugging sixty-pound day-sacks,
students with hangovers and fairy-wings, bald men lollop-
ing, matronly women wobbling, a blind man with a hand-
written sign taped to his back, politely requesting you gave
him space as you passed.

Many were raising money for some worthy cause.
Others were here for reasons more personal and complex
than simply charity, and certainly more noble than my
non-specific twitching about getting older. These were the
people whose participation in the race seemed to be all about
contemplating, even tasting for a moment, another's more
profound physical struggles; the kind of hardship for which
you did not get a commemorative medal and a free energy
drink. One woman in her forties, pretty, with short dark
hair, came past wearing a black T-shirt emblazoned back and
front with large white letters that read, 'In Memory of Our
Beautiful Daughter, Ellie'. Then I spotted a girl with a vest
saying, 'For My Nan', followed by six or seven young men
and women with matching laminated photos stapled to their
backs, showing a woman laughing in an armchair and with
the caption, 'For Aunty Joyce'. Then came a man wearing
the tabard of a head injuries charity that said 'In Memory of
Shane, July 1979 – March 2010'.

The crowd, I realised, was full of ghosts. Were these

runners trying somehow to repay the awful, fatal bravery of the now-dead people denoted on their backs, with some kind of staged, physical ordeal of their own? It seemed that just as the gym has become the twenty-first-century church – even if you neither go very often, nor try very hard when you do, it is good to be a member – so this motley clutch of joggers had more in common with a medieval pilgrimage than a running race. For some, this had clearly become a rite built around death and illness and losing people, all this sweat and pain a way of paying tribute to a courage that surpasses all others in its Everyman quality.

You may recall that I made a big fuss a few pages back about how *true courage* (whatever cant that may yet turn out to be) must be propped up by free will, requiring a degree of dynamic choice rather than pure, Darwinian expediency. But I doubt whether young Ellie or Shane or Aunty Joyce enjoyed a great deal of choice when it came to their last days or moments. They met with the universal betrayal; for there is not a body alive that will not, sooner or later, visit this old treason upon the soul, brave or timid, that governs it. What is more, if Death is the endgame, let us not forget that beforehand comes Dying, which can be a nasty business indeed. Or there is Not Dying, which can be awful too, occasionally even worse. As for bravery in this bind, here is an adversary quite unlike an IED or a bullet, a Rottweiler or a fighting bull, an inescapable enemy trapped within that fickle body of yours. And most of us must at some point confront it.

※

'Fuck, fuck, fuck, fuck, fuck, fuck, *fuuuuuuuuuuuuck*, fuck, fuck, fuck, fuck, fuck.'

'Nnnnnnnnnnnnnnnnnneeeeeeeeuuuuuuuuuuuuughhhhhhhhhh.'

This is what the acme of everyday female courage sounds like if, that is, we are to believe the radical feminist Andrea Dworkin. She made a seminal speech to students in New York in 1975 entitled 'The Sexual Politics of Fear and Courage' and in it, Dworkin declared that 'No phallic hero, no matter what he does to himself or to another to prove his courage, ever matches the solitary, existential courage of the woman who gives birth'.

It is certainly true that giving birth is for many women the most physically testing, often viscerally fearful experience of their adult lives. Perhaps this is not surprising, given that until the mid twentieth century childbirth killed one in a hundred women who attempted it. Labour or childbed fever killed (to name but a few) two of Henry VIII's wives, Mrs Beeton, Alice Roosevelt and the woman for whom the Taj Mahal was built as a mausoleum. Even the first true feminist, Mary Wollstonecraft, could not escape this exclusively feminine quietus ten days after giving life to Mary Shelley. I could go on, but the point is this: while historically there were other horrors like smallpox, typhus, cholera and tuberculosis that killed as many or more women than childbirth, the mortal poetry of losing your life in the process of bringing forth a new one seems to have been etched on our collective consciousness as women. That, and the fact that even within the cordon sanitaire of a modern, well-equipped, First World hospital, giving birth remains, for a great many women, very, very, *very* sore. So painful in fact that, as of 2011, the National Institute for Health and Clinical Excellence (NICE) in the UK declared that it was appropriate to offer an elective caesarean to any woman suffering irredeemably from 'anxiety about childbirth', despite an otherwise normal pregnancy. Now and for the first time ever, British women who wish to become mothers are no longer obliged to face down the curse of Eve.

A few months before these new guidelines were implemented and while every mother without a sound medical excuse was still expected (on paper at least) to attempt labour, I visited the maternity unit at Southmead Hospital in Bristol. Of the seven hundred thousand or so lives that begin every year in Britain, around one in a hundred of them begins at Southmead. All three of my sons were born here, but what of the other women and of the midwives who usher in around sixteen new lives a day, often with an exhortation to their mothers to be brave? With the good offices of the Society of Timid Souls in mind, jostling with a few gory recollections of my own, I returned to Southmead's Central Delivery Suite for the day.

I met nine midwives, eight of them women, an operating theatre technician and a consultant obstetrician, both female, as well as two new mothers and a labouring one, too. Just as the army had been an overwhelmingly, although not exclusively, male environment, this place proved to be governed by women. Neither outfit would care to be accused of chauvinism as such, and nor is this what I am suggesting, but there is nonetheless something telling about a milieu so attuned and bespoke to a particular gender *in extremis*. And here the warriors most certainly were the women. Interesting, then, that among a number of the midwives I spoke to, there seemed to be a lingering doubt as to what bravery had to do with this at all. Their view seemed to be that some combination of necessity, normality and, on the whole, a happy outcome neutered much claim to courage on behalf of the labouring woman. Yet at the same time, everyone acknowledged the absolute centrality of fear. Perhaps this contradiction was just more of the self-abnegation that had made feminists from Wollstonecraft to Dworkin rage, but at the same time, it offered a glimpse of something fascinating and complex about the sexing of courage.

Take Julie Norton, for example. A midwife for nearly thirty years, she hesitated when I asked if the process of birth required some level of bravery from the labouring mother. She had been unequivocal in her view that the way to counter the fear of childbirth lay with pain relief rather than any approach that emphasised the psychological. I had then asked a question about how physical courage is often seen as a masculine quality, and she had replied quickly that women are '*definitely* better with pain, aren't we? I think we deal with things much more openly,' she said, 'Men just keep it all in, don't they?' But at this point, or perhaps because of it, Julie suddenly seemed to lose patience with me and with the whole idea that giving birth might require a quality as muscular as bravery.

'It used to be normal, didn't it?' she suddenly said, briskly. 'We're making it sound like something that it's not. It's Nature, isn't it? You're seeing it as abnormal and a brave thing to do. I don't see it like that. I see it as a process that we all have to go through if we want children. Birth is just for one day in your life and it is pain where you're going to get something at the end of it.'

I had taken up residence in the nerve centre of the place, the staff coffee room by the central midwives' desk. The atmosphere here and throughout a quadrangle of ten delivery rooms and two operating theatres was muted. Shoes squeaked on the lino. A murmur of soprano voices was punctuated now and then by a phone ringing, or the un-oiled wheel of a tea trolley. Then, lest you forgot where you were, came the occasional and muffled screaming of a woman or the first mewl of a child. In the coffee room itself, midwives in scrubs milled about on short breaks, eating, texting, flicking through *Grazia*. On one wall, there was a huge white board describing the status of each labouring woman and people would stand looking up at it.

---

'If I can get her sewn up, then I can get on with the other lady.'

'No, she's got to keep pushing for a bit.'

'They're *all* going to deliver soon.'

'I hope so.'

A doctor and some students walked in wearing theatre scrubs and in mid-conversation.

'So they repositioned the sheath,' one of them was saying, 'the abdominal sheath.'

'The what?'

'That white thing. Otherwise, she'll get hernias.'

On the other side of the room, one of the midwives was microwaving some soup. 'I did some nice twins yesterday,' she said to a colleague, and, in silence, they both watched the soup go round.

The next two midwives I met were pregnant themselves and seemed more willing to identify a requirement for some sort of collective grit among the birthing sisterhood. 'There are,' said one of them, cosily, smoothing the fabric of her scrubs over her belly, 'so many ways these ladies can be classified as brave,' and she ran through a perfunctory list of worst-case scenarios.

Numerous psychological studies both in midwifery and palliative care have identified a strong link between the experience of pain and fear. Still, several of the staff seemed keen to point out that while there were often medical reasons for some labours to be tougher than others, the position of the baby and suchlike, also some labouring mothers were, if you will, simply braver than others.

One midwife said, 'I do come out of some [delivery] rooms and think, "She is a bit wimpish." ' Another mentions the women who 'come in and they're screaming and screaming and they're just not generally coping with it. Or they want an epidural at nought centimetres and they're not prepared at all to cope with anything. They don't feel they should have to, either.'

'And do you equate that with a lack of bravery?' I asked.

I can hear a woman shrieking down the corridor.

She paused and said, 'Yeah, I guess so.'

None of the women I talked to seemed entirely comfortable with the bravery idiom, but there was one person whose ideas about birth conformed to the neat superlatives so liberally deployed in other more obvious arenas of courage. Ricky Perrett was the only male midwife on the team and he clearly thrilled to the excitement and the glamour of labour-ward life. 'What I love about the job is the adrenaline rush I get,' he said. 'As soon as I hear that emergency bell go, I'm the first one to run out of the room.' Much of the rest of the interview was devoted to an account of a spectacular breech delivery Ricky oversaw soon after arriving at Southmead, but, after some minutes, he concluded with a short paean to child-bearing womankind that appeared to suggest the whole business was entirely voluntary.

'I take my hat off,' he said, 'to every lady who's brave enough to do this.'

'*Because*,' he added, 'men couldn't cope with it.'

'Do you not think so?' I said. 'They cope with lots of things, don't they? They go to war.'

'No,' said Ricky firmly, 'if men had to deal with this, they would have designed a general anaesthetic to be implemented at six months of gestation through to six months post-natal. That's probably a little far-fetched, but yes, I'd be a puddle on the floor if I was in pain. Every day, *every day*, these mums are brave. Every day it is *extreme courage* on their part.'

The labouring mothers I talked to were less coherent on the generalities of feminine courage, but, immediately after or during birth, who the hell would be? Still, I was touched by twenty-two-year-old Abi Wiltshire, in early labour with a little girl.

'Yes, I think I'm going to have to be brave,' said Abi, leaning over with her hand on the bed and breathing noisily.

'Especially when you're in the thick of it,' said her boyfriend, Dave, sitting jiggling one leg in a plastic chair nearby.

'And then,' said Abi, 'when she's here, we've got to be brave all over again.'

In fact, for expectant mothers the risk of death is a minute fraction of what it was a century earlier, and yet for their children-in-waiting, birth remains a dangerous business indeed. Figures from 2008 show that around ten babies are stillborn in Britain every day – that is, around one in every two hundred births – and, although this hospital trust's stillbirth rate is below the national average, delivering them is a reality of the midwife's job. They tend, incidentally, to refer to them as a 'poor' or 'bad' 'outcome' and once I'd cottoned on that this medical euphemism did not refer to high forceps or a nasty episiotomy, I caught a glimpse of a whole other world of pain and of courage.

As C. S. Lewis put it in the opening sentence of *A Grief Observed*, 'No one ever told me that grief felt so like fear.' It is this grief, this terrifying Being-Left-Behind, in this case, without the baby you have carried, which calls for the real bravery. Almost every staff member I met made this point; these were the brave women. 'Nature is very cruel at times,' explained the obstetric consultant, 'and bad things still happen despite all our medical interventions. And I'm amazed by people's courage when things have gone wrong for them. We see people whose baby has died and the courage people have to show to see them get up the next day and face the fact that the baby's not alive ...' She trailed off and, without looking away, gave a little shrug.

❧

In the small hours of 6 March, 2000, a newborn infant and a forty-year-old woman with devastating abdominal injuries were carried, on a tablecloth, into the Dr Manuel Velasco Suárez Hospital in San Pablo Huixtepec, a small town to the east of the Oaxaca–Puerto Escondido highway in southern Mexico. The baby was fine, but so Dr Honorio Galvan-Espinosa told me, a decade on, he and his colleagues were shown what lay behind a 'shabby bandage': a long and deep knife wound that ran diagonally down the woman's belly for seventeen centimetres and that had been stitched up with a regular needle and cotton thread. The rural nurse who had brought the woman in, Leon Cruz, said that they were from Rio Talea, a rough settlement high in the mountains, where the injured woman and her family farmed chilli peppers; it was he who had tucked a loop or two of her bowel back into her abdominal cavity and sewn her up. Then, so Cruz told the doctors, they had driven the eight hours to San Pablo Huixtepec. He said that the woman's name was Ines Ramirez Perez and that she had just carried out a caesarean section on herself. The baby she had delivered was the tiny, black-haired bundle now suckling her breast.

Sceptical at first, Dr Galvan and a colleague, Dr Jesus Gabriel-Guzman, proceeded to operate and sure enough, when they opened up the woman's abdomen, they found an incision with irregular edges in her uterus. They 'irrigated profusely, closed the uterine and abdominal walls in layers' and the woman was put on a course of triple-strength antibiotics. Six days later, she and her tiny son were discharged and they returned home to the mountains to carry on life as any other Zapotec mother and child, other than that their story was soon to gain a mythic and global fame.

A month or so after she had been discharged, Dr Galvan

and a colleague had hiked up to Rio Talea to corroborate what they had seen and heard with locals and to speak again with Ramirez. Now certain it was true – every account matched up – they published a paper in 2003 entitled 'Self-inflicted caesarean section with maternal and fetal survival' in the *International Journal of Gynaecology and Obstetrics*.

On 5 March, when the sun was still high in the sky, Ines Ramirez Perez had gone into labour. This was to be her eighth child, her ninth pregnancy. The hours passed, night fell and the contractions intensified, but the birth itself seemed no closer. Ramirez had lost a baby girl *in utero* two years before because of an obstructed labour. In her one-room cabin, in terrible pain but failing to progress, she now began to fear for this son or daughter too. There was no clinic for fifty miles and no telephone nearby. Her husband, the only assistant in previous births, was out drinking. Ramirez told Dr Galvan that she had cleaned a knife she used for butchering animals and sat down. She drank a glass poured from a bottle of rubbing alcohol. Then she began to slice through skin, fat, muscle, across her belly. On the third attempt, she reached her uterus and pulled out her baby boy by his feet. He cried immediately. Dr Galvan said Ramirez had told him that the blood now left her body like the 'kickback from a hose' and that she thought she was going to die. Before losing consciousness, Ramirez wrapped her belly in a jumper and sent her daughter running up the rutted horse track for help. Between two and three in the morning, Leon Cruz had arrived and given Ramirez fluids, stitched and bandaged her, before beginning the long journey to San Pablo Huixtepec. As the medical paper concluded in its closing remarks, 'The maternal instinct for preservation of the offspring can, under unusual circumstances, move women to perform extraordinary acts, disregarding even their own safety and life.'

---

The press soon picked up on the story and it was syndicated around the world. Dona Ines, if not by name, now became famous, her story redolent – in this poor, Catholic country – of the vivid metaphor of miracle. As Honorio Galvan told me, 'I believe in God and for me, He has something to do with this story. However, from the medical point of view, after studying cases such as that of Dona Ines, I am fully aware of what human beings are capable of. And I see it as an extraordinary love story of a mother towards her child.'

Every newborn baby is a miracle of a sort and this particular miracle was named Orlando Ruiz Ramirez. And as I sit here recounting his and his mother's tale for edification of The Society of Timid Souls, I realise that Orlando must be nearing his twelfth birthday. I idly tap his name into my search engine, on the off-chance that Facebook or Twitter has reached a tentacle up through the chilli fields and mountain scree of southern Mexico and into Rio Talea. It has not, as far as I can tell; but I wonder if young Orlando knows that alongside all the reprints of his news story run hundreds of obstetric and midwifery forums, blogs, message boards and online medical encyclopaedias that, with one voice, marvel at his provenance and at the courage, one might even say the *solitary, existential courage*, of his mother.

❧

Which brings me to The Emperor Nero. Not because he was brave or because he was humble, but because there is a school of philosophy espousing both of these virtues that enjoys the closest of links with the histrionic, matricidal, lyre-fiddling maniac. The philosophy is Stoicism and, however the word may have drifted in modern usage from its philosophical moorings, it remains a kind of shorthand for how one might best face down 'the enemy within' – that innate physical frailty that has played arch foe to every Timid Soul that ever lived.

Stoicism itself was born in the third century BC as a scheme of thought embracing logic, physics and ethics. It came from within a kooky group of Athenian intellectuals who preferred to do their thing out of doors, under a painted porch or '*stoa*'. Their core ethical ideas were later developed first by Cicero and thereafter, in the decadent first and second centuries AD, by the Stoics of Imperial Rome, who happened to include Nero's childhood tutor and later adviser, Seneca the Younger, and also Epictetus, a former slave to one of Nero's aides.

Seneca is thought to have suffered from tuberculosis and in a letter to a friend he described his despair at prolonged ill health: 'Often I formed an impulse to kill myself,' he wrote, 'but the age of my most loving father stopped me. I thought not of how bravely I could die, but of how bravely he would not be able to bear the loss. And so I ordered myself to live, for sometimes it is an act of courage to live, too.'

And this Stoical endurance is not just an idea, not if you buy into Epictetus's *Discourses*, anyway. Indeed, endurance can be a modus vivendi for those saddled with this perennially unreliable vessel, the body; and a way of living that is not only practicable but which serves as a balm and a consolation too. Marcus Aurelius quoted Epictetus as saying, 'Thou art a little soul, bearing about a corpse'. Hardly a cheery article of faith, but the point is this: to live in a full understanding of the bleak reality of the human condition was not, so said Epictetus, simply a process of passively, gloomily yielding unto it. On the contrary, it required an engagement with what the philosopher calls *prohairesis* or volition, a re-introduction to the grim proceedings of dynamic free will and choice, in a way that could prove ultimately uplifting:

I must die. But must I die groaning? I must be imprisoned. But must I whine as well? I must suffer exile. Can anyone then hinder me from going with a smile, and a good courage, and at peace? ... Show me a man who is sick and yet happy, in peril and yet happy, dying and yet happy, in exile and happy, in disgrace and happy... Is not the subject teachable? It is teachable. Is it not within our power then? Nay, it is the one thing of all others which is in our power.

The idea that unavoidable suffering may be elevated by a choice to suffer bravely turns out to have been an endlessly rich philosophical, theological and psychological seam. Whether it is Thomas Aquinas on the 'spiritual pleasure' fortitude can give the brave man, the 'self command' raised up by Adam Smith, or the meaning to be found in suffering according to the concentration camp survivor, Viktor Frankl, these are all, in the end, a way of making the best of a bad job.

And besides, however the polemic may rage (oh yes, against the dying of the light), an established social protocol remains: that if someone has been ill, injured or has died, then it is polite and it is proper, whether true or not, to say that they have been Very Brave. This etiquette is learned from the cradle and it prevails in our house too. One of my kids has stuck to his bedroom door a round, orange and much-treasured sticker with a picture of a teddy bear in the middle of it. It was dished out by one of the nurses after a visit to A&E to fix up some playground bump and it announces proudly to the world, 'I WAS BRAVE'.

I was thinking about that sticker the day I visited St

Christopher's Hospice on a suburban street in south London. The whole place was full of dying people, waiting in the cappuccino queue, playing Monopoly with family in the outpatient room, sitting in a circle of high-backed chairs in the gym doing a breathlessness workshop with the physio, or lying in bed, watching red double-deckers rumble up and down Lawrie Park Road. Everyone here should have one of those stickers, I thought, but they do not give them to grown-ups, do they?

St Christopher's Hospice opened in 1967, the brainchild of Dame Cicely Saunders, a former nurse with pioneering ideas about the care of the dying and now widely hailed as the architect of the worldwide hospice movement. 'These patients are not looking for pity and indulgence,' wrote Saunders in a paper in the *Nursing Times* in 1965, 'but that we should look at them with respect and an expectation of courage ... and we will see an extraordinary amount of real happiness and even light-heartedness.'

Recently renovated and all light and space and calm, the hospice Saunders founded is now considered an international flagship of modern palliative care, and anyone who has watched someone they love fall away from them in one of the more usual drab places where the old and ill go to die will probably find themselves, as I was, a little envious and sad when they set eyes on St Christopher's. Yet, however impressive and redemptive its philosophy, the sparkling facilities, the taboo-busting openness or kindly, enlightened staff, the place remains, as I mentioned, *full of dying people*.

And dying does not look much fun to me. My own lovely father had done it just a few months before my St Christopher's visit, thanks to a succession of strokes that wrought a kind of carpet-bombing of his brain. As I had sat beside his bed in a nursing home in Northampton, I recalled the first moment that, as a little girl aged five or six, I realised my father was fallible. It was 1978 or thereabouts and McDonalds had just opened on Kensington High Street in London. Daddy said he would buy us some real American milkshakes and we made a special trip downtown. My sister and I waited in the car, kneeling up on the leatherette of the back seat and watching through the rear windscreen for him to emerge. He walked back towards the car grinning at us with four shakes, two for us and one each for my mother and him, stacked up two high in each hand. On reflection, it was a silly way to carry a milkshake. Halfway across the pavement, they tumbled, slicking pints of pink and brown froth across the concrete. I can still feel, in the pit of my stomach, the regret and slight embarrassment I saw on Daddy's face, blended with our own childish disappointment. He disappeared to buy some more shakes and carried them out more sensibly this time, but the queasy feeling stayed with me for the rest of the day, and I have never forgotten it. Now, as he lay in bed surrounded by a metal railing and no longer able to see or swallow or speak, he held my hand very tightly, less as he might have held it in the past, as a squeeze of affection, or to help me climb a high step, than as some unwitting expression, as I read it, of the extremity in which he now found himself, as one might hold on to a vital scrap of paper or a fifty-pound note in high wind. He died two days later.

It was perhaps because of this that I felt the predicament of the St Christopher's patients I talked to that day rather more keenly than I might have done at another time.

One of them was Cardiff Scott, an outpatient, only just fifty years' old and built strong and stocky. He discovered he had an aggressive form of bone cancer in 2008, when a girlfriend playfully pulled him by the legs off a bed and one of his vertebrae, so he told me, smashed like 'a packet of crisps'. Wearing a T-shirt with a golden sunset, silhouettes of palms and the word JAMAICA printed across it, Cardiff told me how he had moved to Britain in 2000. We had met by chance in the art room at St Christopher's, where I had just watched a group of ten very ill people, including Cardiff, make a large, cheerful collage together. It offered a strange contrast to the grim monotony of Cardiff's tale as it unfolded, via a lengthy account that was all times and dates, names of drugs, wards, and doctors, everything explained according to the days of the week on which each detail occurred. 'And by Sunday afternoon about six o'clock ...' he would say, or, 'that was on the Tuesday morning'. Perhaps this is how you measure and mark time when time feels short. At the worst moments, Cardiff could not walk or even turn in bed, his pelvis disintegrating, and he was given weeks, even hours to live. And yet somehow nearly three years later he is still here and he is even moving about on crutches. He told me that he did not 'feel' like he was going to die, 'not today, not tomorrow, not this week, not this year' and that he had spoken out to the doctors who said otherwise: 'I said I don't want you telling me that I am going to die. Don't tell me that. Because I am a man who believe in God [sic] and I don't believe he is ready for me. I know I am going to die *at some point*. When, I don't know. Some nurses say to me, they say *you don't seem to know what is going on*. I do. I do know what is going on. But if I am afraid of dying, I am still going to die. And if I am not afraid, I'm still going to die. So what's the point? Enjoy yourself. Have a little drink, have a little chat. And that is why, Polly, I *fight* myself out of a wheelchair, I *fight* myself from using a commode at home, I *fight* to use the toilet, I *fight* myself to make a cup of tea, I *fight* myself to walk. Fighting is how you cope. *Fight* until you die.' He spits the word 'fight' across the room.

I was reminded of the time I spent with the soldiers of 1 Rifles and stuck by the irony that while soldiers prefer not to talk about 'fighting' as such – they refer to 'contact' with the enemy, or an episode that is 'kinetic' – all that martial, bellicose talk seems so common as to be almost trite when it comes to serious disease; and never more so than with the ultimate Enemy Within, the 'invader', cancer.

Fighting was one form of courage here, for sure, but so was *not* fighting and not everyone bought into the beefed-up idea about combat.

'I don't think it *is* a fight, as such,' Alan Hopkins told me, mildly. Sixty-seven years' old and with Dickensian whiskers, round cheeks and one of those mouths that smiles naturally at rest, you nevertheless got the impression that Alan was clinging on. 'The only thing I keep stressing is *don't give up*. It's no good saying, *it's a fight, it's a fight*. It's not. You've just got to get through it.'

Alan's wife of forty-six years, Maureen, was being treated as an outpatient at St Christopher's for oesophageal cancer. 'If I panic,' he told me, 'then she's going to be worse, so that is why I'm staying positive.' He didn't look very positive. 'Even if there isn't any hope,' he added, 'you've still got to put up that face, you know, you've got to. If I don't do it, then she's going to go to pieces.' Clearly, as C. S. Lewis wrote in that passage about grief and fear, the people who are dying are not the only ones who need to be brave.

It is tempting, is it not, to imagine that we were somehow better equipped to face all this in the past, before the marvels of modern medicine cocooned us from a cognisance of our physical frailty? Many have proselytised lately about how we as a society have 'Forgotten How To Die' (like we used to be good at it). The hospice movement is all about finding 'better' ways of dying, a 'good death', if you like, just as philosophers have long discussed a 'good life'. And theirs is a sound response to the way in which the dying and their families have, in latter years, been encouraged to clutch at heavy-handed medical intervention, in order to buy hours or days, postponing the inevitable or cloaking it with euphemism, rather than seeking a more calm and candid end. All such institutionalised denial is surely the marker of a craven age and Epictetus or Seneca would no doubt have approved of us recalibrating our expectations in this regard.

And yet I cannot help thinking that, however shielded we may now be from the afflictions and pestilence of old, human beings have always been frightened of dying. People live longer now than they used to, yes, but they do all still die *in the end*; that has not changed. Consider for a moment an immaculate little speech in Shakespeare's *Measure for Measure*, written more than four hundred years ago. In it, a young gentleman called Claudio, languishing in a cell on the Viennese equivalent of Death Row, laments, 'Ay but to die and go we know not where,' before launching into the most vivid litany in all English literature of the possible horrors or blankness that may lie beyond the grave. He concludes:

> The weariest and most loathed worldly life
> That age, ache, penury and imprisonment
> Can lay on nature is a paradise
> To what we fear of death.

And he promptly begs his sister, a nun, to buy his reprieve by having sex with the man who sentenced him. OK, so Claudio is no paragon of courage, or virtue of any kind, but you cannot help seeing his point about dying.

'I think the human instinct is always to survive, isn't it?' was how Nigel Hartley, the Director of Supportive Care at St Christopher's put it. The best counsel Nigel said he had ever been given, in a twenty-five-year career, was that at those times when something awful is happening (like you are dying), then sometimes, the only thing to do is 'the next thing'. He added, 'that actually you can't do anything *other* than the next thing, whatever that happens to be. You can't suddenly leap months ahead. You just have to take the next step and maybe that's how people live when they're dying. *You do the next thing.* It's as mundane as that. It's life in its most basic sense. Because the next thing might be a step. It might get down to the fact that actually the next thing is taking the next breath. Until suddenly there isn't another one.'

If you ask me, this is a damned fine, a *microscopically* fine definition of the human courage impulse.

Nigel and I were sitting in his office downstairs from the wards. The whole wall above his desk was covered with pictures, leaflets and photos, personal stuff, rather than hospice business. Towards the end of our conversation, Nigel pointed out a picture of an orang-utan pinned halfway up the wall.

He went on to tell me about a woman who had come into the hospice for the first time a few years before. She was just forty-five and suffering from chronic obstructive pulmonary disease, which causes airways in the lungs to constrict. She was in a wheelchair and on constant oxygen. She arrived first thing in the morning but, so Nigel told me, 'they couldn't get her into the building.' For a lot of people, he explained, stepping inside a hospice is 'admitting something'. So the woman was initially in the car park and eventually staff persuaded her into the garden, where she stayed until two o'clock that afternoon. One of the nurses eventually called Nigel and said, 'Look, we've been sitting with this woman all day. We've got half an hour before her taxi arrives, could you come and sit with her?' So Nigel went out and there she was, so he told me, 'with a fag on and an oxygen bottle, struggling to breathe'. She was very distressed and 'sobbing', saying to Nigel, 'You must have seen people die. What's it like to die? What's it going to be like when I have my last breath? Is it going to happen today?' She had been doing this all day and, at first, Nigel was at a loss, but after a while he leant forward and, touching her arm, he said,

'Can I stop you?'

---

There was a moment's silence.

'And then,' Nigel told me, 'I heard myself say to her, "What makes you laugh?" Immediately I thought, "Shit, what the hell have I said that for? What a ridiculous thing to say to a distressed woman." '

But quick as a whip, she replied.

'Orang-utans,' she said.

Nigel paused. 'Well monkeys, chimpanzees,' he said, improvising, 'they all look the same to me. What's different about orang-utans?'

'No, they're really funny,' she said.

The woman went on to explain that she had an eight-year-old son and that they lived alone together. She said that they had adopted an orang-utan at a monkey park, sending money every month and in exchange receiving photos and anecdotes about their adoptee. 'And they're really so funny.' She continued for some time until suddenly she stopped.

'Of course, orang-utans abandon their children,' she said. 'How can anyone abandon their child?' and she spiralled back into despair.

Her driver arrived soon after and Nigel said goodbye.

'And I thought I'd never see her again,' he said, but some days later, one of the nurses said, 'There's someone here who wants to see you.'

'And I went up to the outpatient centre and there was this woman, waving at me.'

Nigel walked over and she said, 'I've got something for you.'

She pulled out an envelope from her handbag and passed it to him.

'Can I open it?'

'Yes,' she said, 'open it.'

Inside was the picture of the orang-utan.

'My son and I were on the internet for hours last night,'

she said, 'trying to find you a really good photo of an orang-utan.'

'Oh thank you,' replied Nigel, 'that's really kind.'

'As we were looking,' said the woman, 'I realised that even though orang-utans abandon their children, the children survive.'

'It was,' Nigel told me, 'one of those extraordinary moments where she was saying "Yes" to letting go herself. And actually there's nothing more courageous than realising you can let go of your child. She died two days later.'

❧

I say! I say! I say!

A man goes in to see his doctor, and after some tests, the doctor says, 'I'm sorry, but you have a fatal disease.'

'That's terrible!' says the man. 'How long have I got?'

'Ten,' says the doctor.

'Ten? What kind of answer is that? Ten months? Ten years? Ten what?'

The doctor looks at his watch. 'Nine.'

This is how an American computer scientist, Hal Finney, opened a 2009 entry on an academic community blog, in which he revealed that he too had just been diagnosed with a fatal disease. To those that knew him, this was very Hal, low-key, droll, to the point; but the diagnosis itself was no joke. Indeed, it is hard to think of a worse one. Hal Finney was told he had a degenerative motor neurone disorder called ALS or Amyotrophic Lateral Sclerosis, and the fact that it is fatal is just one final, devastating ornament to what it does to you first.

Hal Finney's is one of those names one would never encounter in the normal run of things, but, among the cognoscenti of Silicon Valley and beyond, it is much respected.

This is the man who wrote much of the code behind one of the pillars of the free internet, one of a discreet handful of master craftsmen behind the technological revolution that changed the world.

Hal had studied computer sciences at Caltech in the mid 1970s and during his freshman year, he met Fran, tiny, dark and pretty, with an oceanic smile. They had married straight after graduation in 1979, had two kids and moved to Santa Barbara. Life was good. As Hal's career as a programmer progressed, he got into cryptography and wrote much of the code for the groundbreaking open-source encryption software known as Pretty Good Privacy, or PGP. When PGP became a major company, Hal had a great job there. He was, it seemed, at the height of his powers.

Having turned fifty, Hal decided in his leisure time to take his personal fitness more seriously. In 2007 he began to run long distances, building a techno-geek's training programme with much graph analysis of data about his speed, distance, and so on. Then 'all of a sudden', so Fran tells me when I met the Finneys in the spring of 2011, 'things started to go wrong'.

Almost overnight, Hal's graphs went weird, the rate of sporting improvement suddenly falling away. This was at the beginning of 2009. At first, the doctor said that such a lull was part of the aging process. But by March, his speech had become slurred, so they returned to the doctor and the tests began. It was in June that a neurologist friend first mentioned motor neurone disease, and uttered three letters that Hal had not heard assembled into an acronym before: 'A', 'L' and 'S'. This, said the friend, was 'the worst-case scenario'. More tests and in August, a definitive diagnosis of ALS came back. It was at an early stage – Hal was still working and running – but this was a disease, he was told, which did not hang about.

Sometimes known as Lou Gehrig's disease, after the famous New York Yankees player struck down by it in 1939, Amyotrophic Lateral Sclerosis causes nerve damage and rapidly progressive muscle atrophy, paralysis and ultimately respiratory failure. The disease takes from its sufferers, with alarming speed, the ability to walk, talk, move, eat and eventually even to breathe. Most die within just two to three years. In the meantime, ALS does not affect the higher brain functions, the ability to think, reason and experience emotion, and there is little pain, all of which puts its victims in a unique philosophical position. As another prominent ALS sufferer, the historian Tony Judt, had told a journalist seven months before his death in 2010: 'I'm just a bunch of dead muscles, thinking.' By virtue of this mental clarity retained while physically dying, it is hardly hyperbolic that the condition is often described as being 'buried alive'. I recalled one of the long-serving nurses at St Christopher's Hospice saying that she considered motor neurone disease as 'the worst thing to get' and that she always thought of the ALS patients as being the very bravest of all.

Besides, there are always 'exceptions', *luckier* unlucky folk, those diagnosed with ALS for whom the disease progresses more 'indolently'. Hoping to be among them, in September 2009, a month after the bad news, Hal and Fran ran the Santa Barbara Half Marathon together, if only to make the point that they could. But, at this race, the ghost running with Hal Finney was to be his own.

Fran shows me a photo of the two of them crossing the finishing line together. They are beaming, sweaty and pink-cheeked, their heads thrown back in relief and they are holding hands, raised up in triumph. 'But it wasn't a triumph,' says Fran. 'For Hal, a half marathon used to be nothing, but this one, it took a lot out of him. I did not know at the time, but that was the last long run he ever went on in his life.' She pauses and then, shaking herself free of the thought, points to the figures in the photo saying, 'So I'm there, saying, "Yeah! We did it!" and there's Hal going, "Oh this is so hard. I can't believe how hard this is."'

Hal himself interjects in this story, for I am in dialogue with both of them. In the first of our two interviews, which come six weeks apart in March and April of 2011, Hal is just able to speak, a series of muffled grunts and groans unintelligible to my ear, but which Fran, who stands behind him, half-leaning on his shoulders half-hugging him, then 'translates'. This brake on communication keeps Hal's answers to my questions short, but the man's eyes are like nothing I have ever seen. This first interview is only by webcam, but even here his eyes dance with warmth and energy and animation. It is as though he is peeking – impishly and entirely against the rules – over a high wall designed and built to shut him out, but not, thankfully, quite able to do so.

'I never recovered from this race,' is what he says and he opens his eyes a little wider to emphasise how very lousy this turn of events was. Fran explains that the evening following the half marathon, Hal's muscles seized up and he couldn't move. It was a week, she says, until he was limping again. It was as though he had in a single day unwittingly squandered some finite physical resource. 'I miss running and it was a sudden and unexpected loss.' He gets emotional for a moment and then musters himself. 'But the key to understanding my reaction to this is that I am very adaptable. Once I was no longer able to run, I viewed it as a chapter in my life that was over. Like if you've been living in a really nice area and then you had to move away. You regret it, but then you go on to find ways to enjoy your life in your new circumstances.' So running gave way to walking, and then walking with sticks, and then to a wheelchair, later a motorised power wheelchair. He does not go out much now.

A month after the race, Hal Finney wrote the blog entry that opened with the joke about the doctor and went on to announce to the wider world that he had ALS. He entitled it 'Dying Outside' and this was what now began to happen to Hal with pitiless speed: 'Even as my body is dying outside,' he wrote, 'I will remain alive inside.' This was both a threat and a promise, for here on his blog post, Hal Finney swore, in the clearest of terms, to do what 90 per cent of ALS sufferers do not do: that is, to choose to live. In practical terms, this meant that before respiratory failure was imminent, Hal would opt by prior arrangement for tracheostomy and mechanical respiration in order to stay alive. This way, survival with ALS becomes a long-term possibility, as evidenced over forty years by Stephen Hawking. Hal wrote:

> It seems then that calling ALS a fatal disease is an over-simplification. ALS takes away your body, but it does not take away your mind and if you are determined and fortunate, it does not have to take away your life. ... I hope that when the time comes, I will choose life. ... I may even be able to write code and my dream is to contribute to open-source software projects even from within an immobile body. That will be a life very much worth living.

The power of communication, says Hal, has been the one thing that is most difficult to adapt to losing. 'Luckily Fran can still understand me most of the time,' he says and Fran translates the line for me. Then she explains how hard it is if Hal attempts to articulate an unimportant non sequitur, or an out-of-the-blue thought, which can be tricky to understand without the context; and so he edits himself differently these days.

I ask whether it feels like a battle sometimes.

'I delegate the battle-fighting to Fran,' says Hal and he smiles.

'Yes, I feel that it is,' says Fran, 'it *is* a battle. Hal adapts. I fight and Hal adapts. And you need both, but I've been frustrated because I haven't been very successful in this battle. It has always been the case in the past that if I try hard enough or fight hard enough or work hard enough, I get my way, but it seems like this one is more difficult.'

I ask them about courage, hers and his.

'I don't have a choice about being brave or not brave,' says Fran. 'I just need to be there.'

Hal adds, 'I don't really view myself as brave. I'm just surviving,' but Fran mentions his not uncontroversial determination to live, even if it means artificial respiration, the place where the majority of ALS sufferers draw the line.

'I think it's bravery to choose to stay on and I'm really happy Hal has that attitude because' – Fran's voice begins to wobble – 'I don't have the bravery right now to deal with it if he chooses not to stay. I'm terrified and I want him around.'

Still, this decision is a long way off, months or even years. Or that is what Hal and Fran thought, until less than a week after this, our first conversation. Then suddenly Hal began to experience laboured breathing, his symptoms dominoed and on 18 April he had an elective tracheostomy. The upside of this highly invasive procedure, which amounts to hacking a large hole in the windpipe at the front of the throat, was one of increasing the chance of long-term survival, by facilitating connection to a respirator. The downsides were manifold and vivid: no speaking, no eating, unholy discomfort.

'Short-term sucks,' says an exhausted-looking Fran and she laughs a mirthless laugh, when I visit a week and a day after Hal gets out of hospital.

That the Finneys even allow me across the threshold of their home in Santa Barbara at such a time is testimony to what decent, open people they are. This was the week I was to be in California interviewing for the book and of course, no question, I must come by and see them as planned. When I get there, it looks like hell. The house, an open-plan single-storey villa in a nice suburb, is full of medical equipment, with the family furniture pushed back against the walls. Hal is up, dressed and in his wheelchair, but he is clearly very uncomfortable. Periodically, Fran has to use a small device to suction mucus, which he cannot shift, out of the opening in his throat and those eyes of his look a little desperate at times. An automatic machine clicks on for several seconds every now and then. At one point, after a terrible suffocating cough, the white flannel pegged in front of Hal's throat wound is flecked with blood. Now it is no longer possible to speak and anything Hal wants to say he types onto the screen of an iPad with a short, black, prodding stick, clutched in a crumpled hand.

'Right after this surgery,' writes Hal, letter by letter, 'I questioned if dying wouldn't have been much simpler.' Then, he pushes a button and an automaton voice reads the sentence. Fran adds that the first thing Hal communicated afterwards was that 100 per cent of the time he was trying to suppress his urge to cough, 'he couldn't move and his whole existence was trying to suppress the coughing.' Hal jabs with his stick on the touch screen and looks up at me. 'There's a plastic tube in my throat that's irritating,' says the voice.

The couple are both plainly still reeling from the shock. 'We didn't know it was going to be like this a year ago,' says Fran. 'A year ago Hal was *walking with a cane*.'

Hal is typing again. We wait for him.

'I didn't realise I would lose speech so completely. I've been essentially mute for two weeks.'

'Was it frightening?' I ask.

'More frustrating than fearful,' Hal types. 'I do feel fear when mistakes are made or someone is hurting me and I can't make myself make a sound. But I have trouble getting myself to feel afraid about the long term. I figure things will work out OK.'

'Hal is *so* reassuring,' says Fran, her eyes filling, 'When I learned that Hal had ALS I was so panicked and Hal's reaction was, "don't worry, don't worry, we have time," and we have had some time.' She laughs. 'We haven't had as much time as I was hoping, but we have had time, a year and a half. Still, I can't think about the long term, Polly, because it does scare me, so I'll let Hal give me the courage that he has.'

Sitting there, I realise how symbiotic their two forms of bravery are. This is a kind of collective courage in miniature, built around this marriage in which each mettle would be impossible without the other – Fran fighting, Hal adapting, Fran caring, Hal enduring. This seems to be how they have both instinctively wrung some element of choice from circumstances that neither would ever choose.

Hal is typing again. 'It's about accepting what happens and making the best of it,' says his computer voice. 'We are all born with a death sentence. Focus on what you can do and can control.' He looks at me, as the voice repeats his words.

'I hope for two or three more years,' he says. 'Any more will be a bonus.'

I get not the merest whiff of anger or sense of injustice from Hal Finney and I say so.

'Sometimes, I get angry while we're out driving,' he types and we wait, 'Not at fate.' He grins.

I finish by asking about the extraordinary existential position that comes with ALS, the one that means your fall is not softened by any loss of mental clarity.

'We don't want his fall softened!' says Fran quickly.

Hal has been typing.

'I will still be "me" to the end,' says the voice.

I ask whether surviving this is in some sense about *throwing* your intellect at the situation.

'Oh, Hal doesn't *throw* anything,' says Fran laughing. 'He just adjusts. He works with the situation and as the situation changes, he works with the new situation and as that changes, he works with the new situation. He looks at his options and he makes choices. If his options change, he makes new choices.'

'And does that,' I ask, 'have something in common with how you write code?'

Hal types. 'A little bit,' comes the answer. 'I like to write code that is small and clean.'

Fran adds, 'Hal used to write elegant code.'

❧

After my visit, Hal's ALS progressed 'dramatically,' so he wrote to me in the middle of 2012. 'It has been constant change, but slow enough that we can adapt.' Fran told me that Hal could no longer control his facial muscles, make sounds of any sort, or use his hands. He was fed through a tube into his stomach and used the ventilator at night.

'I do not seek out mental challenges as I once did,' he wrote. 'Survival takes all my energy.' This and the remaining fragments of communication that were still possible for Hal were undertaken with the help of eye-gaze software. 'But life is still good,' said Fran, 'and although I don't like to look ahead, there are lots of happy times, mostly happy.'

'Because you're together?' I asked.

And to this, they both replied, 'Yes.'

Just before Christmas 2012, Hal emailed me – in person for the first time in many months – to say that things had 'somewhat stabilized.' He was even writing some code, 'although I'm probably fifty times slower than before. Still', he wrote, 'it gives me real pleasure'. This, as he had predicted, was 'a life very much worth living'.

---

# 4

# Elemental

If people think Nature is their friend, then they sure
don't need an enemy.

'A Precautionary Letter to the Next Generation',
Kurt Vonnegut

Are you sitting comfortably? Then I'll begin.

Once upon a time, there was a farmer. The farmer had two
sons, one intelligent and able, the other stupid and lazy. The
intelligent and able one, the elder of the two, did much to
assist his father. But even so, if there were any task to accomplish after nightfall or that might lead his footsteps through
the dank gloom of the cemetery or some other dismal place,
then the boy would say, 'Oh no, Father, I would rather not go
there! It gives me the creeps!'

The fearful boy's younger brother – the stupid and lazy
one – was much bemused by this sentiment. Whether it rose
from the lips of his sibling or was uttered by another in the
village, the boy could not for the life of him understand what
these 'creeps' were. So one day he addressed his concerns to

his father, who just happened to be mid-lecture about his youngest son's need to learn something other than idleness and folly.

'Yes, Father, I will gladly learn something new,' said the boy, 'I should like to learn how to get the creeps. That is something I know nothing about.'

And so it was that with howls of derision still ringing in his ears, the boy left home to learn fear.

*The Boy Who Left Home To Learn Fear* is one of those fairy tales from the Brothers Grimm that has not made it into modern childhoods. For, instead of a cogent moral tale with a sound lesson at the end, there follows a surreal and grisly catalogue of distortions, all hanged men, hellcats and mutilated bodies that tumble from on high. In turn, the eponymous boy visits upon them either disturbing violence or equally disturbing indifference; yet, come what may, 'the creeps' still elude him. At the end, a princess, whose hand the boy has won thanks to his 'bravery', tips a bucket of minnows over him as he sleeps and he awakes exclaiming, 'Oh, I've got the creeps! I've got the creeps! Now I know what the creeps are!'

This odd little story appears three times in different forms among Grimm's fairy tales and although the narrative itself mutinies in the face of a neat allegorical reading, *The Boy Who Left Home To Learn Fear* nonetheless stands as part of an old continuum: one that links an understanding of the nature of dread (and how to overcome it) not with birth or death, but with the messy, hormonal business of growing up. Rites of passage that test a young man's courage crowd the annals of anthropology too; from tribal Papua New Guinea to the wine-dark Aegean, the Amazon Basin to the streets of South Central LA, all over the world and forever, boys have been leaving home to learn fear; and I dare say, one or two girls have too.

For a century or more, psychological science has looked for a normative developmental model for the ebb and flow of fear through childhood, in an attempt to understand the common reasons why and how fears are acquired and then overcome, as well as sifting those intrinsic to growing up, from those that are out of the ordinary and damaging. There have been literally hundreds of studies of youthful terror, across a wide spectrum of methodologies. Some focus on age or on gender, others on socio-economic factors or cultural difference. Throughout, there are strong threads: particular thresholds in childhood when one set of infantile fears gives way to another; and the marked difference in the reporting of fear between boys and girls as they approach their teens (a product, it is believed, of social conditioning). Another paper appeared recently, published by a team of psychologists at Erasmus University in Rotterdam (Muris, Mayer, Schubert, 2010) and this time researchers have chosen the opposite tack, instead examining how *courage* develops in childhood. They called the paper 'You Might Belong in Gryffindor' (the next line being, 'where dwell the brave at heart!', in case the *Harry Potter* song has passed you by).

In this study, in order to test personality type and basic anxiety levels, a range of questionnaires were issued to 327 Dutch schoolchildren between the ages of eight and thirteen, as well as a bespoke self-report scale called the Courage Measure for Children (CM-C), and a series of imaginary courage scenarios that the children were then asked to rank in order of bravery. Finally, each child was asked to describe the most courageous thing they had ever done. Over 70 per cent felt that, at some point in their short lives, they had done something brave. One kid wrote of cycling home through a dark wood at night, another of stealing money from Mum's purse, another of fishing a small brother out of a swimming pool. Above all, here was a group already alive to the ideal of courage, if not quite the nuance, and, particularly among the boys and the less innately anxious children, actively eager to step up to the plate.

And so, inch by timorous inch, each child navigates the earliest fears of infancy, learning that the world is bigger than the room they are in, or the house that is home, or the street on which their house stands, or the town that lies beyond the street; and on it goes. This coming of age, this daring to look beyond the end of your own nose towards the wider world, and some self-sufficiency within it, is all about learning to be brave. Taken to its natural conclusion, this particular part of growing up, and the bravery that accompanies it, reaches some kind of climax when faced with the wider world at its most untamed, its rudest and roughest, its most elemental. We have looked at the Enemy Within, but this is the Enemy Without. Yes, Timid Souls, I do hope you have brought some stout shoes; for I am talking of earth convulsed, winds that roar, mountainous seas, oceans of fire – and of how to face these elements as one small man or woman.

❧

For as long as I can remember, way back into early childhood, I have had a recurring dream, or rather a recurring nightmare. The setting and the story varies, but one part of the slumberous vision – the bad part – has remained the same for more than thirty years. At some juncture in the dream, which always begins in carefree mood, I glance behind me or out of a window and I catch a glimpse of what appears to be the shoulder of a distant hill or some bank of dark cloud above the horizon. I turn to take a second look and now the nightmare really begins, for it is neither a hill nor a bank of cloud, but a vast wave, epic in scale and advancing fast. Sometimes this realisation alone is enough to hurl me into wakefulness; at other times, I must wait until the wave towers over me, black, roaring and foaming, and I gulp one final breath before it consumes me and I jolt awake, clammy and clutching the duvet. Do not ask me why this of all images has lodged so firmly in my frontal lobe – I have no idea – but it is to me the quintessence of fear.

Which is why I found myself a bag of nerves in the press pit at the Billabong XXL Global Big Wave Awards in the spring of 2011. This is one of the biggest dates in the surfing calendar and I had blagged a ticket to the event some months before, hopeful of how these men and women who rode walls of water sixty-, seventy-, even nearly eighty-feet high might enlighten the Timid Souls of our Society. I had even flown out to Los Angeles to attend, but the one thing I had failed to do was to prepare myself for the large cinema screen on the stage in front of the press enclosure, which appeared to be playing my nightmare over and over again to a soundtrack of thumping dance music. The effect rendered me unable to exchange even the basic pleasantries with my fellow hacks, as I stared at the screen with a facial rictus that I hoped might pass for admiration and held on to my note-taking pencil tightly.

Aside from the presence of one jittery English stowaway, Billabong XXL was an out-of-the-box awards affair, held at a large venue in Anaheim, Orange County, not an hour from downtown LA. There were limos, red carpet, banks of photographers, lasers sweeping the sky and bouncers with headsets using gold ropes to control different VIP areas, like drovers at a cattle market. The big trophy of the night, The Ride of The Year 2011 (like the Oscar for Best Picture), was raised on a plinth in the welcome enclosure and pneumatic girls in improbable heels hung around it. The guys in the crowd exuded studied informality, all pressed shirts and jeans, Vans and Ray-Bans, even though the sun had already gone down.

During the ceremony itself $130,000 was to be dished out to the bravest and the best. The spectacle relied on the two-thousand-strong crowd watching video footage of the world's biggest storm swells being surfed, the acme of a niche sport that has grown exponentially since the late 1980s. There are, you see, a few tracts of ocean around the world that offer, on a handful of the wildest days in each year, individual breakers so huge that one can barely believe they are real. Each monstrous wave has a character of its own and the surfing community has given each of them a name to match – *Shipstern Bluff* off Tasmania or *Cloudbreak* in Fiji, *Prowlers* in Irish waters or *Pico Alto* (High Peak) in Peru. At the awards ceremony, each break summoned a different reaction from the crowd too. The one that seemed to make them gasp, cheer, whistle, whoop more than any other was called *Jaws*, which thunders onto the reef off Maui in Hawaii. A montage of vicious wipeouts drew long 'Ooooooooo's from the audience, as surfers on screen disappeared into an assortment of waves that looked, frankly, like The End of Days. One particular tumble into the jaws of ... well ... *Jaws* even caused a few of the devoted to cry out as though in pain. I just felt a little sick.

Some minutes later, *Playboy*'s Playmate of the Month for April tottered onstage to present the much-celebrated surfer Shane Dorian with the gong for Monster Tube (that is the tunnel created by the breaking wave and the offshore wind); Dorian in turn used his speech to thank the wave itself (*Jaws* again), as a Hollywood star might thank his agent or his mother. Next a Frenchman, Benjamin Sanchis, took the prize for the biggest wave of the year, telling the crowd, 'Everybody is scared, but nobody is showing it.' Then he grinned, toothily, and waved an enormous cardboard cheque for $15,000 at the cheering crowd. The host went on to introduce another big wave colossus, Greg Long, who had emerged as a huge name in 2009 at the tender age of twenty-five and who now took the stage beaming a pearly white smile, as the compère quipped, 'That's why I love Greg Long! He smiles at darkness and fear!' The crowd went wild with delight.

Then something strange happened. In the middle of all the cheering and punching the air came a tribute to a reputedly fearless big wave rider called Sion Milosky, who had died a little over six weeks before the ceremony. Wiped out at the notoriously deadly Californian break, *Mavericks*, and pinned underwater by two consecutive waves, Milosky had drowned. If big wave surfing is going to kill you, this is the way that it does it. And so we sat and watched a compilation of Sion's life as a surfer, full of slow-motion images of him paddling up to the camera, all tanned muscle and invincible smile, laughing and then taking off into a mountainous sea. The video ended with a full-frame caption that said 'LIVE LIKE SION' and all around me men and women wiped tears from their eyes. Then Milosky's wife, beautiful and brittle in her grief, came on stage, her arms around their two small, golden-haired daughters and she accepted her husband's posthumous award for the Best Overall Performance of 2011. Mrs Milosky was not smiling.

I wondered for a moment whether 'Live Like Sion' was the most salutary advice one could give this particular audience, but no one else seemed troubled by the irony. Before there was further time to brood, the mood had lifted, hip hop was banging out of the speakers again and the next winner, a Brazilian called Danilo Couto, was whooping and flapping another oversized cheque in the spotlights. He paused for a second to pay tribute to his brother in arms, saying that Sion had been, 'A real human being. A *man*.' And then he held up his arms in triumph once more and the party continued.

---

❧

There is a ship's captain in Eugene O'Neill's *Mourning Becomes Electra* who murmurs that 'The sea hates a coward'. And he is not alone in ascribing some kind of epic will to the daunting wilderness that covers seven-tenths of our globe. Joseph Conrad wrote of its 'irresponsible consciousness of power', Herman Melville of 'some hidden soul beneath'; Jacques Cousteau even bragged 'I make love to it'.

Of course, we all know that oceans do not really think or intend or desire, and yet something about the mystery of the sea's ceaseless and infinitely varied motion makes the cold, damp facts curiously hard to accept. In centuries past, young men would run away to sea, pitting their will against the mighty will of the ocean. It was a dangerous, romantic project that, if it did not kill you, would make a man of you. As the author of *Moby-Dick* wrote in a letter, 'At sea, a fellow comes out. Salt water is like wine, in that respect.'

Naturally, this rite of passage loses its poetry in an age of plane tickets that cost 50p and cargo ships the size of towns. So in its stead has come the new daring of extreme ocean sports, free-diving, ocean rowing and so on, all latter-day expressions of the old 'sea fever' and none more vividly so than those big wave riders I had watched celebrating in Anaheim that night.

Ahead of the awards ceremony, and to avoid the 'stoked/pumped/awesome' atmosphere that would surely prevail that night, I had spent the day driving up and down the Pacific highway to meet two of the leading illuminati of the sport. I wanted to find out whether embracing their especial form of courage was a good way to go about coming of age.

Just after breakfast, I dropped in with Greg Long, the so-called 'giant killer', widely believed to be one of the best big wave surfers of the moment. He was staying at his mum and dad's house in San Clemente, an affluent surfer's enclave halfway between LA and San Diego, where he had grown up, the son of the local lifeguard. We sat on plastic chairs in the sunny back garden and discussed how a southern Californian boy from a nice family might, in the Brothers Grimm phrase, *Learn Fear*.

'The act of riding a big wave is very elemental,' said Greg, with a messianic smile, 'It's totally different to small waves and every single time, there's always that sense of fear. And that's part of the driving motivation – it is *essential* fear.'

Greg Long had his first taste of big waves at fifteen on a trip to Hawaii in 1999 and he fell, in his words, 'deeply in love'. Do you recall the matador, Rafaelillo, whose technique with a charging bull was good, but not so entirely outstanding as to make him famous; and do you recollect how instead he made his name by fighting the most dangerous bulls, the Miuras? Well, if one is to take at face value Greg Long's own account of his early career as a professional surfer – and he is clearly modest – then Greg is, in this respect at least, a little like a Rafaelillo of the waves. If he was going to shine, then it would be within the kind of surfing he loved best of all, on waves like a Miura bull, colossal, unpredictable, dangerous as hell.

This affinity for the cruellest seas is not just a young man's game either. Mike Parsons is almost twenty years older than Greg, the nearest thing the big wave scene has to an *éminence grise*. Mike is feted for the most famous big wave ride of all time. It is not the tallest wave ever surfed – although Mike also held that official world record at the time we met – but it is certainly the most widely known. You may even have seen it, for this was a video that went viral on the internet in 2003 and has been viewed by many, many millions since. Variously credited to a range of different surfers or different waves and called everything from *World's Biggest Wave*

*Ever Surfed* to *Man Surfing Tsunami*, it is in fact just Mike, towing into a sixty-four foot wave at *Jaws* in Hawaii. There follows an astonishing helicopter shot that begins below the lip of the wave and tracks Mike's eighty-second descent of a wall of water so unconscionably huge that I found myself watching the video over and over again, like some creepy fan.

'Yeah, that's probably the ride of my life,' said Mike laconically, over a fruit smoothie in the San Clemente juice bar where we met. Having watched the film so compulsively, I had been expecting some kind of titan, so I was surprised by how slight and unassuming Mike Parsons was in the flesh. Friendly, polite and rather precise, he told me about his twenties trail-blazing the big offshore breaks of southern California, unknown back then in the 1980s.

'To be in that moment,' he said, 'where you're weightless and free-falling and you think the wave is going to hit you but you just make it, you get this crazy rush come over you and this feeling of accomplishment that's indescribable. You just think "wow, I want to do that again" and you chase it. Pretty much, I've chased it for the rest of my life, that feeling.'

This language of addiction ran right through the conversations I had with both men. Greg talked about the chemical make-up of adrenaline as the 'addicting factor' of the sport. 'It's a drug,' he had said. Mike grinned and said he was 'addicted 100 per cent', later describing the idea of *not* surfing dangerous waves as going 'cold turkey'. Perhaps even a Timid Soul, given a taste of this courage, could get hooked.

Yet, in reality for big wave surfers like Greg and Mike, this means a lot more chasing than surfing. There are perhaps only six days of truly epic waves per winter season, which means that anticipation has a huge role to play. In the absence of real practise, mental preparation becomes central to success, or even survival. In young Greg Long's case, this amounts to an obsessively close calculation and rationing of risk, as well as a kind of mental visualisation that has more than a whiff of the warrior code about it, deeply meditating upon every good and bad possible outcome in order to prepare the mind for battle.

'And so what can go wrong?' I asked him breezily.

'Everything,' came the reply, followed by the Greg Long smile.

It was with a grave face that Mike Parsons told me about the worst wipeout of his life, the one that nearly killed him.

'I fell backwards and the lip of the wave pushed me to the bottom and I was completely convinced I was going to drown,' he said. 'You're being crushed to the bottom and rolled and tumbled and dragged and thrown and ripped and torn. It feels like your body is in a blender. And then it will let up for five seconds but it comes back. Twenty seconds under, five seconds up, twenty seconds under, five seconds up, up and down and up and down and up and down – over and over. Your lungs really hurt and it's really hard and you think you have to have air and then you get to a sort of euphoric state where it doesn't hurt as much and then it comes back again – that you really, *really* want air – and I think that's the point where you're very close to blacking out.'

'Your primal instinct as a human being is to keep breathing,' is how Greg put it. He can hold his breath for up to four minutes. 'You can go days without water,' he went on, 'weeks without food, but you can't last more than a few minutes without taking a breath. So a huge part of riding these big waves is mentally getting your head around the idea that you're not going to be able to breathe for a certain period of time and being OK with that.'

I had not, I will be frank, expected to hear such a Zen definition of courage from a twenty-seven-year-old surf dude.

'But there is some sort of curve there,' pointed out the older man, 'where you hit your absolute max of believing you can ride those waves and survive, *I'll go for it*, and then things happen and you realise the reality of it.' Mike shifted a little. 'I've pulled a friend out of the water, dead, and for me, that's when it changed. I realised that you don't always come up.'

'The way I see it,' said Greg, 'if you are doing this sport for long enough and you continue to push yourself as hard as you can, it's only a matter of time before you find one of those waves that is going to take you out.'

I realised that if Mike Parsons and Greg Long had taken to the seas in their teens, albeit twenty years apart, as adrenaline-chasing Boys Who Left Home To Learn Fear, then they had found fear indeed and in the process had been forced to grow up in the starkest of ways.

For Mike, the day came on 23 December 1994. He was surfing the infamous Californian break, *Mavericks*, with his friend Mark Foo. The pair of them wiped out. Mike Parsons came up. Mark Foo did not. It was Mike who lifted his dead friend out of the sea and took him back to land.

'I was 30 years old,' he said, 'and for me that was probably the height of my courage in big waves. I had a very difficult time for about a year to get back the amount of courage that I had before that day. I had terrible nightmares and I had a tough time the first few times I was confronted with really big waves.'

For Greg Long, the horror was fresh. It came in 2010, less than a year before I met him and at the end of a year that had seen him win the two biggest awards for big wave riding in the world, as part of the biggest and best winter the sport had ever had. Greg was halfway through telling me about the El Niño storm tracks and how that made incredible waves, when suddenly he looked decimated.

'And that was all ...' He cleared his throat. 'I mean basically my confidence ...' He stopped again, gathering himself. 'Being totally honest, the whole rug, my confidence in big wave surfing, was just pulled out from underneath my feet the day my best friend passed away.'

This was a surfer called Noel Robinson. Robinson had wiped out in the water with Greg at Puerto Escondido in southern Mexico in May 2010 and he never came back up. Like Mike, Greg recovered his friend's body.

'That was' – Greg paused – 'probably the saddest day of my life. It rattled me to the core, so that this whole last year, even now, I've had this sort of mental block. I carried on surfing big waves, but it was just that edge, that mental confidence of "hey, I'm physically and mentally capable of doing this", I had personally lost it. Even still, I just have this sense of caution in all of my actions that wasn't there before.'

However devastating, these deaths were not only the wages of this kind of growing up but also the very substance of it, the heart of the danger that seems to make this so compelling and compulsive. Perhaps if either Greg or Mike had quit surfing big waves at this point, then their friends would have somehow perished in vain.

'After Mark died, I had to build back up riding big waves and it took a long, long time,' is how Mike put it. 'I went on to ride the biggest waves of my life, but it was a much more calculated approach after that. It's a kind of maturing and just realising that there's a lot to live for.'

The year that followed, as I watched the big wave calendar from a warm, dry desk in England, I saw that Greg Long was there again, charging every huge storm break, every contest, surfing massive wave after massive wave. In the autumn of 2012, he won the major Wave of the Summer award at Puerto Escondido, in the very waters that had killed his friend. I recalled him saying, 'Riding big waves is really what makes me happy, being in the ocean, all the beauty and glory. People get stuck in a state of mediocrity, but I think that we are all here to be nothing short of amazing and great.'

Mike Parsons had turned forty-six the spring I met him, an old warrior of sorts, his rites of passage to manhood complete and wisdom apparently achieved. 'I've definitely passed my curve,' he had said to me near the end of our lunch, 'I don't feel like I've got anything I have to prove. But the ocean is the only place that's humbled me just to the core. It's the only place that I've ever been that over-whelmed and felt like a little teeny spec, you know? You have those spiritual moments in the ocean. I mean surfing in general does that. I think if everyone in the world surfed there wouldn't be fighting and blowing each other up. And I really believe that.' Then he finished his smoothie, gave me a Californian air-hug and we went our different ways into the sunshine.

❧

'If you do not know how to die,' wrote Michel de Montaigne, 'do not worry. Nature will tell you what to do on the spot, fully and adequately. She will do this job perfectly for you. Do not bother your head about it.'

Choosing to take on Mother Nature at her most lethal may be one way to quash the childish timidity within, but is there clearer moral recompense (and truer courage) if the elemental violence that engulfs you does so quite against your own will; moreover if still you hold your ground not just to prove that you can, but to save a life; not to preserve your own breath, but that of another?

The ancient Judaic principle of *Pikku'ah Nefesh* ('regard for human life') is a sacred injunction laid out in the Talmud, one which pre-dates and even outranks the Sabbath laws. And lest you be bowed, cowed and generally *put off* by the sheer numbers of those in every sort of peril around every corner, the impossible enormity of an impossible task, you might recollect that *Pikku'ah Nefesh* assures us, 'He who saves one life saves the world entire'.

❧

The dream that woke Ruth Millington's travelling companion, Michael Runkel, so he told her later, was of being in the middle of the ocean and of being caught in a massive wave. His eyes snapped open in the darkness. The room seemed to be quivering; no, *it was quivering*; now it was shaking; now lurching violently; now rising and falling a foot at a time.

What woke Ruth was Michael's hands around her ankles in her sleeping bag, dragging her off the bed and his screams above a noise more deafening than any other Ruth had ever heard. It was like she says, 'having twenty locomotive trains just underneath the ground and this terrible thundering, grinding and crushing noise.'

Michael was screaming, '*IT'S AN EARTHQUAKE.*'

Ruth, a British lawyer, and Michael, a German photographer, were old travelling buddies. For this trip they had met up the evening before – Christmas night, 2003 – at Akbar's Guest House in a back street of the UNESCO World Heritage city of Bam in Iran, an extraordinary two-thousand-year-old Silk Road citadel, encircled by a maze of tiny, sixteenth-century mud-brick streets. Earlier in the year Ruth had quit her high-flying job at an investment bank in the City of London, 'burned out', so she says, at the age of thirty-three. She had begun travelling to far-flung places, to get back in touch with herself, to grow up a bit, to learn about what she calls 'the *real* world'. Ruth and Michael had decided to meet for Christmas in Iran, as adventurous backpackers will.

It was dark when Ruth got to Akbar's Guest House and she was tired from the journey, so the two friends had a quick supper and Ruth went to bed in the room they shared.

The intricate beauty of Bam could wait until the morning. Around eleven o'clock, just as she was nodding off, there was a slight earth tremor. Michael, who was talking to some people in the courtyard outside their room, popped his head around the door saying not to worry and that there had been tremors all afternoon.

'OK,' said Ruth, ever the seasoned traveller. And she fell fast asleep.

The earthquake struck at 5.26 a.m. Seconds later, Michael yanked Ruth into consciousness.

'If you can imagine,' she says to me, 'it's like being in a deep sleep and waking up in a washing machine which is spinning and pitch black. I couldn't see a thing. I stood up, fighting to get my sleeping bag off. I could feel the ground underneath my feet literally leaping up and down and Michael screaming at the top of his lungs, 'We've got to get out!' and I was still having difficulty hearing him because of the noise that was coming from the ground and the crashing metal roofs, smashing glass, the sounds of a building literally disintegrating. I was thrown about fifteen feet across the room on to the other bed and suddenly the room came in on me. I felt bricks smash onto my head and I lay there thinking, 'if I don't move now I'm going to die'. It was very clear, like a decision 'live or die?' and I chose to live. Suddenly everything went into slow motion and I just remember sticking my hand out in the dark and Michael's hand was there pulling me up.'

As a human being, you are supposed to be safe on terra firma; you are literally in your element, but not so tonight. A surreal horror ensued. Together they struggled with the door of the room against the shifting rubble and once outside, Ruth tells me that she ran forward with her hands in front of her and almost immediately her fingers felt a wall of rubble and debris taller than she was. She scrambled to the top.

'Suddenly, the noise all stopped.' Ruth clicks her fingers.

'Literally like that. Absolute silence. There was this white dust hovering in the air and it's all around me and I remember turning around to Michael and going, "where's the hotel gone?" There was nothing there.'

Then the wailing began. 'It was like a humming, but actually, when you listened again, it was a very, very low wailing and it came from all around the city. It's one of the most horrendous noises I've ever heard. It just filled the air and it went on all day.'

Around half of the population of Bam had been killed in the preceding two minutes, twenty-five thousand of the forty-three thousand residents of the city. The vast majority of the survivors not only lost their families, but were also injured, many seriously so. The quake registered 6.3 on the Richter Scale, not as high as some, but, owing to the fabric of the mud-bricks from which the city had been constructed all those centuries before, almost the entirety of the old city had dissolved to fine earth and either crushed or suffocated people in their beds.

Remember that cryptic line from *The Waste Land*, 'I will show you fear in a handful of dust'? Well, that day in Bam, here was 'fear in a handful of dust', alright, but, where many or most would be immobilised by the scale of such a predicament, Ruth Millington – the faintly bossy, inquisitive, curly-haired Lawyer Who Left Home To Learn ... well, if-not-exactly-Fear-then-certainly-*Life* – was, it transpired, entirely galvanised by it. For the next nine hours, she and Michael Runkel would dig nine people out of the rubble with their bare hands and save seven lives.

It began when Ruth spotted a Belgian man bent over on the ground a few metres away. He was shouting, 'Natalie! Natalie!' and Ruth saw what she describes as 'one of the most horrific sights I've ever seen': just the crown of a head, hair and blood, the rest of the body buried downwards in the rubble, 'and I could hear this woman suffocating.' Ruth makes a hissing, gasping sound. 'I literally froze for a couple of seconds and then I went, "right, get her out" and I went straight towards her and knelt down and we were just scrambling like dogs to get to her face.'

It now dawned on Ruth, who knew no more formal first aid than that learned on a course at the bank several years before, that there were other people, Lord knows how many, under the ground on which she crouched, barefoot in her pyjamas. So she asked the young man whose girlfriend had just been retrieved from her would-be grave to carry on digging her out, promising to keep coming back to check on them.

It was still not yet six o'clock. It would be dark until eight, which made locating people a process of yelling down into the black ground and then listening for muffled screams in reply, but judging the distances involved or whether you were standing on top of someone was well nigh impossible. 'I've never prayed so hard for light,' Ruth says.

At length, the earth, its anger spent, did what the earth is supposed to do. It turned on its axis and morning broke.

With no sign of organised help, even down on the main road, the two friends divided the pile of rubble, each beginning to dig for survivors at either end, as the sun began to touch mounds of ochre rubble for as far as the eye could see. Just one wall of Akbar's Guest House, the tall Persian facade, stood in front of the rubble pile on which Michael and Ruth stood, surrounded by gas cylinders, electrical wires, air-conditioning units and window frames. Ruth says she now realised how 'bloody lucky' they had been and she recalls one of these window frames that looked like a crucifix standing in the devastation. As the sun rose, the roads filled with cars and motorbikes that had driven in from the surrounding countryside to look for family and friends and now the rush-hour growl of engines joined the wailing as the soundscape of the stricken city.

But the light meant that now Ruth and Michael could truly get to work, digging people out. The account that follows from Ruth is full of bizarre, horrific images: two coughing heads sticking out of the rubble, pointing like the faces of Janus in opposite directions and tethered together by a metal bedstead; a young woman in a black hijab holding a baby and rocking back and forth wailing; a German man, head down in the debris and screaming, only his feet sticking out; Ruth, in her words 'managing' some local people enlisted to help her dig, as I imagine one might manage a team of junior lawyers on a big acquisition; a bed frame beneath a wall shuddered by aftershocks and Ruth's intuition that 'there's someone underneath that, but where's the head going to be?'; then the dust and the gravel and the matted hair; the two men, gradually freed to the neck and then to the waist, who as soon as their arms were liberated began to shriek uncontrollably; the salvaged bed sheets used to carry the injured down to the road; and everywhere, *everywhere* bodies wrapped in blankets, children, adults, 'hundreds and hundreds of them,' says Ruth.

As the hours passed, time and again Ruth would liberate a face or a head, scraping rubble from nostrils and mouths, and say 'I'm not going to abandon you' but that she would be back to continue digging when she had made sure that no more people were drowning in the rubble.

'It was like I was doing a business deal,' says Ruth, 'I was so calm. I was calculated – I don't mean that in a nasty way – but I knew exactly what I needed to do. I had to do x, y, z and there was no emotion there. Ironically, Michael and I have always been slightly competitive and there was a slight competitive element between us which actually enabled us to be more successful in what we did. It may sound a little bit strange, but it's a quality that we used to actually enhance what we were doing.'

Michael and Ruth finished digging around three o'clock that afternoon, confident that they had accounted, alive or dead, for everyone in the hotel and now they had to get the injured of Akbar's Guest House to hospital in Kerman, nearly two hundred kilometres away. So Ruth looted some water from a shop, while Michael considered hot-wiring a car and eventually they harangued a Jeep driver into taking them to Kerman. From Kerman, they were transferred to Tehran and ten days later, Ruth and the people she and Michael had saved were home.

I ask Ruth how she weighs what the outside world reads as her courage and her answer further shakes any simple ideas I may have entertained about the nature of free will and how it rubs along with bravery.

'I never even felt like it was a choice,' she says, 'it was just something I did automatically. I know I was brave but,' – she pauses – 'you always think it's someone else that's brave, you know, I just thought it was something that I had to do and I don't even mean it in a modest way; it was just something I did and if I was in that situation again, I hopefully would do the same. And if that is bravery then so be it, it's bravery, but I've never really quantified it as that.'

I wonder out loud whether Ruth is troubled by the multitude she could not save.

'I don't feel guilty about not being able to save the whole of Bam, if that's what you mean,' she says with a certainty that surprises me. 'You have to have a reality and I worked to the best of my abilities with the limited amount of resources – well, there weren't any resources – we had one shovel and I used my hands – and I saved these people's lives. I am proud of what we did.'

❦

In the Old Testament, when the people of Yahweh get too big for their boots, or in the Qur'an, when Allah is displeased, God goes about setting the world of men to rights with tempests that crack rock, earthquakes, wildfire. Certainly, the human mind often struggles to understand how anything, other than a wrathful God, could account for the elemental violence of planet Earth.

After the Bam earthquake, in 2005 a team of researchers at the Iranian Institute for Health Sciences Research in Tehran (Montazeri et al, 2005), tracked the psychological aftershocks of the disaster, a veritable deluge of psychiatric disorders and depression which beset the souls of survivors rendered timid by the cataclysm. Interviewing just under a thousand of 'the saved', they identified severe mental health issues among 58 per cent. A second paper published two years later by psychiatrists at Kerman University (Ghaffari-Nejad, et al, 2007) found so-called 'complicated grief' in more than two-thirds of the surviving population in Bam, people for whom fear and sadness were somehow magnified by how very common it was to feel this way. According to news reports in the years after the quake, many sought solace in opium, the use of which is semi-respectable on the city's ruined streets, but which was blamed, in this epidemic form, for hampering the reconstruction effort, both of city street and of soul.

❦

Of the elemental braveries I have investigated on behalf of the Society of Timid Souls, each one a rite of passage, the tale of Fleur Lombard is in many ways the least dramatic. The element she took on required no wilderness, neither meteorological nor tectonic tumult, in order to be a true foe. It may appeal to the most timid of the Timid Souls to learn that Fleur's sad story takes place in a supermarket. But do not relax just yet, for fear can hide in unexpected places, and bravery too.

Twenty-one-year-old Fleur Lombard had been a fire-fighter for two years when her team, Blue Watch at Speed-well Station in Bristol, got 'a shout' just after half past twelve on Sunday 4 February 1996. They had spent the morning, as they did on Sundays, cleaning the engine house, check-ing equipment and then stringing up a net across the yard and playing volleyball in the winter sunshine. Fleur, the only woman on Blue Watch, loved working with men, the fast-talking banter, the competition. Whatever some of the fire-fighters' wives might think of it, Fleur, blonde and pretty, was one of the lads.

When I met Fleur's parents, Roger and Jane Lombard, a respectable Derby couple admittedly somewhat rattled by their daughter's initial decision to join the fire service, her father told me that when asked about the best bit of her new job, she had said, 'It's going through the streets in the dark and the wail's on and you can see the blue light flashing off all the shop windows. It's bloody exciting!' I expect most firefighters would identify with that. Fleur too, her mother and father were keen to stress, was very concerned with being treated with scrupulous equality, not being mollycoddled for being female.

'I suppose you could say that if I had a concern,' said her father, Roger, 'it was that she got herself into the situation in which she eventually came unstuck and she stuck it out for longer than she should have done, just to prove that she could.'

The shout that Sunday afternoon was to a supermarket called Leo's at Staple Hill, five minutes' drive from Speedwell.

There was little indication of the scale of the incident, so just one engine with four or five on board rolled out of the doors. Ten minutes later, a second call came through. Again the siren sounded, the lights flicked on and the printer rattled out the location 'Leo's' once again.

Fleur and a more experienced firefighter called Rob Seaman, who had mentored her during her probationary period at Speedwell, were assigned to breathing apparatus that day. These are the firefighters who lead the way, suited and booted, into the flames themselves and, in the back of the second engine as it swung out of the yard, Fleur and Rob scrambled into their kit.

I met Rob Seaman fifteen years on from that day at a small, retained fire station on the banks of the Severn river, where we sat upstairs in an empty classroom and drank strong tea. 'When we turned out of the station,' he told me, 'about a minute into the journey, we were going towards Staple Hill and you could see a lot of thick black smoke and you thought "bloody hell, this is a big fire" and also it was a Sunday, it was open, there might even be people inside.'

Fleur had turned to him at this point and said, 'Oh God, it would probably have been a good day for me to go sick', and they had laughed. Remembering this now stops Rob mid-flow and he looks out of the window for a moment.

When they arrived at the supermarket, with its aisles and chiller-cabinets built into an old Victorian warehouse, the fire, which had started in a storeroom at the back of the shop, was already coming through the roof. A fire engine was pumping an arced jet of water down into the flames.

As the first team briefed the Station Officer, a policeman approached Rob and said, 'The manager's just told me he doesn't know if all the shoppers are out of the shop.' The dynamics of the incident turned on that moment. Now Rob and Fleur were told to go in and lay a guide line to the back of the store, a slim, sixty-metre rope with tabs on it, strung at waist height and showing the way in and the way out in low or zero visibility. Fleur would carry the bag, from which the guide line would reel out, as well as the communications headset that allowed contact with the team outside the building. Rob would follow her tying off the guide line. Ideally, a hose team would also come to give Fleur and Rob some cover from the flames, but this is where the briefing was sketchy and the hose team went in a different direction into the store.

Rob and Fleur entered the building and began to grope their way down the left-hand aisle, past the trolley park and down through the wines and spirits. At first they were able to talk to one another, but the further they got, the noise of the fire got louder, things popping, breaking, small explosions, until they were shouting across to one another. It was getting hotter, too, and darker, as the smoke blackened towards the source of the fire.

'We got down to the corner of the store. There was a big fridge unit, milk and butter I think. Everything in it had started to melt and it was all mushy. And I said to Fleur, I shouted to her and said "It's getting really hot in here now. We haven't got any water, we need to think about getting out." And she said "Okay." And I'm still trying to tie off, conscious that we need to get this done so the other team can come in and search off it'.

Suddenly, Rob heard Fleur shout, 'Evacuate! Evacuate!'

They turned towards the door, the fire really roaring now and tiles flying off the roof. 'Black, black smoke,' says Rob, and unbearable heat enveloped them from above, two sure signs of an incipient flashover.

A flashover, Rob explained to me by drawing a graph in my notebook, is the point at which a fire in a room becomes *a room on fire*, the flammable gases in the air igniting. Bent double below the scorched air and now gripping one another's waist straps in the darkness, Fleur and Rob fumbled as fast as they could back along the wines and spirits aisle.

'To this day, I think there's about a minute that I can't recollect whatsoever,' Rob said, looking down at his big hands, capable in so many other situations. 'Unless I choose not to remember it. I don't know. I don't know. Eventually I remember coming to, face down on the floor of the aisle. My tunic had ridden up and I'm sort of burning all around here,' he shows me his wrists, 'my ears too. And my first thoughts were "What's happened? Where's Fleur?" I was scrambling around for her and then it cleared a little bit and I was grabbed by some firefighters and pulled out.'

'Have you got Fleur?' he asked them.

'No, she's not out yet.'

Rob grabbed the hose and went straight back in with another firefighter, Pat Foley.

'It wasn't long at all, within thirty, forty seconds, I saw her. And as soon as I saw her I knew she was dead. She was completely still. Her helmet had gone, her face mask had gone, her fire kit had gone from there to there,' – Rob pointed to his shoulder and then his waist – 'completely burnt away. Almost, I mean, you could see her breast. And I've seen people who have died in fires before, not firefighters, and the way that their mouth is and the way that they're trying to breathe, and the way that the mouth is burnt into a position where the superheated gases have gone down and killed them instantly.'

Fleur was in a crouching position, her forehead against the wall. Rob picked her up from behind. Her breathing apparatus fell off, the straps burned through. He and Pat Foley carried Fleur out of the building, covered her body and Rob collapsed.

'Well my whole world has just ended, at that point,' said

Rob and he paused for a long time, 'because I knew she was dead. And to this day I still feel the same way. I felt I had a responsibility for her. One because she was a woman, two because she'd been in the fire service less time than me and was less experienced in life in general, as well. I mean you'd hear about firefighters dying, but it's a job and you expect to go home after your shift. You didn't expect not to go home.'

Rob Seaman was awarded the George Medal for his courage that day, and Fleur Lombard, the first and only British female firefighter to be killed in the line of duty, a posthumous Queen's Gallantry Medal. There had never been any shoppers inside the burning store.

After the Staple Hill Supermarket fire, it was discovered that the fire which killed Fleur Lombard had been started deliberately by a new security guard at the store. It was suggested at his trial that he may have done something similar at his previous job too, where upon 'discovering' a fire he had 'bravely' put it out and was praised by the Avon Fire Service for his action. This time, the young man's bid to counterfeit the kind of courageous kudos that firefighters like Fleur Lombard and Rob Seaman enjoyed for real had got horribly out of hand. He served seven years for arson. And this was, I suppose, his rite of passage.

❦

For Roger and Jane Lombard, as perhaps for any parent in their situation, the loss of their golden girl is little diminished by the years that have passed. 'You can see that it is not far below the surface,' Roger says to me, more than once. Sitting drinking coffee and eating neat sandwiches with the couple in a small, formal dining room, there were no outbursts, or free-flowing tears, but the Lombards' on-going pain is palpable. They tell me about the police officers coming to the door; the race (unsuccessful) to get Fleur's sister on the phone before the news hit the radio; the torrent of media interest that followed; they tell me how much Fleur loved the job, how proud they were of her and about the thousand-strong crowd at her funeral in Derby Cathedral, where her coffin was carried in on a turntable ladder.

I realise, talking to them, that neither Mr nor Mrs Lombard had left home to learn fear. They had not faced down some physical, elemental menace, an angry sea, an earthquake, an inferno. There was no coming of age here and yet now they needed courage more than ever before. Recalling the moment they learned of their daughter's death, Roger turns to Jane and says, 'I think the police left, didn't they, and I said to you, "Are you alright?" And you said, "Yes, are you alright?" and I said "Yes".'

And he half-smiles at her and adds, 'Both lying.'

# Limelight

The audience intimidates me. I feel asphyxiated by its
breath, paralysed by its curious glances, struck dumb by
all those strange faces.

Frederic Chopin, aged 25, to Franz Liszt

The evening of my visit to Fleur Lombard's parents, her
father Roger emailed me to add something he had been too
choked to relate during the day:

'I think probably the hardest thing I had to do,' he wrote,
'and I sincerely hope it is the hardest thing I ever have to do,
was to face the throng of reporters outside the house on the
"morning after". I remember thinking "Right, well I've got
a demonstrably very brave daughter and now I'm going to
bloody well do this so she can see I can be brave too, and say
what she would want me to say in a way that she would want
me to say it, without looking like either a weeping prat or
an unemotional zombie" and marching off down the drive
to do it. I still don't know how I did it. I said the "hardest
thing" but I suppose on reflection and at the risk of being

immodest it was also the bravest thing I've ever done and perhaps there's a thought for you.'

As it was, I had been wondering about what the difference might be between the courage of someone facing a bona fide danger – a bullet, a bull, a tumour, a wave, a fire – as opposed to the courage of one who feels fear brought on by circumstances in which there is no actual risk to life or limb. We have already agreed – to a ripple of relief among the Timid Souls – that some degree of fear, or at least an awareness of it, is concomitant with bravery. Even Aristotle, who on the face of it favoured courage as a trait of character as much as a behaviour requiring willpower, nevertheless acknowledged fear as a kind of magnetic North from which to locate its plucky opposite. His doctrine of the golden mean positions the virtue of courage (*andreia*) at the midpoint betwixt fear (*phobos*) and confidence (*tharsos*), preserving the righteous man both from rashness and from cowardice. Yet what exactly is happening if any real practical or even moral necessity to be brave is stripped away and one is left with purely the *feeling* of terror to be overcome?

Think back, if you will, to 1942 and to that icy January on West 73rd Street; recollect those trembling pianists and the actors and singers who joined them to form Bernard Gabriel's Society of Timid Souls. With no peril to fall back on, the nerves experienced by those original Timid Souls and others like them who choose to step into the limelight, are like an ornate confection of fear itself. The acute dread so many performers must daily overcome is arguably the most 'real' part of the whole enterprise: braving the risk that having stepped out of the crowd, fearful enough on its own, that you then proceed to look ridiculous, laughable, or simply that your one talent deserts you when you need it most.

The fear of public humiliation runs deep and, however different from an illness it may be, it remains another Enemy

disclaimer. Indeed, each micro-constituency within the performing arts seems instinctively to imply that there is something that makes it especially terrifying *for them*. A flute player told me that it was because she had to sit still in the orchestra and could not physically uncoil her nerves by rushing around onstage. An actor said that it was because he had to be so emotionally naked in order to inhabit his character. An oboe player said that the problem lay with the unpredictable caprice of the instrument's double reed. A horn player said it was because the horn is so loud that there is no hiding in the ensemble. A ballerina said it was because if a dancer fluffs the choreography they not only look silly but risk pain and a possible career-threatening injury. And on it goes. What they say is true of course, but it seems that, a little like love, there is something about the intense experience of stage fright, whether you are topping the bill at the Met, or skulking in the ranks of some provincial orchestra, that makes it feel like you are The Only Person On Earth Who Really Knows What This Living Hell Feels Like. There is also something of the shame that seems to go hand-in-hand with stage fright that causes each sufferer to search for some reason why they in particular have succumbed, while their colleagues are singing/playing/acting/dancing, apparently quite unruffled.

Renée Fleming wrote candidly in her autobiography some years ago of the crippling stage fright that beset her in the late 1990s as she hit the height of her career. Months of mounting nervousness, triggered by a marriage break-up and a heavy workload, climaxed at La Scala in Milan in 1998, where Fleming was singing the lead in Donizetti's *Lucrezia Borgia*. In many Italian opera houses portions of the audience have more in common with the aficionados of the Spanish bull-ring crowd than with the culture vultures of London or New York and nowhere is opera closer to a blood sport than at La Scala. Here a much-dreaded faction called the *loggionisti* sit in the uppermost gallery, booing and catcalling at any singer who does not meet their exacting standards. Known for their forensic knowledge of the repertoire as well as their bruising vendettas, the *loggionisti* have visited baying displeasure upon many a famous name, even booing Pavarotti for apparently spending too long away from his homeland. Quite what Renée Fleming's offence was is unclear, but certainly her opening night as Lucrezia was not the luckiest of performances. The tenor had dropped out and been replaced at the last minute. Then the conductor fainted with a thud at the end of Fleming's first aria. Finally, at the end of her final cadenza, which deviated somewhat from La Scala convention, the gods erupted and Fleming was booed to the gold-fretted rafters. It lasted for the whole of her closing scene and afterwards, she wrote, 'I began to shake and I shook for days.'

There followed a year of abysmal stage fright. Fleming never missed even so much as a rehearsal, but her memoirs are full of Kafkaesque images to describe the turmoil within: she calls it her 'dark night of the soul' when she would find herself 'going into the tunnel', 'drenched with sweat' and 'consumed with terror'. 'Every cell in my body was screaming, *No! I can't do this!*' she writes, 'you feel as if you will die.'

It is heady stuff. Operatic, even.

Yet when I talk to Renée Fleming, either time has healed or some need to deliver high-octane confessions abated, for her account is more measured, more grown-up somehow.

'It was just a very difficult time,' she says. 'You know, the mind can only take so much and then it says, "OK, I don't want to do this any more. This is too much pressure".'

We talk about how the pressure increases as your career takes off and how heavy the weight of expectation can become once you are famous, as well as how very public the critique of your shortcomings; how important it was to have 'wonderful people' around you.

'During the worst period,' she tells me, 'my voice teacher stood in my dressing room and walked me to the stage. And thank God, because in retrospect I think if I had somehow quit or said, "I'm just going to take some time off and get on top of this", I'm not sure when and how I would have gone back.'

I ask about the stigma that surely must come with stage fright when you are as celebrated as Renée Fleming, how cloak and dagger you need to be about the fear.

'No. *You just have to sing well*,' she says, 'That is all people are concerned about. But also I didn't talk about it back then. I didn't talk about it until I was in control of it again and it was behind me.'

Renée Fleming's former manager dubbed her 'Mother Courage'. It is a grandiose soubriquet for someone who simply sings, but there is little doubt that Fleming has been forced to teach herself a certain form of bravery. For it is at the very moment of faltering, of incipient timidity, that one can see most clearly what the performer's bravery is all about. Besides, I find myself feeling rather honoured that Renée Fleming turns out to be one of us Timid Souls.

'Do you ever get nervous now?' I ask.

'Oh sure. There are still high-pressure engagements and I'm very happy when they're over,' she says, and then qualifies, 'I'm always comfortable once I get on stage. It's the week or two in advance or the three days in advance when I suffer. And I've always had this strange coping mechanism, in a sense a sort of "deal" with myself that if I suffer enough in advance, then I can perform well.'

This is, of course, one of the dominant myth-cum-clichés of the artistic life, but it is also the very definition of 'virtuoso'. The word's etymology lies in the seventeenth-century notion of purchasing musical mastery with many 'virtuous' hours. There is even a long obsolete usage of 'virtue' dating back to thirteenth-century Norman French that takes 'vertu' to mean 'valour', the 'vertueux' a virtuoso of courage. Clearly, however remote the artist and the warrior, there is some primordial, shared DNA here.

Towards the end of the interview, Renée Fleming makes one point about the differences between real and perceived jeopardy that particularly stays with me. It comes as we discuss a psychological study of opera singers in London in the 1980s that found steeper levels of performance anxiety among singers with voices in the higher registers, tenors and sopranos. Technique or temperament, I wonder out loud.

'No,' says Renée Fleming, 'I think it's the level of risk. We who sing high have a great deal of risk, tenors most of all because the *raison d'être* really for a tenor is a brilliant high C or a brilliant high tone. And sopranos have the same pressure to a slightly lesser degree. But, you know, every voice type has difficulty.' ('Difficulty', I have worked out by now, is one of Fleming's euphemisms for fear.) 'One of the things I've discovered,' she concludes, 'is that whoever *perceives* that they are under pressure will have more difficulty than whoever doesn't.'

Whether you are crossing enemy ground under fire or singing Donizetti, there is no escaping how very subjective fear can be; and bravery too.

❧

And the list of stage-fright sufferers goes on. *And on.* Caruso. Olivier. Adele. Sylvie Guillem. Ian Holm. Daniel Day-Lewis. Vanessa Redgrave. Richard Burton. Robbie Williams. Mikhail Baryshnikov. Sheila Hancock. Neil Shicoff. Tommy Cooper. Vladimir Horowitz. Kenneth MacMillan. Glenn Gould. Maria Callas. Lady Gaga. As for the audience, we are relieved to discover that our cultural paladins are Timid

Souls too. It takes the edge off the untouchable, spangly frivolity of it all.

All of which made it surprising how very difficult it proved to persuade these people, so loquacious on the subject of stage fright, to talk about its opposite – stage courage, if you like. Despite the provenance of the Society of Timid Souls, a surprising number of actors, singers and musicians immediately declined requests for an interview on this subject. I had found that skydivers do not mind talking about bravery, nor matadors (heaven knows). Soldiers are OK about it too, and cancer patients, but I got the impression that there was a sheepishness about any claim to be brave on the part of these performers, as if it might betray some vanity. Fear without real jeopardy seemed to be a source of some shame, almost as though it diminished whatever mettle might be summoned to overcome it.

One eminent English veteran actor – you would know him – took the trouble to ring me to explain.

'You see,' he said, 'many people would say that actors are just people who didn't get enough attention as children and that is why they need to dress up in other people's clothes and shout in the evening. And some of that is true. *I* think we contribute something to society, but I would not wish to stand next to a firefighter or a disaster survivor and say we are brave.'

He wished me luck and that was the end of that.

❧

It is certainly true that one decides for oneself – or one's psyche latches on to – what *is* a big deal. Pray silence, if you will, for A Tale of Two Timid Souls.

On a Tuesday morning doused in watery English sunshine in October 2008, a twenty-eight-year-old man called

Billy Cross drove to the edge of a park near Tamworth town centre in the Midlands. More than five thousand miles away and not a great many weeks later, another young man of similar age, also pale and a little too lean, called Seth Herbey, left his suburban home in Napa, California and drove a few blocks to his local grocery store.

Both men filmed what happened next on their mobile phones.

'I've got a feeling I'm going to be pretty fucking nervous during this,' says Billy, sitting in the car, darting uneasy looks out of the window. Next he is walking. All you can see is his deadpan, pasty face and the shoulders of a red and white jacket, framed from beneath by the camera phone he holds in his hand; beyond his spiky haircut is a boundless, blue sky.

Seth also begins in the driving seat of his car. 'OK,' says he, sounding forcibly chipper. 'Well, I'm getting ready to go into a grocery store. And I'm not going to buy anything. I'm just going to walk in, see how I feel in there. You know, it's been months since I've been able to go into a grocery store. So – here – goes.' And he smiles at the camera, one of those smiles that is more about deploying the appropriate muscles than it is about smiling.

Billy Cross has just lit a cigarette. He is crossing the park towards Tamworth main shopping precinct and you can hear the sound of leaves crunching beneath his feet and kids playing in the distance. 'I don't feel comfortable at all,' he says, 'I feel really dodgy.' The picture suddenly cuts.

Seth has hung his camera around his neck to avoid attracting attention, so the footage that follows in the grocery store makes disturbing viewing. It is full of irrational losses of focus and there is a violent shaking motion. You can hear piped muzak and the hum of refrigerators, with some toggle on Seth's clothing clicking loudly in the foreground, the squeak of his sneakers on the floor, and the sound of his breathing, nightmarishly close.

'Whoa.' Billy is back in the car and pulling hard on another cigarette. 'Now that was unexpected,' he says, 'to feel as bad as that, so soon. I decided to turn around almost instantly. I had a major fucking scary thought.' And the camera cuts again.

Seth Herbey has stopped by some racks of boiled sweets. 'I don't feel too bad,' he murmurs hoarsely and then on we go, past the orange juice, the eggs, the pasta. The shop tannoy sounds indistinctly.

Lest you are waiting for something to happen here – for someone to pull a gun, or a bomb to go off, some encounter of drama and significance for Billy or Seth – I should suggest at this point that you stop waiting. Because nothing is going to happen. Nothing, except that you are witnessing, in real time, two truly Timid Souls teaching themselves to be brave. For Billy and Seth suffer from agoraphobia, a fear less of open spaces, as is commonly thought, than of settings in which excessive anxiety or a full-blown panic attack might occur and from which an 'escape' would prove difficult, intolerable embarrassment inevitable.

The word 'agoraphobia' comes from the Greek for marketplace, *agora*, and fear, *phobos*, so it is fitting that the large-scale modern consumer experience – malls, multiplexes, car parks, fast-food joints – have become a fulcrum for the twenty-first century agoraphobic's terror. This fear, with its symptoms of dizziness, breathlessness and dread, typically grows into a complex pattern of avoidance behaviour that can result, as it did for Billy and Seth in 2008, in sufferers becoming housebound, unemployed and unemployable.

You might wonder what this has to do with limelight and stage fright, but stay with me.

Billy's film continues, narrated to his camera phone in

Proustian detail. Vacillation eventually gives way to a small epiphany – 'Fuck it,' he says – and he walks the five minutes to Tamworth's main multi-storey car park. For Seth, several aisles of freezer cabinets are conquered before he whispers, 'I'm feeling a little anxiety,' and together we hurry out of the store.

Both Billy Cross and Seth Herbey uploaded these two 'exposure therapy' videos and dozens more like them onto YouTube. This online phenomenon, relatively new at the time, has grown exponentially since – part confessional, part inspirational, this is self-administered, communal, extempore stress inoculation. Its clinical efficacy may be hard to measure, but it bears more than a passing resemblance, does it not, to the techniques of the original Timid Souls? The fact that the action is in some sense 'performed' seems to be a key part of why it works. 'I do think of you people who are watching these videos,' Billy says at one point, 'I think of you as being here with me.' It is as though 'acting' the bravery can ultimately be self-fulfilling; the gaze of the onlooker, once your nemesis, is now your saviour.

So how should one weigh the differences between conquering 'real' or 'perceived' fear with 'real' or 'perceived' bravery? As Kierkegaard observed in 1841 in the university thesis that would launch him as the first great existential philosopher: 'It requires courage not to surrender oneself to the ingenious or compassionate counsels of despair that would induce a man to eliminate himself from the ranks of the living; but it does not follow from this that every huckster who is fattened and nourished in self-confidence has more courage than the man who yielded to despair.' Or as Yeats asked sixty years later in an unpublished lecture: 'Why should we honour those that die upon the field of battle? A man may show as reckless a courage in entering into the abyss of himself.'

✤

There turns out to be no mention of Bernard Gabriel's Society of Timid Souls – I have looked – in New York City's historical archives. I could find just one obscure, out-of-print memoir of a violinist and wealthy patron of the arts, who recalled *en passant* how Bernard Gabriel had 'cured' her as a nervous young musician. Later I came upon an amateur archivist's 1997 interview with an elderly New Yorker who, more than six decades earlier, had shared a piano teacher with Bernard Gabriel. She said his name had been 'Cohen' back then, the son of a Russian Jewish violinist with the New York Philharmonic. He took up the name 'Gabriel' some-time in the 1930s and she recalled some kind of 'theory' he had developed about how 'heckling' might remedy 'self-consciousness' in the performer. But, tantalisingly, that was where the recollections ended. Even the building where the Timid Souls originally met, Sherman Square Studios at 160 West 73rd Street, does not seem to have held the memory either. It went on to become well-known as home or work-place to a host of stellar names from the world of music, including Leonard Bernstein, Ginger Rogers, Liza Minnelli, Barbra Streisand and Lotte Lenya, but there is no further mention of the Timid Souls. Bernard Gabriel himself moved on too, continuing a lively career of playing recitals alongside various other ventures, like The Try Out Club on Monday evenings for rehearsing new material. In 1951, he even set up a new stage-fright club called 'Previews For Performers', but it seems never to have struck quite the chord that the Timid Souls did in those months after Pearl Harbor. In the end, Gabriel moved into radio, hosting a popular classical music show that aired into the 1970s.

The one place where the Society of Timid Souls has rever-berated at least a little is in a portion of the psychological literature concerning stage fright, or as the clinicians prefer to term it, 'Performance Anxiety'.

According to a clinical psychologist based at Harvard Medical School (Powell, 2004), around 2 per cent of the US population suffers from performance anxiety, although neither of the two diagnostic classifications of mental disorders, ICD-10-Chapter V and DSM-IV, distinguishes it from social phobia or social anxiety disorder (such as that experienced by Billy Cross and Seth Herbey). This performance anxiety afflicts not just performers, but also people who cannot speak up in class or in meetings, cannot present their own work, or take professional exams, those who cannot complete a thesis or a report because of a paralysing terror of being embarrassed by their own performance. For around a third of them, there is co-morbidity with generalised anxiety or depression, but the other two-thirds are perfectly 'well' aside from their performance anxiety. More to the point, significant levels of queasy discomfort are positively the norm for anyone who has ever had to make a speech at a wedding or a presentation at work. It is as-near-as-damn-it a universal fear in the modern First World.

This was why I found myself flicking through the publicity material for Toastmasters International® ('Where Leaders Are Made'). Here I found lots of nice glossy photos of good-looking people with great teeth, smiling confidently at the camera. If you did not know that this was an organisation that runs more than 12,000 clubs with more than a quarter of a million members across 113 countries worldwide – every one of them aimed at overcoming fear in public speaking – then you might be forgiven for thinking it was an ad for a dentist. They made such an inspiring line-up – so relaxed, so happy – that you could not wait to join their club and become a bit more like them.

None of which much prepared me for my visit to my own

local Toastmasters club, Voice of Wales, which meets every other Thursday in the small Welsh town of Usk. No one here looked much like the people in the publicity photos. Instead there were cardigans in muted colours, a certain amount of awkward dentistry, a couple of cheap blazers too and some odd eyeshadow. On a table sat a large plate of custard creams and an urn of tea.

I had been told that I would be visiting on A Very Special Evening as it would mark the end of one Voice of Wales Presidential term and the beginning of another. There would be a number of visiting dignitaries from other Toastmasters clubs as well as the Area and District Governors. Alongside the usual speeches and table topics, I was assured, there would be pomp and there would be ceremony. 'Please ask for me when you arrive,' the incoming President had emailed me the night before. 'I will be the nervous one doing the headless chicken impression.'

I arrived at The Sessions House, home by day to Usk Town Council, on a golden July evening. The small book-lined chamber where the meeting was to be held was filled with dust-flecked shafts of light. A large yellow Toastmaster's flag attached to two poles was propped on the far wall, in front of it a wooden lectern and then rows of plastic chairs. There were about thirty of us there, of all ages. Everyone I spoke to had joined Voice of Wales because they were scared of public speaking and had some personal or professional reason to overcome that timidity. I looked around me; here was a society of timid souls alright and, although everyone looked happy to be among kindred spirits, the smiles were tense and you could almost taste the adrenaline.

I was handed a running order that broke the whole evening down into increments of one, two, three and five minutes and the meeting followed it rigidly. As these increments ticked by, it dawned on me that this protocol was the only thing keeping the simmering fear under control. The 'Sergeant-at-Arms' opened proceedings delivering a 'Call To Order', at which point all informality ceased – that was down to take two minutes, and it did. Then a 'Welcome', which took five. Next the Past President handed over to the New President who then made the 'President's Address', five and seven minutes respectively, and on it went. The Presidents, outgoing and incoming, said uplifting things about 'rising to the challenge' and wore little medals around their necks, embossed with a blue enamel 'T'. Small silver cups were dished out to the worthy in assorted categories and there was lots of clapping. Twenty-seven minutes in, the so-called Grammarian, a man in a grey jumper called Andy, stood up for three minutes to introduce The Word of The Day. He had been inspired, he said, by *Sesame Street* and so The Word of The Day would be, we learned, any word beginning with 'V', 'but not "very"' he said, wagging a finger. A couple of Toastmasters giggled hysterically.

Next, the Area Governor, a woman called Charlotte who reminded me a little of Delia Smith, took her sixty-second slot to introduce the three main speakers of the night. There were to be three prepared speeches, each seven minutes long, each a milestone on the way to becoming a Toastmasters Competent Communicator. This journey is marked by making ten speeches over many weeks according to a strict set of internationally fixed guidelines and you could tell where each speaker was on that journey by the letters and a number on their name badge: CC1 all the way up to CC10. After that, the sky is the limit; you can become an 'Advanced Communicator', if you want, or a 'Competent Leader', and so on until you are a Distinguished Toastmaster, a DTM, which seems to be a bit like having a DSO.

'You must,' Charlotte told them, 'fulfil the objectives of each speech and control any nervousness you may feel.'

First, a rather shouty woman held forth about a child she sponsored in Latin America. Another stepped up to decry space travel as a waste of money. The third opined as to why it was important not to prejudge people upon first meeting. Each speaker soberly shook the hand of the last speaker as they stepped up to the lectern; each began with their best shot at a bright smile and the formal salutation, 'Toastmasters, Madame Toastmaster, Welcome Guests, Friends'. And each time, I found myself holding my breath with the rest of the audience. It was like that moment in *Gladiator* where Russell Crowe rakes his hand through the Colosseum sand. Then one by one, they began to address us. Each held the lectern with studied authority, even though their eyes still looked scared; each began to prowl the stage back and forth, as they had been taught, using lots of those gestures that involve holding the upper part of each arm close to your body then gesticulating loosely from the elbow. I think it was supposed to look authoritative and relaxed – and, gradually, it began to. I recollected an army sergeant a few months before yelling at the young soldiers he was training, '*Come on! Show me your war face!*' and I recalled how part of Being Brave is actually just Looking Brave, *Acting Brave*. At Voice of Wales, it was more like '*Show me your Cicero face!*'

Next we took a break, with some biscuits and orange squash, during which everyone was asked to score each speaker on a pre-printed Toastmasters International ballot sheet with perforated sections for each speech. At the end of the break, another Call To Order (two minutes) was followed by an Introduction to the Evaluations of the three speeches (one minute) and then by the Evaluations themselves (three minutes apiece). These were generally benign and encouraging – 'very nice eye contact', 'I loved it when you said "sapphire blue ocean"' – with a pointer or two towards improving performance – 'try not to clasp your hands together' and so on.

The assembled company was then invited to Evaluate the Evaluations on the perforated ballot sheets. A short hair-raising section of improvised speeches from the floor on 'Table Topics' ramped the adrenaline sky-high again before there were yet more Evaluations, as well as reports from the Timekeeper, the 'Ah Counter' (who counts utterances of 'er' and 'ah' per speaker) and the Grammarian on his favourite usage of words beginning with 'V', as well as some other words he liked, such as 'gobsmacked' and 'glaciation'.

'Apologies to Andy,' said one Toastmaster wit, 'for popping out in the middle of his evaluation. I had to make a Visit. That's another "V" for you!' And everyone laughed, apparently giddy with relief that we had all survived.

Then there was more clapping and at the appointed hour, everyone dispersed into the twilit streets of Usk, a little braver than they had been two hours earlier.

❧

After the business with the actors and singers who did not wish to be interviewed, I was less surprised by how difficult it was to persuade their therapists to talk. For in London, New York, LA, and other cities where the creative industries cluster, there turn out to be a considerable number of private clinics and therapy rooms specialising in performance anxiety, stage fright and the associated drug and alcohol dependencies. Clearly, for a shrink, there is a buck to be turned here and 'discretion', in the form of levels of secrecy more suited to espionage than to entertainment, seems to be very much part of what they are selling.

At length, I persuaded one such therapist to meet me, on the condition that I would print neither a name, nor his/

her gender. It would be usual in reporting such a meeting to eschew details of particular cases or anything that might compromise patient confidentiality, but apparently even *the area of London* in which he/she had his/her clinic was also too hot to handle. The interview itself – for which I was bundled in and out early in the morning before the working day began – turned out to be a soup of innocuous generalities about childhood pressure and perfectionism, a narcissistic desire for attention and then the fear of that attention, as the veteran actor had mentioned. There followed some observations about the shame of losing one's nerve – which presumably accounted for the furtive manner in which we had met – and, finally, a few Sufi breathing techniques.

There was just one part I found truly surprising. The therapist told me that he/she treated all kinds of performers, but that a significant majority of his/her patients turned out to be orchestral musicians. Moreover, *every one* of these had, upon presentation, been taking beta blockers in order to manage their nerves.

'I shouldn't have said that really,' he/she said at that point and we drew swiftly to a close.

Percentages differ according to the study as to how many orchestral musicians suffer from severe performance anxiety, from 16 per cent (Fishbein et al, 1988) to 21 per cent (van Kemenade, van Son & van Heech, 1995), to a survey of more than two thousand orchestral musicians (Lockwood, 1989) that found that an astonishing 24 per cent have experience of the most severe forms of performance anxiety. A survey of 56 orchestras (James, 1998) found that 70 per cent had suffered or do suffer from anxiety severe enough to impair the quality of their performance. For 16 per cent, this happened more than once a week.

Here was fear indeed and I had not expected to find it in such a place. Had I given it much thought, I would have assumed that the decorum of the setting and the ensemble nature of the performance somehow soaked up any fear, but these recent figures, by any standards, were on an epidemic scale. Which makes sense of why high levels of silent drug use have become so very much part of how many orchestral musicians prop up their courage. Forget about rock stars in rehab; take a look in the orchestra pit.

It seems to have started quietly in 1966 when *The Lancet* published the findings of a study into the effect of beta blockers on anxiety. This article was the first to suggest that drugs typically prescribed for heart conditions or hypertension might also be used in the treatment of stage fright. Here was a pill you could pop that took away the debilitating physical symptoms of fear – nausea, dizziness, sweating, breathlessness, shaking – with all their devastating effects upon the fine motor control required to play an instrument, but which, unlike alcohol or tranquillizers, previously the recourse of many a nervous musician, left your wits and your performance apparently undimmed. The beta blocker of choice was propranolol, marketed under the name of Inderal. A little over twenty years later, a survey by the International Conference of Symphony Orchestra Musicians in the US revealed that 27 per cent of its musicians had used Inderal to mitigate their stage fright. An as-yet unpublished study of 357 musicians across eight premier orchestras in Australia (quoted in Professor Dianna Kenny's recent book, *The Psychology of Musical Performance Anxiety*) set the figure who used propranolol to manage their performance anxiety at nearly 30 per cent.

'I wish that I could have that sense of pleasure and enjoyment of playing in public without being medicated,' said Ken Mirkin, a gentle, beetle-browed viola player with the New York Philharmonic, as we sat in his apartment a couple of blocks from the Lincoln Center.

'I don't know why I have such a sense of panic over it,'

he said. 'I've spent years in psychotherapy and also behavioural modifications, doing bio-feedback and hypnosis and breathing exercises and yoga, visualisation, everything possible and basically the only thing that ever really helped was the Inderal.'

Ken was one of four professional orchestral players I met who take propranolol to steady their nerves, a practice that one of them, a flautist, said was 'as common as masturbation – if you say you don't do it, you're a liar'. Another, an oboe player, said, 'A lot of people look down on it but it's not a performance-enhancing drug, it's a performance-enabling drug. It doesn't practise your scales for you. It just lets you be the musician you are.' The third, a principal French horn, said, 'If playing the right notes in tune is cheating, then I am all for it,' and he laughed.

Of the four, all of them in their fifties and a quarter century in the profession, it was Ken Mirkin for whom the use of propranolol seemed to be the most central and most current. It was he who said, when I asked when he last took some, 'Oh, probably about a couple of weeks ago.'

Ken Mirkin was fifteen when he had his first, shocking experience of stage fright. Admitted to a prestigious summer music programme, Ken entered a masterclass with a famous cellist. 'I put the bow down on the string and it just bounced across the strings "b-r-r-r-r-r-r-r-r-r-r". I said "I'm sorry" and I stopped and I took a breath and said "OK, I'll start again." And it just happened again. I remember I started crying a little and everything was just spinning like I was going to pass out. I had never experienced anxiety like that before. And that set off a whole snowball effect for me. It was so humiliating, what happened in that masterclass, and I was just so afraid of it happening every time I played that it was a self-fulfilling thing. From that moment on, I had a lifelong battle with performance anxiety.'

Still in his teens, Ken started to take Valium for every audition, including the one that won him a place at America's finest conservatoire, the Juilliard School in New York.

Ken described to me the cycle that perpetuated this. It starts with a sense of humiliation, followed by a fear of humiliation, followed by a fear of the fear – 'people are going to think I'm crazy' – followed by an 'unhealthy' sense that the spectators somehow want to see you fail or fall apart, like the circus audience who have come to see the fire-eater burn himself or the tightrope walker fall. 'I always felt like I was walking on a tightrope,' said Ken.

Ken's father was on Inderal for a heart condition and a fellow student had mentioned its use for stage fright. As Juilliard graduation loomed and Ken was, in his words, 'floundering', he made up his mind to try it. He took four of his father's pills with him to the Aspen Music Festival in Colorado that summer and he did something he would never, *ever* normally do. He entered the concerto competition. He practised hard and then took 10 mg of Inderal an hour before the performance.

'For the first time since I was a child,' he said, 'I had this absolutely complete calm. I just started to play and my bow didn't bounce at all – and I won.'

That autumn, auditions for the San Francisco Symphony Orchestra and the New York Philharmonic followed. Ken took Inderal and was offered both jobs. After a short spell in San Francisco, he took the New York job. For a down-at-heel Brooklyn kid, it was a dream come true, 'like playing for the Yankees' said Ken.

I asked if he told anyone about the little pink pills.

'Nobody except for my parents,' he replied. 'I think in those days, it probably would have been similar to how people think about doping in baseball. Inderal is not going to make you play better than you can. It's not like steroids, but people just didn't know what it was and how it worked and I think they would have just thought that I was not much good. I wanted to be accepted for the player I was and Inderal helped me play to my potential; it couldn't make me play better than my potential but I didn't want people to dismiss me because I was using Inderal. So I told nobody.'

That was thirty years ago and Ken Mirkin has been in the New York Philharmonic ever since, but he has never gotten on top of his fear of performing. Even after all these years, if a piece of repertoire is particularly challenging, Ken takes an Inderal. He told me that he expects to take it periodically all his working life.

'I'd love to never take it again,' he said.

'Do you think that might happen?' I asked.

'When I die,' he replied and laughed a little too loudly.

A bit later, I asked Ken what it was that he was actually afraid *of*.

'I'm not sure I ever figured that out,' he said. 'Maybe just a feeling that I'm not good enough. I don't think I ever really had the confidence to think that I really deserved to be something special.'

'And that's not counter-balanced,' I asked, 'by being in one of the best orchestras in the world?'

'No it isn't.' He shook his head. 'It doesn't. No.'

'Is it exacerbated by being in one of the best orchestras in the world?'

'Maybe,' said Ken.

A number of high-profile musicians – Nigel Kennedy is one example – have spoken up against the use of beta blockers in the green room, saying that it deadens performance. It is certainly a banned substance in the Olympics where its use in archery or shooting would constitute cheating. And while it is clearly not 'cheating' in a performance context, there is no getting away from the fact that this is Dutch courage of a sort. Most telling is that people who take Inderal tend to wish they did not. The oboe player I talked to equated it to taking regular Advil for migraines. Ideally you would not, but needs must. 'You do what you have to do,' said another, grimly. From all of them came sound arguments about how the fear is the rational fear of losing one's job, but a whiff of apology seemed to hang in the air that this dread-without-danger could not be marshalled by willpower alone.

Nevertheless, the mechanisms of courage required to overcome stage fright are necessarily as real and true as the next sort. Near the end of our interview, Ken Mirkin said, with great animation, '[Performing] takes a *huge* amount of bravery because you're putting your soul and your reputation on the line every time you go out.' I had wondered at this only a few days before, but now it rang true. 'Not only is it all of your skill and all the practice that you do,' he went on, 'but it's also this whole emotional part too. So you're putting yourself in an extremely vulnerable position every time you perform. To me that takes a huge amount of bravery.'

❧

In 1995, on the eve of the Rugby World Cup, Nelson Mandela gave the South African team captain, Francois Pienaar, an extract of Teddy Roosevelt's 'Man In The Arena' speech – the iconic exhortation to courage from which you will recall the phrase 'timid souls' originally derives. Here was a man who knew a thing or two about courage anointing the notion that a nation's sportsmen could make flesh such a lofty virtue. It was a vindication of sports fans the world over, who had long cast their idols as the bravest of the brave, as gladiators.

Of course, the adversarial nature of sport speaks clearly to the idea that courage is born of opposition or pressure, with international team tournaments like the football or rugby world cups enacting in miniature all the patriotic valour of war, minus the nasty bits. Yet the other part of sporting courage surely lies with what the most high-profile players must endure in terms of a terrifying wash of limelight. If a full house at the Lincoln Center or La Scala sounds scary, try a roaring, baying crowd of a hundred thousand, half of whom actively want you to screw up, the other half of whom have pinned their every hope upon watching you excel. Add to that banks of cameras on all sides, shooting your every movement in high resolution for second-by-second analysis by a phalanx of commentators, not to mention your employers, and oh yes, if it is one of your more prominent matches, a global television audience of *hundreds of millions*. That you get paid freakish amounts of money for doing this must only go a limited distance towards settling your nerves.

Which is why I decided to track down a man who mediates such terrors. He is one of English football's more shadowy figures, an Italian 'mental strength' trainer called Christian Lattanzio, now part of the coaching team at Manchester City FC. Lattanzio's name hit the headlines during the 2010 World Cup, when he was spotted among the entourage of Fabio Capello, the then England manager. Headlines screamed that at last the English squad had given in to the need expressed by their previous manager, Sven-Göran Eriksson, for some kind of 'mental training' in order to shore up their nerve. The official England line stated that Lattanzio was acting simply as Capello's translator, but feverish speculation ensued as to which esoteric mind arts he might be inculcating in the dressing room.

When he and I met, Mr Lattanzio – a small, wiry man in his early forties with very white teeth and a careful, scholarly manner – seemed keen to play down this mental training of the England squad.

'I want to be as low profile as possible, really,' he said and it occurred to me at first that this might be because he had so transparently failed to teach the English team much in the way of 'mental strength' – or courage, by another name – given how they were trounced out of the World Cup amid howls that they had lost their bottle. However, Lattanzio assured me that he was indeed translating for 'the boss', Fabio Capello, and that the mental strength coaching was, so he said, 'very minimal'. He referred to a presentation he had delivered for the squad on the subject, but said that no player had been obliged to take up the offer of mental coaching. 'The boss,' said Lattanzio, with his strong Italian accent, 'believes in giving freedom to the players and to let them decide whether they want to enquire further or not. And if they don't it's fine; if they do, I am at their disposal twenty-four seven.'

Lattanzio was vague about any further detail – possibly he was contractually required to be – and I could not work out why, having agreed to this interview, he appeared to be flannelling. Then he suddenly said, 'I am very cautious, because I think there is a lot of misconception about this kind of work' and he looked me in the eye.

It dawned on me that Lattanzio's circumspection might be less about how this played in the public eye, so much as how it played within the Premier League community, especially among the players. The last thing he seemed to want to do was to be seen to be proselytising from the rooftops about 'mental strength'.

'I believe,' he said, 'that the definition of talent must include mental strength somewhere along the line, because I've seen players, technically and physically very, very gifted, certainly capable of playing at the top of the game, but they never made it because of mental issues. And I'm not talking here about clinical problems, but simply about being able to be disciplined and coordinate their actions. But the definition of talent, in many countries, and in England it seems to be the same, is about what can you produce with the ball on your feet, rather than to have the mental strength.' And he looked a little saddened at this.

Christian Lattanzio is not exactly a lone voice on this subject – Carlo Ancelotti, one of the most sought-after managers in the sport and former manager at Chelsea FC, appointed a sport psychologist as his number two during his tenure at Chelsea – but to focus on the inner workings of the player's head is nevertheless to swim against the tide.

Which perhaps explains why there was something almost furtive about our meeting in a small box room with a vacuum cleaner, at the back of the media centre at the MCFC training ground. The centre stood away from the main training block in the middle of a car park packed with expensive cars; occasionally some tall kid of athletic build wandered past wearing a huge Rolex and drove off in one of them. At one point, a car valet service set up a gazebo and started noisily jet-washing a vast blacked-out Mercedes right next to our small window. No one seemed to notice that we were there and perhaps our apparent invisibility made Lattanzio relax a little. For he began to talk about the stigma that can attach to suggesting one might *learn* one's courage in this most macho of sports.

'There is a concept in psychology called anchoring,' he said, 'and I am amazed how this has been used in a negative way towards introducing sports psychology. The perception is that if you come from outside and you come dressed in a different way, that you don't belong. It looks like you are there to solve a problem,' – I noted that Lattanzio was wearing the standard blue and black MCFC training kit – 'now, players tend to anchor that figure to a problem solver and therefore, they think "I don't want to be seen as a problem, so I don't want to talk to the guy". So I think that if you are in-house and you have more of a coaching role, you are seen as somebody that is here anyway, then I think you can better offer that support. But the first thing still when I go to some seminars is "Oh, I would like you to talk with a couple of nutters that I've got at the club", – he laughed – 'and I always say "Well, probably I wouldn't be the right person. I want to work with the ones that are doing well". Like physical training, you don't train physically only when you are injured, but you train every day.'

I had inched as close as I was going to get to the truth of Christian Lattanzio's job spec and so we turned instead to talk of how a footballer might actually train his mind to withstand the terrifying rigours of performance.

'We can consciously only concentrate on a quite limited number of things,' said Lattanzio, 'but if you start to think about billions of people watching, the way that the press write about you and how the opposition treat you, then you are using some channel that you will not be able to use to perform. People say you have to be focused, but I don't think that we *cannot* be focused. I think that the brain works in such a way that we *always* focus; we just might not be focused on the right things. So you need to have a plan, a simple one, that can bring you back to where you are supposed to be mentally.'

The plan ran something like this.

'I always work on the formula that is *performance = preparation + the state you access during the game*' – Lattanzio drew an imaginary diagram with his finger on the table – 'The preparation is always the way they train, the way they eat, the way they rest, the way they conduct their life. And the interesting thing is that when the referee blows the whistle the only thing that you can control is your emotional and physical state, because you can't do anything about the way you've prepared. It is difficult to change your mental state during a high-pressure situation because things move too quickly, but it is possible by changing the physiological indicator of the mental state, muscular tension and breathing or by visualising a positive experience, although of course that requires training.'

Here was that old trick again, the one that I had observed with the would-be orators of Usk, the big wave surfers of San Clemente and many others besides – that if you can enact the semblance of imperturbability, go through every motion of calm and poise, whether you are a whiskery librarian from South Wales or a global football star, then *looking* brave may yet take you half the way to *being* brave. Just as Don Quixote aped valiant knights of old, tilting at windmills and sheep, risking and enduring ridicule on all sides, and yet emerging still a brave man, so the curious business of performance illuminates a certain path to courage. Without danger, there is no automatic presumption of courage, but if fear sets in, it still takes real bravery to overcome it.

Towards the end of our conversation, just before Manchester City's afternoon training session, Christian Lattanzio said this:

'For a Premier League player, every time that the ball comes to his feet, he's under pressure because of the pace of the game and because everyone is looking at him. For me, the courage is to be able to receive the ball and play, not hide at difficult times in the game, when your team's not doing well but still you want the ball. To be able to ask for the ball and to show that you can do what you're supposed to do, *to play* – because it's very difficult when things are not going well to keep showing that. The bravery for me comes from being able to absorb and to metabolise the negative experiences and transform them somehow into positive ones. It is to come out and to take your responsibility.'

Six months after this conversation, Manchester City won

the Premier League. But now, Timid Souls, step back from the stadium. Remove from your mind the roar of the crowd and forget the handsome pay packet. Read those words of Christian Lattanzio again, starting at 'For me, the courage ...' You may wish to replace one or all of the words, 'ball', 'play' and 'game'.

It sounds scarcely different from another sort of job, does it not, that a fit, young man might do, another sort of courage he might learn?

# 6

# Maŋ (II)

*J'ai vécu.*
I survived

The Abbé Sieyès, when asked what he had
done during the French Revolution

Imagine this. You are standing in the desert. You are an eighteen-year-old soldier. You signed up three years ago, when
you were scarcely more than a child, but this is your first
war. The combats you are wearing are patched and came in
packaging marked with the name of the last war your country's army fought in this desert. You were only six back then.
You have spent the last month in a desert camp not far away,
waiting and training and watching your country's leader on
satellite TV arguing the *casus belli*. Every few days you drive
in convoy up to the border between one tract of desert and
the other and then you drive back again. A few of you crack
jokes about coming on holiday. But one day, a Friday, you
cross that border and, along with many thousands of others,
you have become, overnight, an invading army. Monday

comes and your brigade is assigned a mission. You are to look for the enemy's armoured division in what your seniors term 'virgin territory'. This is how you pass the week: by day, you patrol down long, straight, desert roads waiting to see if anyone or anything shoots at you and periodically they do; by night, you sleep on the sand with your buddies inside a square of your parked vehicles. It is very hot; you smoke a lot of cigarettes and eat a certain quantity of boil-in-the-bag burger'n'beans, but you have yet to really taste war.

Until now. It is Friday again, your eighth day in theatre. You are standing in the same desert as before, but you are surrounded by blood, flames, gunfire and screaming. This is to be your first and your last day of war.

✤

Before I go on, I should mention incidentally how very difficult it is to write or speak of these things without being drawn into that old habit of glamorising the whole dirty, bloody business; of finding order, meaning and nobility where there may in fact be little or none. And strangely, it is courage, of all things, that plays will-o'-the-wisp here – one moment, alive and true in a material act of humanity, the next, little more than an idea, a fluke, even a game or a lie.

In John Steinbeck's great novel, *East of Eden*, comes a jewel of war rhetoric. It is delivered in the form of a father's pep talk as he prepares his reluctant son for enlistment:

> "I want to tell you that a soldier gives up so much to get something back. From the day of a child's birth he is taught by every circumstance, by every law and rule and right, to protect his own life. He starts with that great instinct, and everything confirms it. And then he is a soldier and he must learn to violate all of this – he must

learn coldly to put himself in the way of losing his own life without going mad. And if you can do that – and, mind you, some can't – then you will have the greatest gift of all. Look, son," Cyrus said earnestly, "nearly all men are afraid, and they don't even know what causes their fear – shadows, perplexities, dangers without names and numbers, fear of a faceless death. But if you can bring yourself to face not shadows but real death, described and recognisable, by bullet or sabre, arrow or lance, then you never need be afraid again, at least not in the same way you were before. Then you will be a man set apart from other men, safe where other men may cry in terror. This is the great reward. Maybe this is the only reward. Maybe this is the final purity all ringed with filth."

There is a twist, of course. For Cyrus Trask, the speaker of these sage words, is a fraud, a man whose experience of war was, like our teenager in the desert, a single devastating engagement. However – quite unlike the teenager, as I would discover – Cyrus went on to build a life upon his soldierly acumen and yarns of his many battles. The question remains whether Trask's fabrication devalues the poetry and wisdom of what he says. Those interested in courage should pay particular attention to that 'final purity all ringed with filth'. Because courage is what he is referring to, of course.

And so, as I considered war once again – and this time from the perspective of the individual, aside from the group – I found myself wondering whether this 'purity' is what binds bravery and conflict together. Or whether that is just a fantasy peddled by a fantasist, propping up an old fiction for which so many fall. Is this about 'pure' courage or simply what a Timid Soul will do to stay alive?

❧

Last spring, I drove the long, straight road down over the moors towards the most westerly tip of England to visit Christopher Finney GC. We sipped Nescafé in a small bright sitting room, as his baby daughter tootled about the floor with some large rubber alphabet letters and then proceeded to lie face down on her father's chest and go to sleep, rising and falling with his breath, as he talked of terrible things. For Chris Finney was that boy in the desert, a young armoured vehicle driver with D Squadron of the British Blues and Royals. The year was 2003 and the desert lay in southern Iraq.

A week after crossing the border from Kuwait, Chris's troop, a convoy of five armoured reconnaissance vehicles, was on its way to help another troop that had 'found' the missing Iraqi 6th Armoured Division north-west of Basra. Eighteen-year-old Chris was at the controls of the lead Scimitar. On the way, the convoy slowed almost to a standstill to weigh up what threat, if any, might be presented by a small settlement of mud houses behind a bank and next to a waterway.

'Then out of nowhere,' said Chris, 'came the biggest bang ever. I was looking through my driver sights which is about the size of a letterbox and I didn't see anything other than a massive spark, a flame. I didn't know what had happened at all. Then Alan' – this was the gunner, Lance Corporal Alan Tudball – 'was screaming on the headsets. I thought we'd been shot at by an RPG and that Alan was scared basically' – Chris laughed as he said this – 'So I was thinking "bloody hell, shut up, will you"?'

The bang was in fact a 30 mm round shearing through the top of the gun turret, straight through Alan Tudball's left thigh and out through the floor. It was luck of a sort, Chris pointed out, that the Scimitar had not been issued with the standard belly of anti-mine under armour, for if it had, the round would have bounced around inside.

The command came over Chris's headset to 'Reverse!

Reverse! Reverse!' and Chris followed the order, inadvertently flinging the commander issuing it from the top of the vehicle into the sand. The fall yanked the officer's headset off and communication between them was cut. Another loud bang followed, as Chris hit the vehicle behind.

'I thought "oh no, they've done us from the front, they've cut us off from the back and now we're all going to die," he said. 'So I opened my hatch up and I stuck my head up and there were three people running away from us across the river and I was convinced they were Mujahedeen, so I thought "Right, they're having it."'

Chris ducked down to grab his rifle from the bracket behind the driver seat, but these brackets were stiff and the back of the cabin, an area packed with ammunition, was a wall of flame. Chris gave up, another fragment of malformed luck, for the three figures were the driver of the vehicle behind, his own commander who had fallen off the Scimitar and the overall troop leader, all running for cover.

Chris's helmet was tethered to the vehicle radio, so he pulled it off, scrambled out and stood on top of the Scimitar for a moment, no helmet, no gun, his body armour open because of the heat.

'I was just looking for direction. Because I was so junior. It's very much like the junior ranks and the troopers are the kids and the seniors are the grown-ups. The lads were even saying "oh the grown-ups are coming, put your fags out." It was almost, if you wanted to put it like that, *the grown-ups will look after us, it'll be alright. I'll just do what they tell me to do and it'll be fine*. It wasn't until we actually got attacked that I thought "Bloody hell, no one's going to tell me anything."'

Realising how exposed he was, Chris jumped down and saw Alan Tudball struggling to get out of his hatch. He shinned up onto the burning vehicle and leaned in to help Tudball out – 'it just gave me something to do, to be honest, while we figure out what's next'. Alan was stumbling and holding his head, then he fell over.

'Alan,' Chris had said, 'what's happened mate, what's wrong?'

'Morphine,' Alan had replied, 'get me morphine.'

Chris did not realise that Alan also had a head wound, meaning the morphine every combat soldier carries in his right leg pocket could kill him. So Chris was working out how to get to Alan's morphine without dragging the injured leg through the dirt, when he spotted an aircraft immediately above. 'That was the first I knew there had ever even been a plane,' said Chris. It opened fire.

'I used to have a game on the PC,' Chris told me, 'called *M1 Tank Platoon II* and at the time I thought the sounds were shit, totally inaccurate. But I can tell you they are exactly what an A10 sounds like and I knew only America had A10s. The second it started firing I thought of that game. It was so low you could see the pilot, his head and his helmet. I just thought "I'm dead".'

Chris grabbed Alan, who was unconscious, and tried to haul him out of the line of fire.

'Then my whole right arm shook and I was dragged to my knees,' said Chris, 'and I thought that I'd hurt Alan and he'd reached out at my leg to stop me, so I stood up and turned around. Alan was a mess. He'd got shot in his head and in his arm and I think his chest and he had blood coming out his ears, his mouth, and his leg was already smashed up. I thought he was dead and no one was doing anything about it' – Chris shook his head, still apparently finding this hard to believe – 'So I lay down next to him and put my arm around him and I said "Come on mate, wake up," and then he didn't, so I cried a little bit, and then I stood up and I looked down at my boots and thought I was going to be in the shit because you don't join the Household Cavalry and get away with dirty boots and I realised what was making them dirty was blood and I thought "where's that come from"?'

Chris had been shot in the buttock and was bleeding heavily. On the hillside above, he saw the coloured smoke used to indicate friendly fire. Then he spotted Alan's headset hanging off the side of the Scimitar.

The official account of the incident says that Trooper Finney now 'calmly and concisely sent a lucid situation report by radio'. His exact words, so he told me, were, 'Hello, fucking anyone. It's Chris. Alan's dead. I've been hit. Come and get us, you wankers. Over.'

Chris lets out a short hollow laugh. 'I don't know how much you know about speaking on the radio but you're not meant to swear, you're not meant to say names. It was like the worst radio message you could imagine. And the fact was that everyone within a ten-mile radius had seen what happened. I didn't need to say it really, but at that moment I felt I had to.'

The Scimitar behind was now burning ferociously too and Chris could hear someone inside it. Realising that the gunner, another good friend, Matty Hull, was trapped, Chris climbed up on top of the vehicle to try and get him out.

'You could hear rounds starting to cook off and ping around inside, it was pretty horrible' – he paused, then told me quietly how a soldier appeared from one of the rear vehicles and persuaded him to climb back down.

'And I thought "yeah, you're probably right, that's just stupidity".' Chris looked out of the window for a moment. 'So we got off and I tapped the side of the vehicle and I said "Ta-da, Matty". And that was that.'

Chris said this last part so quickly that I did not catch it at first and I asked him to repeat it, which he did, word for word, and then there was a long silence.

This is where Chris Finney's moment of war came to an end, although the incident itself would become infamous.

First aid arrived; Chris and Alan were taken to a tracked ambulance. It was only the next day on the hospital ship that Chris found out Alan Tudball had survived. The body of Matty Hull was not recovered until the following day. It was reported that two Iraqi civilians who were waving a large white flag were also shot dead by the A10.

Thanks to what happened on 28 March 2003, Chris Finney is the youngest person ever to be awarded the George Cross. It would have been the Victoria Cross, of course, with which the George Cross ranks equally, had the attack come from enemy guns.

I asked Chris if there was something about his youth or inexperience that had made him act as he did.

'Maybe,' came the one-word reply.

'Would a more seasoned soldier have been running across the field with the others?'

'Perhaps, yeah.' He glanced down at his baby girl who was beginning to stir on her father's chest. 'In the same way that she'll go and play with fire but I won't, because I know it's going to hurt me. Maybe.'

It often seems that the most prestigious war medals are associated with the times when things go badly wrong. As for Chris Finney, he seems to read blunders as the reality of war. And I do not wish to misrepresent him – he was not bitter; he was certainly not anti-war or anti-military and he was chary to blame anybody for what took place: 'I'd say shit happens,' he said. He said he had 'inner peace' about his conduct that day and he was 'very proud' of his medal, too, notwithstanding some scepticism as to whether what he had done was actually brave – 'the Household Cavalry are good at writing citations,' is how he put it. Even so, Finney's whole account of that day was deeply (if unwittingly) woven with a narrative of blunder. This seemed to be how he had made sense of it: from the absence of under armour that stopped the first A10 round from potentially killing everyone in the vehicle, to the awkward rifle bracket that prevented Chris from gunning down three of his own cohort; from the second attack that stopped him administering potentially lethal morphine to a friend with a head wound, to the jammed gun-turret hatch that trapped Matty Hull. On all sides, helmets and headsets were wrenched-off, and among the pilots in the air, misinformation and muddled radio frequencies confounded. People fell over, ran when they should have stayed, stayed when they should have run. Right down to the patched combats from the last Gulf War, it was, as Chris called it in the old British military slang, 'a cake and arse party'. And yet the man himself had been outstandingly brave, not least because of his persistent and instinctive humanity in the most inhuman predicament.

The final gaffe is perhaps that the very medal which might have redeemed the episode by recognising Finney's courage – a final purity to be drawn from the filth, if you go with Steinbeck – may be the very thing that ended Chris's military career. He told me how the weight of expectation that accompanied a medal as prestigious as a GC became a burden, something he could not live up to, a performance he could not repeat. 'I'm not an actor that can be in another film and I'm not a writer who's got my latest novel coming out and has got this skill that can go on and on and on. It was literally a couple of minutes in a desert eight years ago. It doesn't mean I'm a good soldier. It means I'm a good friend. And maybe stupid. I don't want my whole life to be judged on that.'

That is why in 2009 Christopher Finney left the British Army. He now runs what I like to think of as the bravest garden centre in the west (of England) and despite it all, as he and his small daughter waved me goodbye from the back door, he struck me as a happy man.

You can purloin valour, apparently. Nick it. Pinch it. Nobble it. Steal it. But should dishonesty begin to stir within you, I had better warn against this particular larceny. Because to Steal Valour – in America at least – can land you in jail for a whole year.

Xavier Alvarez's problem was not so much light fingers, as an unfortunate habit of making things up. This was a man who reportedly touted an array of exotic whoppers, from one about marrying a Mexican film star, to another about playing hockey for the Detroit Red Wings, even one about rescuing an American ambassador during the Iranian hostage crisis. His big mistake, however, was to tell the board of the Three Valleys Municipal Water District in Los Angeles County, to which he had been elected in 2007, that he was a retired marine who had won the Medal of Honor, the highest military award in the country. 'I got wounded many times by the same guy,' Alvarez claimed in open session, 'I'm still around.'

The story was a fabrication. When the truth came out Alvarez was vilified in the local press and turfed off the water board. However, thanks to the Stolen Valor Act of 2005, signed into law by George W. Bush at the end of 2006, it was now not simply pathetic or insulting to peddle such rot, but illegal too. This was a piece of legislation that broadened an existing federal law prohibiting the unauthorized wear, manufacture or sale of awards and decorations of the United States Military. It now also became an offence to falsely claim to have received a US Military award or decoration. Moreover, there were double the penalties, from six months to one year's custodial sentence, if the award about which you were telling tall tales happened to be the Medal of Honor.

All this may sound Pythonesque, but apparently Medal of Honor phoneys were seen to be becoming something of a blight, Timid Souls of a sort driven to desperate means by a desire to be seen as brave.

As for the case of United States v. Alvarez, the appeal process dragged from 2010, through 2011 and into 2012, thanks to a tortuous and surreal debate about the nature of veracity, falsehood and their relationship with First Amendment liberty. Surely an American citizen had the constitutional right to hornswoggle as much as he liked, cried one side, so long as it was not fraud, defamation or incitement. On the contrary, argued the other, how could a government raise up the soldierly virtues as worth a hill of beans, if you then allowed charlatans of all shapes and sizes to debase those virtues with their counterfeit claims. 'What about unfaithful spouses?' hollered one side. 'What about Holocaust deniers?' bellowed the other.

At length and to dismay in certain quarters, the Alvarez conviction was upheld by the Supreme Court, and so there it was – you could fib to your wife about that pretty girl at the office, you could add as many mendacious flourishes as you thought you could get away with to your CV, but courage, particularly of the military sort, would only hold its value as a moral currency if folk like Mr Alvarez were not allowed to go around lying through their teeth about it. The tacit message seemed to be that without a kind of gold standard, upheld in the sanctity of the Medal of Honor, then heaven knows what courage might become. It is hard to think of another virtue that would be legally deemed so susceptible to taint; equally, it is hard to think of another virtue a man might be so eager to lie about.

There is no problem, however – you will be glad to hear this – with branding one of the best-selling first-person shooter video games of the last ten years as *Medal of Honor*. No problem with that at all.

Back in Chepstow, one of the serjeants of 1st Battalion The Rifles mentioned this *Medal of Honor* game to me (the latest version of which is set in Afghanistan). We were talking a few weeks after he and the other soldiers I had met earlier in 2011 returned from fighting in Helmand. The battle group, which included various cohorts from other parts of the army and navy, had suffered ten fatalities during their six-month tour in Nahr-e Saraj, five of the dead from 1 Rifles. There had been around eighty casualties severe enough to be flown home, one in ten of these with so-called 'life-changing injuries', including three double amputees. Their Commanding Officer called it 'a steady drum beat of attrition'. The question I had asked the serjeant was about whether a soldier injured or killed on operational duty in a war zone is demonstrably courageous simply by virtue of the fact that they were there and that the risk had been borne out.

'You're a civilian, OK,' he said, 'and you go into a Careers Office. No one's forced you to go into that Careers Office. You've done it off your own back. And you know what you're in for. I mean, in this day and age, with *Medal of Honor* games, Xbox games and all the media coverage, if you don't know what you're going to get yourself into, then you're a mug, isn't it? [sic] It's nothing about being brave. You're just doing your own mental game of 'I want to go and do that. I want a piece of that. I want to be a part of that.' And you know the consequences.'

This conversation was part of another two days I spent at Beachley Barracks, in the same acid-yellow classroom as before, talking to each of the infantrymen and women I had met in March the week before they went to war. Yes, thank God, everyone I had met did come back, although, while I had passed these months in the usual civilian fashion, many of 1 Rifles had, so the saying goes, Been To Hell And Back.

The soldiers and their commanders told me about searing

temperatures up to 50°C, a disconcerting so-called '360° battle' with insurgent forces on all sides, no clear battle lines and, at the peak of summer, a landscape thick with crops four or five feet above their heads. Improvised Explosive Devices (IEDs) remained the weapon of choice for the enemy side, although they had graduated to devices with little or no metal content, undermining the efficacy of those much-rehearsed drills with metal detectors. New drills were rapidly developed *in situ*. The regimental serjeant major said he reckoned of the IEDs they *did* find before they detonated, around 80 per cent were discovered by 'ground signs' alone. One multiple commander told me about finding such a bomb when he simply spotted some grass out of the corner of his eye lying the wrong way on top of some other grass. Another described two dozen plastic Coke bottles, each of them filled with home-made explosives and with a pressure plate taped to the top, each powered with a battery pack, the part that would give a Vallon reading, dug-in a few metres away. All were buried within a couple of hundred metres of one particular checkpoint.

Of the five Battalion deaths in the course of the April to October tour – that is around one to a hundred men deployed from Beachley – four of them were killed by IEDs. Not that the trauma was equitably shared out. One young Rifleman, this his first deployment, managed to get through the whole thing without seeing anything bloody first-hand. Another seasoned colour serjeant, on his third Afghan tour, was visibly shaken by the 'harsh' things he had witnessed this time, present when two of the three double amputations took place – 'it was injuries that you just thought *Jesus Christ, how is he still alive?*' he said and he shut his eyes for a moment.

The cumulative account of that summer in Nahr-e Saraj offered other insights too: the Commanding Officer brushing the teeth of one of the most severely injured men in the hospital at Camp Bastion; a serjeant promoted to fill the place of a friend killed the previous evening, now running forward and rummaging in a flooded ditch for a live grenade hurled at his first patrol in command – he throws it away, it explodes safely and they patrol on (Deacon Cutterham would later receive the Conspicuous Gallantry Cross for this); a young lance corporal opening a parcel of water balloons sent from home and the riotous water fight that ensued that hot afternoon at the checkpoint; a corporal on the last war of his twenty-year army career standing in a corner of the patrol base, folding the kit of an old and now dead friend to be sent home with the body; or the unmistakeable sadness of one of the older soldiers at the promotion he has won upon returning home, the one that will now take him away from all that was meaningful and vital about the front line.

I was pretty sure you got none of this on a console war game.

Outside the Green Zone, these were months of big news: Osama bin Laden had been shot dead; President Obama had announced the drawdown of US troops by 2014; the tenth anniversary of the war itself had come and gone. These macro events, while clearly of some significance among the upper ranks, seemed barely to have registered with the Riflemen on the ground. Their focus was close: the next patrol; their mates; the number of weeks to go until R & R (the two-week break every soldier gets mid-tour); or the 'chuff chart' countdown until it was time to go home; in other words, *survival*.

Lance Corporal Hayley Ridgeway, the petite twenty-three-year-old medic who had gone to war with a lucky teddy from her mum and a sweet wrapper from her kid brother, had an extraordinarily tough tour – everyone said so, from the commanders to the junior soldiers, all of them with a certain hushed respect for how 'a female' could be so brave.

'There's quite a lot to tell you this time,' she said to me, as she took off her beret and sat down.

---

Hayley was based at a checkpoint in the south of Nahr-e Saraj called Shaparak, home to the twenty-five men of 8 Platoon C Company, with Hayley as their team medic. The CP itself was not big and conditions were tough there, with very basic facilities. The men took it in turn to patrol, as often as three or four times a day, and every time they went out, they took their only medic, Hayley, with them. As the summer fighting season got underway, a major ISAF (International Security Assistance Force) offensive to the north seemed to trigger a change of enemy tactics. CP Shaparak, which had been fairly quiet until then, now became the focus of an intense IED battle right outside the gate. The dozens of primed Coke bottles were theirs and much more besides. 'We were riddled with IEDs,' said Hayley. In late July, one of the platoon and a good friend aged just nineteen lost both his legs and part of one arm. After that, the mood darkened.

'I know we're meant to say "Oh we're doing a good thing",' said Hayley, 'but everyone was down, of course they were. Every time we went out of the gate we were scared. It was horrible.'

On 12 August around teatime, as the day was beginning to cool, one such routine patrol girded themselves and stepped out of the gate heading for Dactran village nearby. The line of nine men and Hayley was just a hundred and fifty metres from the checkpoint when there was a massive explosion. This was the situation Hayley had most been dreading, so she told me before the tour – treating her own friends. Out of the dust, emerged the interpreter at a sprint, part of his hand blown off and shrieking. As he passed, she heard a voice calling 'Hayley, Hayley, medic, medic.' Struggling to her feet – a rock seemed to have hit her knee in the blast – Hayley went to work, checking each man as she passed up the line. Arriving at the platoon commander, twenty-four-year-old Lieutenant Dan Clack – 'the Boss' Hayley called him – she saw that his leg was bent off to one side. Straightening it up before anyone could see it, she checked him. 'And he wasn't breathing,' she said. 'He didn't have a pulse and I thought "well I've got to do something".' Hayley put up an intraosseous drip, used in the most severe trauma, and then she heard someone else screaming. Leaving Dan Clack in the care of three of his men, Hayley followed the noise. Her friend Lowy had been peppered with ball bearings and had instinctively run for the nearest treeline before collapsing. Through the smoke and dust, she found him, gave him morphine, and removed three ball bearings from his neck. The remainder of the patrol had less urgent injuries. Together they now loaded Dan Clack onto a quad bike that had been sent out from the checkpoint and they drove back. Hayley said she could remember running behind the quad and not being able to keep up. She realised that she was limping but 'I wasn't going to check,' she said.

Back inside Shaparak and knowing that the medical helicopter would not be there for another twenty minutes, Hayley looked at 'the Boss'.

'We're going to start CPR.'

'What, is he dead?' said one of them.

'It doesn't matter,' said Hayley, 'We're going to get him back.'

And for a moment, she did get Dan Clack back. Dan began to be sick. Removing the airway tube from his mouth, Hayley whispered in his ear, 'When I put this back in your mouth I want you to clamp down on it'. And he did, Hayley said, 'so I knew he was listening to me'. His pulse returned and when she asked him to squeeze her hand, he did.

'The only thing I wanted to do then was get every single person to say something to him so that if he didn't make it, at least he knows his friends are there. Because he wasn't the boss, he was our friend. So I got all his Rifleman to line up and I said "Just say something to him. Anything." So they were like "Come on Boss. You've done it this far, you can do it." Or just calling him every name under the sun and saying "Just stop being a weasel". We used to call him Snagglepuss, because he slept an unbelievable amount. And people were just shouting that to him "Oh, come on Snagglepuss, there's plenty of time to sleep. You can't sleep now.'" Hayley looked down and fiddled with a toggle on her uniform. 'Every single lad said something to him.'

They were still doing CPR when the helicopter arrived. Four of the five injured men, including Dan Clack, were placed on board.

'And as we handed him over,' said Hayley, 'to be honest, I thought I'd done it. I thought, if I could bring him back, that was it, he'd stay back.' Hayley paused for a moment. 'I really thought we'd got him back.'

Dan Clack died on the helicopter. The surgeons at Camp Bastion said that there was no way he could have survived, his jugular severed by a single ball bearing from the explosion. Technically Hayley should not have been able to resuscitate him at all. 'Well I promise you I did,' she said, 'I'm not making it up.'

The brave postscript to this is that all the while Hayley herself was badly injured. A ball bearing had split her kneecap, the metal lodged so deeply that there was a moment when the doctors thought the leg would have to be amputated. She was evacuated from CP Shaparak that evening and three days later was back in England. It took three operations to remove the ball bearing and save her knee. On 18 August 2011, the body of Dan Clack was the last ever to be repatriated with due ceremony through Wootton Bassett – future repatriations were moved to RAF Brize Norton. In March 2012, Hayley Ridgeway was Mentioned in Dispatches for what she did the day he died.

———————

'Yeah, so that was the twelfth of August,' she said to me at the end. 'The worst day of my life.'

Before I left Beachley Barracks, I asked everyone what it was that made all this bravery and loyalty and endurance worth it and I got a strange array of answers. Hayley and the more junior soldiers without exception stuck to the mantra about friendship. The Commanding Officer agreed, adding that the tour had proved it, but he also said how hard it was to get a reporter in the UK to write about the tactical progress ISAF was making. Another senior figure at the Battalion said this: 'Do I think it was worth dying for? I can't picture anything to be blatantly honest with you. I don't think it's worth a life, the Afghan cause. I certainly don't think it's worth three or four hundred that we've lost now. But that aside – OK I've got be careful what I'm saying here – I don't *personally* think it's worth a life, but I think they did die courageously and doing something that they love and something that they enjoy and that they signed up for. They get a full military funeral and it's a very respectful way to go.'

And this, I suppose, may be a 'final purity' of a sort.

❧

There is a famous thought experiment in ethics called the Trolley Problem. It is the brainchild of two of the most prominent female ethical philosophers of the late twentieth century – Philippa Foot at Oxford, whom we encountered earlier, and also Judith Jarvis Thomson at MIT. The Trolley Problem has a close, if not exactly straightforward, relationship with courage of the military variety and indeed, trainee soldiers in the US Army are taught to wrap their thinking gear around this one.

Foot's version (the first) goes like this: a trolley or train is running out of control down a track. In its path are five people who cannot escape. The good news is that there is a spur nearby and by turning onto the spur, the driver, Edward, can send the runaway trolley the other way, thereby saving the five. The bad news is that there is one person tied to this spur. Should Edward turn or not?

The second version (Thomson's) casts it thus: the runaway trolley is out of control as before. Again, there are five poor souls in its path. This time, however, a man called George is on a bridge under which the trolley will pass. George can stop it, if only he pushes the very fat man who happens to be standing next to him onto the track, where his heft will halt the trolley, saving the five but killing the fat man. Is this what George should do?

It is, as Thomson wrote, 'a lovely, nasty difficulty'. The Trolley Problem has been restaged many times by different thinkers, the core dilemma standing testimony to the limitations of pure utilitarianism – the 'greatest good for the greatest number'. For, if you take the utilitarian approach, of course, Edward should turn and George should shove. However, numerous psychological studies of our intuitions on such matters of life and death have consistently shown that while on the whole people tend to favour turning the trolley, potentially sacrificing the person tied to the spur (or some comparative harm), they also feel it is wrong actively to kill, either the fat man or anyone else, their ethical squeamishness related to the level of intentionality to harm.

Which brings me back to courage. Because while on paper it should be possible to calculate a clear path for ethical and specifically *courageous* action (and courage is one virtue that likes to be busy), sometimes the ethical, the courageous thing is to withhold action. What is more, in the fog of war such dilemmas may be far from clear-cut. That is the point. That is the 'lovely, nasty difficulty' of it and in reality, the crossroads at which the physical and moral courage of many a soldier may part company.

❦

A telephone call.

> – Hello?
> – Tony.
> – Aldo?
> – You're not going to believe this. I'm down. I've lost my foot.
> – Stop messing about.
> – I'm not messing about. I wouldn't mess about with things like this.
> – Stop messing about.
> – Tony, I'm telling you, I've lost my foot.
> [a loud bang]
> – Oh my God.
> [The line goes dead]

On 6 March 2005, Sergeant Alderson left the British Army after twenty-four years in bomb disposal. On 9 March 2005, Mr Alderson arrived in Afghanistan to work for an aid organisation involved in clearing old Soviet munitions and for the next eighteen months, he was, in his words, 'blowing sixty tonne a week'.

At the end of September the following year, this same David Alderson was engaged by ArmorGroup, a large British private security company contracted to the UN. This time the job was to clean up in the immediate aftermath of the short but brutal Lebanon war waged that summer between Israel and Hezbollah. Israeli cluster bombing in southern Lebanon had left large areas littered with submunitions, millions upon millions of bomblets the size of a matchbox that lay where they fell, or dangled from trees. Small but deadly, these bomblets were claiming civilian lives.

Alderson was running one of two teams working around Deir Mimas, an ancient village that stands on an arid bluff surrounded by wadies where fruit and olives grow. The team's task was to look for the submunitions; their team leader, Alderson, would then 'get rid of' whatever they found. The particular problem in Deir Mimas was that the war had ended just as the olive harvest was about to begin and it was proving impossible to keep local farmers, impoverished by months of conflict, out of their olive groves.

On 24 November, Aldo, as everyone calls him, was having a mid-morning break and a brew with the village mukhtar when he heard two explosions in a wady nearby. He and the other team leader, a Bosnian bomb disposal specialist called Damir Paradzik, went to investigate.

At the top of the narrow valley, the team medic shouted down in Arabic and a familiar voice shrieked up from among the trees, the words indistinct. The cries came from a goat herder called Sabah, whom Aldo had got to know and says he 'bollocked' every morning not to take his animals into this olive grove until it had been cleared. 'He's bloody hurt,' thought Aldo.

'Right, come on,' he said. 'We're going down.'

Aldo and Damir dropped down to the old riverbed in the direction of the voice and there they saw four dead goats and in the midst Sabah who was darting about in blind panic.

'Tell him to stand still,' shouted Aldo up to the medic. 'We can't do anything while he's running about. He's making more danger for us all. *Just get him to stand still.*'

Aldo did not have to do what he did next. Slowly, carefully, he walked over to Sabah, checking the ground, checking the bushes. Something was not right. There was no evidence of bomblets, no packaging, none of the spaces cluster bombs leave behind, nothing. Aldo grabbed Sabah who was still dancing on the spot and sent him back up the path towards Damir who was some distance behind. As he turned, Aldo looked; still no sign of what had killed Sabah's goats and nearly killed Sabah.

'OK, we've got him out,' Damir called down.

'Damir.' Aldo's voice echoed off the steep gulley sides. 'There's something wrong here.' He paused. 'I'm coming out the way I went in.'

Gingerly, Aldo began to turn and bang, he was thrown forward with a blast of heat, a tang of carbon.

He says the next thing he remembers is being face down on the ground, his ears 'ringing like mad'. He got into a push-up position. One arm was ripped open but it could take his weight. He looked down, 'checked the crown jewels first' and looked beyond to his feet. One of them was not there.

'Great,' said Aldo under his breath.

'Are you alright? *Are you alright?*' Damir was yelling.

'I've lost my foot,' called Aldo, 'but don't worry'.

'I'm coming to get you.'

'Well just watch what you're doing.'

Aldo pushed himself up against the trunk of an olive tree and, wiping blood out of his eyes, looked up. At the rocky lip of the wady, he could see his team panicking.

'Stand still!' he shouted. 'You're not coming in.'

Aldo lit a cigarette, got out his mobile and made that telephone call to his boss, Tony. The explosion that interrupted the call came from where Damir was picking his way down.

Now it was Aldo shouting up to Damir, who replied that he had lost his leg. He had in fact like Aldo lost a foot, the language barrier and the shock confusing the issue, but immediately the priority changed to Damir. Aldo took charge from his position against the tree, yelling to his team three hundred feet above to line up down the path and pass Damir back up that steep but safe part of the bank.

'*THIS,*' he bellowed, '*IS – A – MINEFIELD,*' lest anyone was in any doubt.

'Well how are *you* going to get out?' yelled someone.

'I've got two choices.' His voice echoed. 'I either wait for another team to come in, but I'm going to bleed out. Or I'm going to have to do something and get out myself.'

Aldo could not go forward, of course, but he could not go backwards either, as it was in his footsteps that Damir had been walking when he was hit. Nearby was the thirty-foot dry riverbank and Aldo called up to his medic that he was going to try and climb up that.

'Look, if I get hit, I'm not going to know anything about it, but at least you can tell people what I was doing.'

The medic nodded and Aldo began to crawl. His out-stretched hand touched something. Another mine. The blood in his eyes meant that Aldo had to disarm it by touch alone, flipping back the lid and unscrewing the clock striker. Then, leaving the disarmed mine for the investigation that would surely follow, Aldo began to climb, the pain now kicking in as he leant for a moment, unthinkingly, not on a foot but on the tattered flesh where it had once been. Within moments, he reached the top. 'I don't know how I did it, but I did. All my men call me 'Tiger' now.'

The Deir Mimas olive grove turned out to be an undisclosed unmarked minefield laid by Israeli special forces a few months earlier to target fighters coming and going from a Hezbollah weapons cache apparently further down the wady. To lay an unmarked minefield is against the Geneva Convention, of course. It took the Israeli Defence Minister more than two weeks to concede that such minefields existed.

For Aldo, having clambered out of what was to all intents

and purposes Hell, it was ambulance, hospital, surgery, repatriation, more surgery, rehabilitation and, seven months later, he and his new prosthetic steel Flex-foot returned to work, and not at a desk. This time he was demining in Uganda. After that, it was back to southern Lebanon for a further eighteen months. Another stint in Afghanistan followed. When, in the summer of 2011, I flew to the northeast of England, and drove to a small town called Saltburn-by-the-Sea, south of Newcastle, to meet David Alderson, he was six weeks back from southern Sudan and just about to depart for Kandahar again, this time for up to two years. The job? In his words, to 'tidy up' after the battles waged around Kandahar over the last year.

There is more than a little monkish austerity about David Alderson when I meet him in person. There is no small talk upon my arrival at his father's council house, home for the weeks that Alderson is in the UK; there is no tea, no talk of the journey or the weather, no flummery of any sort. There is a courteous hello, followed by a silence, as I settle and unpack my tape recorder and notebook in a neat, plain sitting room with scratchy chairs. On the walls are one or two of the military equivalent of school photos, a flowery plate that is also a clock and a framed certificate from the Royal Humane Society honouring Alderson's courage in the Deir Mimas minefield. On the coffee table, there is one of those heavy cut-glass ashtrays you used to get in British pubs and Alderson chain-smokes throughout the interview. While he volunteers the specifics of his story, what people said and did in forensic if impassive detail, endeavouring to draw Alderson into the psychological hinterland beyond his extraordinary tale is something of a losing game.

I ask him, for instance, what it is that he enjoys about the job. 'You're saving lives, aren't you?' he replies. 'Our job is try and save life, not get rid of it.' He flicks his ash and looks up at me for my next question. Much of the interview goes like this. It is not evasion as such, just plain speaking of the plainest variety. What is very clear however – and also strangely monastic – is his dogged sense of vocation.

'I've always had no fear, you know what I mean?' he says. 'I don't know why, but even as a young kid I wanted to be bomb disposal.'

Alderson's father, who is watching TV in the kitchen next door, was also in the army and his son signed up at sixteen, adamant that he would end up in EOD (Explosive Ordnance Disposal).

I ask about Alderson's mother and he tells me his parents divorced when he was a child.

'Did you have a close relationship with her?' I ask.

'No, not really.'

I ask how many bombs Alderson has diffused.

'I've done that many,' he says, 'I've lost count.'

'Thousands? Tens of thousands?'

'Tens of thousands. Hundreds of thousands,' he replies.

'Before 2006 had you ever been injured?'

'No.'

'Had you had any close shaves?'

'No, nope.'

'So it's possible to be pretty safe doing this?'

'Yeah. The way that we look at it is if you respect it, it will respect you,' he says, 'It's just about sorting it out, because a lot of people will run away, but somebody's got to do it, otherwise the world would come to a grinding halt. That's why I say we're a special breed.'

I ask how he thinks that 'special breed' learn to live with the risk.

'You just get used to it. There's not many of us that are still married.'

There is an old joke in bomb disposal that EOD stands for Every One Divorced.

'It's because we're away a lot. It just gets too much for the wife. They'll be on tenterhooks,' and he lights another cigarette.

'Were you married?' I ask.

'I was married yeah.'

'Have you got kids?'

'I've got two yeah.'

He tells me later that his daughter, aged fifteen, and son, aged thirteen, have just moved to Canada with their mother.

'Does the job get harder to do after you've got children?'

'No, no. In our job you're either dedicated to it or you're not. There's no mediocre. And I've always been dedicated to it.'

'Have you ever had a moment where your dedication has faltered?' I ask, realising that I am looking at the steel pole sticking out of a flesh-coloured prosthesis a little way below Aldo's knee (he is wearing shorts) and into a blue sock and a boot.

'No,' he replies.

'Is bomb disposal to some extent your reason to live?'

'I suppose yeah. I'm very proud of it.'

In talking about what happened at Deir Mimas, Alderson says he has had no flashbacks, no inner struggles with the loss of his foot and ankle, no doubt about returning to work. He is also very clear that he felt unafraid throughout the episode itself; 'as calm as a cucumber' is how he puts it and, having met him, I can believe it.

'I put it down to three things,' he says, 'one was my training, two was adrenaline and the third was survivability, willing to survive. That's the only way I can explain it.'

David Alderson puts me in mind of that line, 'A soldier gives up so much to get something back'. Here indeed is 'a man set apart from other men' but not without paying a price. Perhaps that is why Alderson's courage appears to be triple distilled, as if the water had been removed from it somehow. And while this kind of bravery is certainly austere, it is not nihilistic. Instead there is an almost religious zealotry to the survival here, unshakeable and stripped down to the barest essentials. And if ever Aldo had a Timid Soul, it is long gone.

∗

There is another side to survival of course. No 'great reward', no 'final purity', just *survival*. I saw it more powerfully than at any other time in my life in Kosovo, first in 1999 and again nearly twelve years later – for the civilian drawn into violent conflict has none of the training, physical or mental, that might arm a soldier against the horrors of war. And yet they must needs be brave.

Vjollca Berisha is visibly shaking the first time I see her. It is early September 1999 and a colleague and I are watching camera rushes filmed as part of a documentary we are making for the BBC. We have been following a British police team sent to Kosovo in the immediate aftermath of the war there to gather forensic evidence of war crimes for the UN Tribunal in The Hague. I have already shared with the Timid Souls those absurd paroxysms that gripped me prior to commencing the job, but now this footage, over which we huddle on a small monitor screen, is no laughing matter.

It shows a school gymnasium with the usual climbing bars and ropes. All over the floor, white plastic sheeting has been rolled out and it is dotted with people's belongings, a watch here, a belt there, a cheap brooch, a list written on a piece of paper and tucked into an empty wallet. Taped to the climbing bars are photographs in plastic wallets, each showing a piece of clothing, a cardigan, a child's sneaker, a leather jacket. Each item is encrusted with a thin film of reddish mud, each labelled with a long number written in marker pen on a blue card. A long line of people shuffle past the exhibits and photos, more or less in silence. Occasionally someone catches the elbow of a companion and points to something; the companion shakes their head and they shuffle on.

These remnants have been laid out by the UN investigators, the personal effects excavated from a series of mass graves around the small town of Suva Reka, which lies in a lush wide valley in southern Kosovo. In March 1999, this valley bore witness to a bloodbath that followed the beginning of NATO air strikes on Serbian targets. As the bombing began, Serb paramilitary units reacted with apocalyptic abandon, sweeping down through this valley, killing hundreds upon hundreds of ethnic Albanian civilians. The bodies of most of the dead then disappeared: until now.

The belongings displayed in the Suva Reka gym have been found either on or alongside bodies or body parts exhumed and now waiting unidentified in black body bags at a makeshift mortuary in an agricultural building on the edge of town. One large collection of items, including dozens of shoes and scraps of clothing, was found in the churned mud of an old firing range, from which it seems that many interred bodies had been removed by heavy machines and taken elsewhere, leaving only these items and a few grim shreds of human remains behind.

While the UN process is geared to accumulating evidence of crimes committed, to enumerate and if possible name the dead, there is another agenda here too. Many of the local people in this room do not know what happened to their fathers and mothers, their sons and daughters, but they fear the worst and everywhere you turn, you witness a hunger to reclaim and bury their dead. Everyone in this gym is looking for a sign quite literally from beyond the grave.

'There she is,' says my colleague, pointing to the monitor screen, where a woman and a child have just walked into shot. 'That's Vjollca. And that is Gramoz.'

A small boy aged eight or nine is holding on to his mother's arm with both hands. She seems almost oblivious to him, although they are pressed against one another. Vjollca seems able to look only at the ceiling or the walls, turning her head anywhere rather than look at what is laid out on the floor. She is wearing a black tracksuit zipped right up under the chin and the thin shiny fabric quivers wherever it drapes between the contours of her thin frame. Gramoz's expression is blank, but hers is contorted, as though the muscles of her face were fighting to keep her mouth shut somehow. Presumably if she were to part her lips, even to take a breath, howls might fill the air and never stop.

When this footage was filmed, Vjollca Berisha had just come out of hiding and had returned to her home town for the first time in five months. She and her son Gramoz left on 26 March, two of only three survivors of one of the worst atrocities of the Kosovo war.

Around lunchtime that day, Serbian police in Suva Reka massacred forty-nine members of the extended Berisha family, from an eighteen-month-old baby to a woman eight months pregnant and a ninety-nine-year-old great-grandmother. The men were shot against the wall of the courtyard between their family homes, the women and children corralled into a nearby pizza restaurant where machine guns were fired through the windows and grenades hurled until everyone lay still. Vjollca's husband died by their back door, her two elder children in the restaurant. She and Gramoz survived by playing dead amid a lifeless tangle of those they loved the most and they left Suva Reka slung in a flatbed truck of bodies. Mother and son jumped unseen from the back of the truck outside town and not five minutes' drive from the firing range where the UN later found all those shoes and shreds of clothing, now laid out on the floor of the school gym.

Items belonging to forty-two of the forty-nine dead Berishas are eventually identified among the material excavated from the firing range, largely thanks to the labours of one of the surviving Berisha family, a cousin and former lawyer called Hysni. Hysni Berisha lives up the road from the main family compound. That is how he, his wife and two kids escaped the bloodshed. It was Hysni who, when UN troops finally rolled into Suva Reka on 13 June, ran into the road gesticulating and who led them to the pizza restaurant. Once the UN War Crimes Tribunal exhumations begin some weeks later, he appears at the graveside every day, no sight or smell so shocking to him as the truth of what happened to his family. The day they find nine-year-old Mirat Berisha's school jotter in the pit is, Hysni says, 'the worst day of my life'. But the bodies are nowhere to be found. One day, lest the scale of the crime has eluded us, Hysni hands me a typed list:

| # | Name | Father's name | Surname | Age | Date of murder | Status |
|---|------|---------------|---------|-----|----------------|--------|
| 1 | Hanumsha | Rrustem | Berisha | 80 | 26.03.1999 | Missing |
| 2 | Musli | Sahit | Berisha | 60 | 26.03.1999 | Missing |
| 3 | Nafije | Musli | Berisha | 56 | 26.03.1999 | Missing |
| 4 | Zymryte | Musli | Berisha | 30 | 26.03.1999 | Missing |
| 5 | Afrim | Musli | Berisha | 24 | 26.03.1999 | Missing |
| 6 | Violeta | Musli | Berisha | 22 | 26.03.1999 | Missing |
| 7 | Hamdi | Sahit | Berisha | 53 | 26.03.1999 | Missing |
| 8 | Zelije | Halil | Berisha | 43 | 26.03.1999 | Missing |
| 9 | Arta | Hamdi | Berisha | 17 | 26.03.1999 | Missing |
| 10 | Zana | Hamdi | Berisha | 15 | 26.03.1999 | Missing |
| 11 | Merita | Hamdi | Berisha | 14 | 26.03.1999 | Missing |
| 12 | Hanumsha | Hamdi | Berisha | 12 | 26.03.1999 | Missing |
| 13 | Mirat | Hamdi | Berisha | 9 | 26.03.1999 | Missing |

| # | Name | Father's name | Surname | Age | Date of murder | Status |
|---|------|---------------|---------|-----|----------------|--------|
| 14 | Avdi | Sahit | Berisha | 46 | 26.03.1999 | Missing |
| 15 | Fatime | Maliq | Berisha | 43 | 26.03.1999 | Missing |
| 16 | Kushtrim | Avdi | Berisha | 12 | 26.03.1999 | Missing |
| 17 | Nexhat | Faik | Berisha | 44 | 26.03.1999 | Missing |
| 18 | Majlinda | Nexhat | Berisha | 15 | 26.03.1999 | Missing |
| 19 | Erolinda | Nexhat | Berisha | 13 | 26.03.1999 | Missing |
| 20 | Redon | Nexhat | Berisha | 2 | 26.03.1999 | Missing |
| 21 | Altin | Nexhat | Berisha | 11 | 26.03.1999 | Missing |
| 22 | Fatime | | Berisha | 49 | 26.03.1999 | Missing |
| 23 | Faton | Ismet | Berisha | 28 | 26.03.1999 | Missing |
| 24 | Sebahate | Idriz | Berisha | 26 | 26.03.1999 | Missing |
| 25 | Ismet | Faton | Berisha | 3 | 26.03.1999 | Missing |
| 26 | Heron | Faton | Berisha | 1 | 26.03.1999 | Missing |
| 27 | Shirine | Ismet | Berisha | 16 | 26.03.1999 | Missing |
| 28 | Hava | Ramadan | Berisha | 63 | 26.03.1999 | Missing |
| 29 | Sedat | Vesel | Berisha | 45 | 26.03.1999 | Missing |
| 30 | Dafina | Sedat | Berisha | 15 | 26.03.1999 | Missing |
| 31 | Drilon | Sedat | Berisha | 13 | 26.03.1999 | Missing |
| 32 | Bujar | Vesel | Berisha | 41 | 26.03.1999 | Missing |
| 33 | Florije | Muharrem | Berisha | 39 | 26.03.1999 | Missing |
| 34 | Vlorijan | Bujar | Berisha | 15 | 26.03.1999 | Missing |
| 35 | Edon | Bujar | Berisha | 13 | 26.03.1999 | Missing |
| 36 | Dorontina | Bujar | Berisha | 3 | 26.03.1999 | Missing |
| 37 | Nexhmedin | Vesel | Berisha | 38 | 26.03.1999 | Missing |
| 38 | Lirije | | Berisha | 28 | 26.03.1999 | Missing |
| 39 | Vesel | Shaban | Berisha | 65 | 26.03.1999 | Missing |
| 40 | Sofije | | Berisha | 58 | 26.03.1999 | Missing |
| 41 | Hatixhe | | Berisha | 99 | 26.03.1999 | Missing |
| 42 | Hajdin | Vesel | Berisha | 37 | 26.03.1999 | Missing |
| 43 | Mihrije | Rraif | Berisha | 26 | 26.03.1999 | Missing |
| 44 | Besim | Vesel | Berisha | 33 | 26.03.1999 | Missing |
| 45 | Mevlyde | | Berisha | 26 | 26.03.1999 | Missing |
| 46 | Genc | Besim | Berisha | 4 | 26.03.1999 | Missing |
| 47 | Granit | Besim | Berisha | 2 | 26.03.1999 | Missing |
| 48 | Fatmire | Vesel | Berisha | 23 | 26.03.1999 | Missing |
| 49 | Jashar | Melit | Berisha | 55 | 26.03.1999 | Missing |

Numbers 29, 30 and 31 are Vjollca's husband and her other two children. Next Hysni takes our camera crew to the yard where the men were shot, pointing out the bullet holes in the concrete; and to the pizza restaurant, a horrific place, scorched, pock-marked and streaked with dried blood, a broken ladies' watch and a half melted baby's bottle among the shattered glass on the floor.

That was 1999. A little under two years later, a series of mass graves was excavated at a secure military facility in Batajnica outside Belgrade. In one trench, the burned, decayed and fragmented bodies of 'at least' fourteen women, thirteen men, all in civilian clothing, as well as nine children, including a baby and a foetus almost at term, were found alongside ID documents belonging to several of the Berisha family. When Slobodan Milošević went to trial in The Hague the following winter, the Suva Reka massacre and subsequent cover-up were among the evidence against him. In 2009, after a two-and-a-half-year trial, four Serb policemen were jailed in Belgrade for their role in the killing of the Berishas, although three of the accused walked free, including the commander of the unit who had carried out the attack.

Over the years, I have often thought of Vjollca and Gramoz Berisha and of their cousin, Hysni. That is why, twelve years after the massacre, and with The Society of Timid Souls in mind, I travelled back to southern Kosovo to find out how a person who experiences horror on this scale can find the courage not only to survive but to *live*.

Within minutes of my arrival in Suva Reka, Hysni Berisha was at the hotel to meet me and greeted me like an old friend. For the rest of the day, he drove me around the various locations again: the restaurant (still a ruin); the firing range (now a rubbish dump); the Berisha compound (still empty, but with a noisy family next door, cleaning a rug with a hose and broom, as small children ran back and forth through the spray). In the evening, we went to Vjollca's house in nearby Prizren, or rather her father's house, for although Vjollca works in Suva Reka every day, driving along the very road onto which she and Gramoz jumped from the truck of dead bodies, she has never returned to her own house.

I sat with Vjollca, Hysni and her father in a neat, modern sitting room, a dish of chocolate biscuits untouched between us. On top of the TV was one of those photo frames with three apertures, with Vjollca's husband Sedat in one, her son Drilon in another and daughter Dafina in the third. Vjollca told me again about 26 March, an account punctuated with horrific detail: the gunmen swearing at the crying children; the feeling that kerosene was being poured onto the bodies, before Vjollca realised it was blood; her son Drilon tugging his sweatshirt hood down to try and protect his head from the bullets; a nephew, Altin, stirring on the stretcher they were using to carry the bodies to the truck and being shot again; the men cleaning the blood off the pavement before they drove off. She told me about the other survivor, her sister-in-law Shyhrete Berisha, who now lives in Germany and who whispered that they must jump from the vehicle, 'Or they will bury us alive.' All four of Shyhrete's children had been killed. Shyhrete said she was going to leave them behind, lifted the tarpaulin and jumped.

'I was in a dilemma,' said Vjollca. 'I reached for Gramoz, who was lying on a couple of corpses, nearby. I wanted to see his face one more time. I moved the sweatshirt that was over his face and I saw his eyes – they were open. He was staring at me. "Moz, are you alive?" He said, "Yes". I told him we were going to jump from the truck. He was afraid and said, "No". I just pulled him. There was another child, Mirat, who was still alive and was crying. I begged him to let me help him jump off first and then I would follow with Gramoz. But he started screaming for his mother, even louder. I was running out of time. I got hold of Gramoz, raised the truck cover and jumped. We fell in the middle of the road and within seconds we were on our feet. I grabbed his hand and we headed for the fields.'

One Serb family near the road gave them sugar water and took them to another Albanian house nearby. There they were given first aid and driven to Vjollca's sister's house in the hills where they hid for the rest of the war.

For a long time, so said Vjollca, Gramoz had nightmares and nosebleeds, but he never spoke to his mother of what had happened. 'Never, not a word,' she said.

I asked Vjollca how she herself found the courage to live and she said, 'Only my heart knows how I managed to get on with life, waking every morning to those memories. At the beginning, I wished I was dead. I even tried not to eat or sleep. And time has not healed because there are too many victims. But, what else could I do? Life goes on, whether we like it or not, and we have a saying that man is stronger than stone. Also I had to think about Gramoz and that made me feel stronger.'

Throughout our conversation, Vjollca has been kneading a patch of skin just below one of her collarbones so hard that it leaves large red marks, her face a mask of pain, but at the end she says, 'You will wait for Gramoz, won't you? I am expecting him any moment. He has been at university in Pristina all week. I want you to see him.' Then she adds, 'My face is different when he is around.'

And in he walks, the key to Vjollca's survival: a tall good-looking young man of twenty, with a trendy haircut and trainers. Gramoz kisses his mum and her face erupts in a vast smile that I would never have thought possible. She wrinkles her nose at him and then leaning a shoulder against his chest, turns back to look at me, beaming.

# 7

# Gravity

Each time we make a choice, we pay
With courage to behold the restless day,
And count it fair.

'Courage', Amelia Earhart

Even for those of us in the luxurious position of having been
spared war and genocide, disaster and disease, there remains,
beyond survival, the thorny issue of how to make the best of
one short life. In the wealthy West, the pursuit of the individual goal has become like a religion, as projected identities
and bucket lists of 'dreams' replace the soul and prayers. So
The Good Life as philosophers once framed it morphs into
The Lived Life. For some, this Lived Life might be full of
altruistic vocation – think of Aldo Alderson, or Sally-Ann
Sutton and her reflexive inability to stand by when someone
needs help. For others, the calling might be creative, as for
Renée Fleming, or adrenaline-fuelled as for Mike Parsons.
The inspiration for the choices made can be cultural, as for
Rafaelillo, or spring from love, as for Hal and Fran Finney.

But the point is this: even without the *extremis* endured or sought out by these people, it is true that every Timid Soul seeking their own Lived Life requires not simply self-knowledge but the courage of conviction too.

And so it was that I found myself drawn to one particular constituency who enact this Lived Life more dramatically, more poetically than any other. What they do – and this is what they all have in common – is to challenge the force that glues our feet to the planet: gravity itself. Reclaiming the airy wilderness above our heads, they climb; they jump; they walk tightropes. Of course, once upon a time, you had to be careful that this kind of thing did not tip over into hubris; remember Icarus and those lousy wings? But we do not worry so much about challenging the gods these days. In fact, although most of us remain terrified by the physical experience of great height, our language of aspiration and desire remains tied to the heavens – the sky is our limit, we reach for the stars, our dreams take flight, our ambition soars.

And some folk take this literally. For them, a defiance of fundamental Newtonian law is not only exhilarating but also strangely meaningful, a philosophical exercise in brave living.

❧

At the bottom of the 'Business' page on Alain Robert's website is a section on sponsorship. Monsieur Robert is better known as 'the French Spiderman', an urban climber now famous for his rope-free ascents of the world's most iconic skyscrapers. By this point in browsing, we have already learned what Alain Robert might bring to your convention, seminar or event. This final paragraph addresses how his relationship with your brand might work for you:

*Big businesses and entrepreneurs want to associate their brand names with the image of a man who personifies courage and pushes the limits. Sponsors images are displayed during Alain's events and on his website. If you wish more piece of information do not hesitate to contact us.*

A Swiss watchmaker had gone for it; someone who sold climbing equipment too, as well as a French chain of hair-transplant clinics and Norgil, the country's leading brand of hair replacement products. I, however, was less interested in how Robert, a man now in his late forties, achieved his lustrous shoulder-length locks than I was to discover how anyone in their right mind was able to scale the exterior of more than a hundred of the world's tallest monuments and buildings. He has climbed Taipei 101 in Taiwan (1667 feet), The Petronas Tower in Kuala Lumpur (1483 feet), The Willis Tower in Chicago (1453 feet), The Empire State Building (1250 feet) – and the list runs on. Moreover, he has managed to do this, on many occasions, with nothing more than a pair of soft leather shoes and, slung on the back of his belt, a pouch of chalk powder into which he periodically probes the fingers of a bare hand. Surely such a man should be called on to advise the Society of Timid Souls. And so I clicked the *contact us* link.

Some months later, I found myself in the winding back streets of Pézenas, a small town in Languedoc-Roussillon in the south of France, lost and doing loops on foot, searching for the cobbled lane where 'the human spider' lives. My confusion made me fifteen minutes late and this was the first thing Alain Robert mentioned after I had climbed the ancient spiral stone staircase to his small apartment. He appeared touchy that I had not managed to be more punctual. I grovelled and flattered until the atmosphere thawed and then the interview began, although that feeling of walking on eggshells never quite went away.

Gingerly, I began upon the safe ground covered in many press interviews to date and asked Alain Robert about his childhood in Valence.

'I was not even knowing that I wanted to climb at that time, but I knew one thing as a young boy: I knew I wanted to be courageous,' he said. 'I was very clear about it. But I was not courageous. That was the bad thing. And I remember that I was a bit afraid of everything and lacking of self-confidence because I wasn't really tall and kids, they were teasing me a little bit when I was going to school. They can be really tough,' and he shrugged as if to show this did not bother him any more.

Alain Robert is still a tiny man, five foot four inches off the ground and an extraordinary physical presence, crooked and strangely miniature in scale with bunched, twisted shoulders, tiny delicate hands, long wispy hair and a large craggy face that seems too big for his body. He was wearing a black fleece and turquoise leather trousers that expired at a pair of cowboy boots the colour of double cream and with a generous slice of heel.

'So I was admiring Zorro,' he continued, 'Robin Hood, D'Artagnan and I wanted to be like that kind of hero. Even now if I'm watching Zorro, with Banderas, I like it. The only thing is it's not completely realistic. It was more like a dream than something you can really do, I guess.'

When Alain was eight or nine, he began to identify a heroic path that did not require actual swashbuckling as such. It all hinged on the day he watched a Spencer Tracy movie about a pair of brothers who climb Mont Blanc in the wake of a plane crash to look for the wreckage.

'When I saw it on TV, I found it completely extraordinary. I knew that at least this is something that I would be able to do. At least being a climber seems to be possible, not like Zorro or D'Artagnan, but still like the kind of stuff that you saw on TV.' Alain paused for a moment and nodded towards the huge plasma TV he was watching with the sound turned down as we talked.

With one eye on the rolling news channel, Alain shared with me the gold-plated 'Spidie' mythology about how, as a twelve-year-old, he had been locked out of home and had climbed the seven storeys to his family's apartment. Many a journalist has heard this tale of a Timid Soul Delivered. For my version, he said it was 'like a reinvention. It was the right time. It was the right day. I had a good excuse.' And from there it snowballed. He had little to say about the internal transformation that accompanied his becoming a serious rock climber by his late teens, other than that it was a process of willpower, of wanting to be a climber more powerfully than his fear gripped him. This is why, he said, most people do not overcome their fear of heights – they simply do not *want to* as much as he did. But that does not mean he has not had to pay a price.

A devastating accident when he was twenty, one of four serious falls in his lifetime, is what accounts for the peculiarities of Alain's physique now. His surgeon has told journalists that his patient is 'a medical enigma', and Alain's own website boasts that he is 'disabled up to 66 per cent'. He certainly walks with a pronounced limp and his torso is strangely coiled. Both wrists have been broken three times – 'it is like you take this cup,' he said, tapping my coffee, 'and throw it at the wall' – his nose smashed twice, his pelvis once and on two occasions the impact on his skull after a fall put him in a coma for several days, injuries which have affected his balance long term, the medical definition of 'vertigo'. He showed me his mangled wrists, describing how he cannot rotate them but must swivel at the shoulder, then the feathery fingers of one hand, which are, he said, numb and upon which the muscle has 'completely melted'. He demonstrated how he cannot grip a ledge as you or I might, should (heaven forbid) we find ourselves dangling from one, but how he flexes at the joint just below the fingernail and holds his full body weight from a fingertip.

The willpower to recover from the second of these serious accidents was what propelled Alain into free solo, that is, climbing without ropes. 'For me,' he said, 'the dream, the way of living, my own way, is even stronger than all of those obstacles.' And then he passed me an extraordinary photo of himself, taken some time in his twenties, apparently magically glued to a smooth rock face with the toes of two climbing shoes and his fingertips alone. He is halfway through one of the most extreme free solo routes ever climbed.

For the third time that morning, Alain's mobile rang and he took the call, for he has no manager, answering all emails and calls himself. 'Sometimes I am juggling with many things together,' he said, after hanging up, 'I'm always saying "yes" to everybody and then at the end of the day, I'm completely...' and he mimed a flop of exhaustion.

It was one such 'yes' that marked Alain's transition from climbing rock faces to scaling the glassy flanks of skyscrapers, when, in 1994, a watch company invited him to do just that. When it became clear that permission to climb such buildings would not be forthcoming without the use of safety equipment, Robert was asked if he would mind climbing without official consent and from that moment he was reborn as the daring outlaw of his childhood dream. It was in the guerrilla climb – whereby Alain would simply launch himself up the side of a building and by the time security knew what was going on, he was out of reach – that he truly found his niche. 'When I look at it now,' he said, 'I know why I like it even more than just doing my stuff like climbing a cliff,' – he paused and pushed each cowboy boot off with the opposing toe – 'you can't get forbidden to climb a cliff,' and then the French Spiderman warmed his tiny black-socked feet in front of a small electric fan heater plugged in next to the colossal TV.

For the next fifteen years, Alain free-soloed sometimes as many as seven or eight iconic skyscrapers a year. Sometimes he would be arrested part of the way up, other times detained on the rooftop and fined. Sometimes he would wear his sponsors' logos; other times raise money for good causes. Periodically he would be invited to climb too. On two occasions, he even got stuck and had to be rescued by the fire brigade from the side of a building. And with every death-defying ascent, watched by crowds on the ground, office workers sitting at their high altitude desks, and featured in the global press, Alain Robert became famous.

The audience became an integral part of what he does, in a way that was not so very different from those agoraphobics' exposure therapy videos on YouTube, the publicity powering the courage. When I asked Alain about his celebrity, he said, 'Yeah, I'm signing autographs,' and he grinned. 'I would be a liar if I was saying I don't enjoy it. I do enjoy it. It's like when I think about the little boy, shy with his target to become courageous, it's just like such a long way.'

I wondered how he felt about height, for this was surely the abstraction that had delivered his dream and his celebrity.

'I love it, because,' he paused searching for the words, 'because it can easily take back your life. This is maybe the whole concept. That is why I don't use rope because then I would not be able to appreciate height.'

'Why not?' I asked.

'Because … in fact I am interested in living something dangerous. It's a better life for me. I'm not saying it's a better life for everybody, you know, but for me, if there is no matter about life and death, I'm not really interested. The whole concept is this kind of philosophy about being courageous, being brave, being Zorro. I wouldn't feel like I am a kind of Zorro by climbing with a rope.'

Alain Robert is married with three grown children and I knew that his wife, Nicole, sometimes questioned her husband's need to renew this dream of his over and over again, so I asked him whether the recent deaths of two renowned free solo climbers, each of them after decades of daring ascents, had shaken his confidence in any way.

'No,' he said. 'The good thing is that those people, they have had the guts to live, to lead *their* life, because I don't think that somebody who is serving at the McDonalds is living his dream. It's the kind of life where you are doing it because somewhere you are obliged because you are living in a society in which you need to make money to have some food on the table, to have a roof over your head. We think that we are obliged to do this, but we are not so much, not if you really look at it.'

After the interview, Alain swapped his black fleece for a turquoise leather jacket to match his trousers and we sashayed out into the streets of Pézenas for lunch. At a small pizza restaurant he proceeded to devour a great roundel of cheese and dough, washed down with the champagne that, I had noted, he shares with all journalists who interview him, a demonstration, perhaps, of the high life he leads. I had attempted to order a glass of *vin blanc*, but he looked a little disappointed and said, 'You don't like bubbles?' I changed my order.

Over this lunch, we agreed that I would join Alain for his next 'urban Everest', the recently completed Burj Khalifa in Dubai, now the highest building in the world. He told me that the arrangements for the ascent were still under discussion and that he would call when a date was set. Two months later, as much of the region shook to the most violent paroxysms of the Arab Spring, I spotted on the news that the French Spiderman had scaled the Burj Khalifa, all 2717 feet of it, but with the safety harness and rope required by the building's owners who had contracted him. I had been checking in with Alain during this time, but heard nothing of the timing of this ascent in advance. I did not really understand why he did not let me know, other than that it might have something to do with the use of safety gear after what Robert had told me about being Zorro, being brave, about living that dangerous, 'better life'.

✤

In the archives of British Pathé can be found ninety disturbing seconds of newsreel concerning another French citizen with a vertical dream.

Filmed in 1912, it opens in a public garden in Paris. Near some thin trees and a row of street lamps stands a man, garnished, in the fashion of the day, with a moustache the size of a small squirrel and wearing a voluminous soft cap upon his head. The day is misty and cold, the shapes of the buildings behind as if they have been sketched in pencil, the man's every breath a brume in the air. It is his outfit that is of chief interest to the cinematographer and he performs a manly twirl to show off a bulky all-in-one suit swathing his figure. It is drawn in at the waist in the sporting style, ballooning over each leg like a pair of plus fours and, at the back, there is a sort of knapsack integrated into the shoulders of the garment. When he has completed his twirl, the man stands, shifting from foot to foot for a moment, then takes off his hat, looks inside it and puts it back on again, before looking up one last time, straight down the camera lens.

The next shot shows the same man, this time standing on a dining chair atop a small bistro table at the edge of a curving balustrade. Behind him are some distinctive kiosks with arched roofs. The man has now unfurled the contents of his suit into great swags of dark silk, the upper part of which seems to be held above his head by some sort of hidden frame, the lower portions extending to cover his hands and flapping first to his waist, then as he shakes his shoulders, dropping to his ankles. He wrestles with the strange cloak for a moment, like someone trying to make an unruly bed. Then he turns to the balustrade and puts one foot on it, twitching the fabric and glancing up at a low, white sky. Next, he leans forward a little, and he looks down. If it were possible to watch doubt or terror or both descend upon a Timid Soul in the act of trying to be brave, then this is surely what happens next: for a full thirty-nine seconds, the moustachioed man in the hat stands there, one foot on the metal railing, making a few small fidgety movements with a foot or a shoulder, but mostly just looking down. The steam of his breath counts out the moments – five, four, three, two, one – and then leaning, stooping with his head and now his shoulders, as though struggling to wrench the reluctant body behind them, the man jumps.

The next shot shows the great feet of the Eiffel Tower and between them, like a stone, drops the tiny shape of a man, chased by a flutter of limp silk.

These are the final moments of a French tailor called François Reichelt, wearing an experimental parachute of his own design and manufacture. Asked, a few minutes before his ascent to the first platform of the Eiffel Tower, if he might consider a safety rope of some sort, Monsieur Reichelt told journalists from *Le Petit Journal*, 'I wish to attempt this experiment myself and without dissembling, because I intend to prove the value of my invention.' According to *Le Figaro*'s report the next day, he was smiling just before he jumped the fifty-seven metres to the ground, although there is not much evidence of smiling on the newsreel. An unnamed friend of Reichelt's, quoted the day after his death in *Le Gaulois*, implied that commercial pressures to attract sponsorship before the expiry of his patent on the parachute lay behind the unfortunate tailor's hasty publicity stunt.

Who would have thought that ambition and daring could look so like suicide? Or how subtle the tipping point between antic and horror?

※

And so it was a merciful dose of common sense that came along in the personage of Kent Diebolt.

Kent Diebolt runs a rope access company based in New York and Washington DC that uses men or women on ropes to reach inaccessible areas of man-made structures. If a ladder or scaffolding will not suffice, nor opening a window, you call Kent or someone like him. His particular speciality of more than twenty years is detailed architectural surveys of historic pre-war buildings, unattainable by any other means; in other words, *high*.

Kent and his team have dangled from the spire of the Chrysler Building, the dome of the US Capitol, the rafters of the Cathedral Church of St John the Divine, the gilded rooftop of the New York Life Building, the fretted Tribune Tower in Chicago and many more. For them, such vertiginous height is another day at the office, a professional necessity; as Kent puts it, 'the ropes are just how we get to work. It's about the ends not the means, right?'

People who work at height, like Kent Diebolt's team, find themselves in remarkably similar places to Alain Robert or others who pursue height in search of a thrill or a sense of fulfilment. But is it braver to be up there enacting the sloughing-off of fear, than to be examining the patina on the roof tiles, or looking for cracks in the guttering?

Strangely, according to Kent, these two constituencies have one key thing (and one thing only) in common, a magnificent by-product of the extreme conditions in which they find themselves. And it is not a love of adrenaline, but an intensity of focus that is all but impossible to replicate on terra firma.

'A lot of climbing,' explained Diebolt, 'is a mind game. It's about self-control because you get in these positions where the implications of failure are pretty large. What it's about is *focus* and that's what I tell people when they say to me "you must not be afraid of heights". I tell them I *am* afraid of heights, I have a rational fear of heights and when I'm working, I'm not looking down 42nd Street from the spire of the Chrysler Building and saying "what if" because as soon as you say "what if", you've lost the game. So you focus on the work. You're there to do a job, you've been paid well to do it and you just do the work. And at the end of the day you're exhausted mentally and that's part of the charm of it, that absolute focus. You're out of everything else. *Everything.* And the world has fallen away for the day.'

It all relies on the two ropes of the trusted system, used with little variation throughout the rope access industry, whether on oil rigs or in mountain rescue. Independently anchored, one is the work positioning line, the other the tether that will catch you if you fall. Each is separately anchored to a substantial structure at the top of the building, a steel beam, a chimney, a stairwell. You know your knots are good because you tied them yourself. A friction control device on the rope allows you to move down, mechanical rope grabs to move up, as you sit in a boson's chair, a small plastic seat suspended from the rope, and the fall-protection line comes with you. It is, said Kent, 'really safe' and he enthusiastically quoted the industry's 'extraordinary' Health and Safety record. While others trust boom lifts or swing stages, this group trusts ropes. As Kent's chief rigger, Mike, put it drily, 'It depends whose Titanic you want to sail on.'

The key is a meticulous engagement with the detail, from the planning process onwards, an absolute intolerance of sloppiness or complacency. Kent talks about hiring people who are 'safety-minded', rather than daring or fearless. 'I get emails from yahoos who say "I've been climbing El Capitan and I have my own ropes and I have balls this big" and those guys, we're not interested in them.' He laughed and shook his head. 'We don't even answer their emails or calls. I want people working for me that have that rational fear and I'd like them to have that fear every day. You know, complacency is the devil here. Once gravity takes charge, there is no going back. It's irretrievable. You can't rewind or unwind the scene. We say gravity never sleeps. It keeps you on edge and being on edge keeps you cautious.'

Kent's background is in construction and his was the first business to undertake this sort of work in the US. The team's debut job in Manhattan was inspecting the intricate tile work on the vaulted ceiling of Saint Thomas Church, a cathedral-sized neo-Gothic masterpiece at 53rd and Fifth Avenue. The team had drilled a hole through the tile vault of the ceiling and dropped ropes, tied off to some structural steel in the attic above, down through the hole to the floor of the nave ninety-five feet below. Kent then proceeded to climb up to the ceiling. A bank of industrial lighting was directed upwards to illuminate the work, but just as Kent got to the top of the rope, the church's old wiring gave out and the building was plunged into darkness. Down on the church floor, Kent could hear one of the team heading off to change a fuse in the basement, leaving him suspended in the shadows.

'As I was up there by myself in the dark, I looked down at the pews,' he said, 'and all I could see was my crumpled body broken over the back of the pews and as I said before, you just can't go there. And so I wrestled with myself and got a grip, but I had no work to do and I was up there by myself in the dark for ten or fifteen minutes. It was a moment of terror, my worst moment ever.'

We sat in silence for a second and then Kent busied himself by explaining the relationship between exposure, the amount of air and space around you at height, and your levels of what he called 'comfort' and what you or I might term 'fear'. That explains why dangling from a spire is 'less comfortable' than being attached to the side of a big building with another such building across the street; it is why to hang at the corner of a tall edifice feels worse than being in the middle of one facade. In other words, even if you are a man as practical as Kent Diebolt, fear, as Montaigne once put it, 'ravishes our judgement'; irrationality gets a hold of your amygdala and pokes it hard.

All the same, Kent clearly loves his work, the mysteries of the world experienced at height. He rhapsodised about an exclusivity of access to the most beautiful vistas of the American urban landscape and the intimate relationship he enjoyed with some of its most handsome architecture. This was not just a day at the office; this was a life worth living.

Yes, but is it a brave one? I wondered.

'Yeah, I mean, I suppose it is,' he said reluctantly, 'but it's not a noble bravery, is it? There are many people who say "I could never do what you do" and I say yeah, that's why I have a business. So it's more self-serving than noble, you know?'

At the end of our conversation, Kent turned to me and asked, 'How do *you* feel about heights?'

'Oh I'm kind of clammy-palms rather than sick,' I said, 'an average fear of heights.'

'Right,' said Kent, 'not terrified. So if I offered to give you a day or two of training, would you go off on a building?'

He and I had been sitting talking in a minimalist office in downtown Manhattan. There were books about architecture lying around and Kent himself was a middle-aged urbanite with a nice jumper and rimless glasses. And so I can only put the airy confidence with which I answered this question down to some kind of spell cast by the sensible, grown-up atmosphere.

'Would I?' I said. 'Yeah, possibly.'

An hour and a half later, Kent, and then I, emerged through a wooden trapdoor into the lantern that tops the gold and terracotta pitched roof of the Thurgood Marshall US Courthouse in Lower Manhattan, a few blocks from the Brooklyn Bridge. This was not the 'training' Kent had mentioned – there was no time for that, this week – but we had agreed to take a look at the latest project of Kent's company, which had recently completed a roof survey of the magnificent thirty-seven-storey tower, completed in 1936. The lantern itself was not much bigger than an old British telephone box and, almost six hundred feet off the ground, it was open at the sides with four pillars reaching up to an ornate little candle-snuffer of a canopy. The trapdoor shut and all around me, the aerial roofscape of Manhattan rolled away, in demonstration of Kent's earlier point about exposure. However, rather than admiring the view, which is what we had come to do, I now spent the next ten minutes standing very still, feeling like I might pass out or weep or vomit or worse, alternately freezing cold and boiling hot and entirely blank as to what to do about it. Samuel Beckett described it as 'the butterflies of vertigo', but this was an uglier feeling than that, so physically overpowering that even now I struggle to describe it. Suffice to say, I would go to some considerable lengths to avoid going there again. As for stepping over the edge, however many safety ropes were on offer, oh no. Never. *Ever.* Not in a million years. Not in a month of Sundays. Not in a blue moon.

At length, I calmed down enough to crack a smile and Kent, mildly amused, took a photo of me, inadvertently gripping the glazed tiles of one of the pillars. It was all perfectly safe of course, but this was a good education for a Timid Soul – thank you, Kent – and never again would I conflate any slight scepticism I might feel as to the philosophical rewards of taking risks at great height, with an idea that it was anything other than perfectly terrifying to be there.

❧

As we had walked downtown, Kent Diebolt told me that one of his favourite movies was *Man On Wire*, the documentary about Philippe Petit's tightrope walk in 1974 between the Twin Towers. 'I've seen it, like, five times,' he said, 'an extraordinary guy'.

There seems to be something about funambulism, as French high-wire walkers call their art, that gets this kind of reaction. It seems curiously to bypass all the usual high-altitude machismo, that people either love or hate, while retaining all of the danger and the glamour. This is a circus art taken out of the ring and placed in the natural or urban landscape, with feats that appear not so much gung-ho as poetic. Requiring colossal strength, immaculate balance and nerves of steel, it is nevertheless the delicacy of the spectacle that sticks in the mind, our imagination reading these 'skywalks' less as acts of daredevilry than of almost angelic figures suspended in space.

Wondering if this meditative ethos could possibly be true, I go to meet Didier Pasquette in Paris, a high-wire master known for his spectacular skywalks. Pasquette was first introduced to the wire in his late teens by Philippe Petit himself, whom he describes as 'almost a priest'. He then went on in the late 1980s to be taught by Petit's teacher Rudy

Omankowski at the prestigious Centre National des Arts du Cirque in Châlons-en-Champagne. Alongside more conventional circus work, Pasquette has completed thirty-six '*grandes marches*', such as that between the spindly towers of the vast medieval basilica at L'Epine in north-eastern France, or the traversal of a 430-metre-wire secured fifty metres above the London Thames.

When we meet, Pasquette tells me he is toying with an '*idée folle*' to suspend a wire, the highest ever walked, between two hot air balloons, and yet the man himself cuts a disarmingly sane figure, practical, precise, a little shy. He talks about how you learn to walk a wire first by 'learning again how to walk', revising the mechanics of perambulation you learned as a child, first along a line on the ground, then one metre above the ground, then three metres, ten metres and so on, all the time teaching yourself to 'feel' what is going on with the wire, the wind, the light, your body. In fact, when Pasquette walks at great height, he says he merely imagines that he is just above the ground. The mental state is the same; 'it is a metal wire between two points, that is all.'

Pasquette has brought a new pair of bespoke shoes to show me. Carried in a soft felt bag, they are glossy black leather above with shaped, suede soles. 'You can touch them, if you like,' he said and I do, although I can sense him tense a little as I handle them and relax again when I put them down. Even so, Pasquette is not remotely precious about discussing what can go wrong, telling me he knows that among those who come to watch are a significant minority who have actually come to see him fall. '*When is he going to fall off?*' his wife or friends can hear them yelling from the crowd. 'It's just human nature,' says Pasquette, calmly.

He has fallen off, of course, 'lots of times', although self-evidently never at height. Falling is a key part of the training. 'This is what allows me to know my limits and what

I can and can't overcome,' he says. 'It is a tangible barrier and an essential one, otherwise you would push further and further, I know you would, and then you would fall and die. I have faced death in my own life. My first wife was killed in a car accident. And death is the big unknown for everyone. We have this Christian idea that after death we ascend into the sky. I have to say I have never seen anyone in the sky, but the truth is we are human, we are mortal. One day we will die, we don't know when. I take risks in my job, but you take risks too. Later today, when you cross the road, you don't know what's going to happen. That is what gives spice to life. If you knew when you were born the date you were going to die, that would be hell. When that year approached, you would increasingly put the brakes on living, wouldn't you?'

Sometimes Pasquette is asked to wear a safety cord attached to the wire and he does, although he shares Alain Robert's distaste for protective measures. 'For me being attached removes the beauty from my work,' he says. 'It no longer represents liberty. A tightrope walker should be like a bird. If I am attached, I am not a bird, I am a parrot. A parrot on a pedestal with a chain around its foot. I want the image of the tightrope walker to remain free.'

For a moment, I cannot help wondering how far being a bird is from being Zorro, but Pasquette is in full flood and telling me what it is he loves about wire-walking. 'It is just me and my wire,' he says, 'the wire and the sky, a universe of freedom and space. I don't know what makes it so beautiful. Perhaps because we are above. I am in direct contact with the emptiness, with the wind, with the sound of the city and with myself.' It is intoxicating stuff, especially from a man who is otherwise so mild-mannered. And yet his whole argument seems to hinge on a kind of artistic worship of the ego, a veneration of his own individual urge to do these things, to live this life. It reads like the very opposite of the collective courage of soldiers, somehow.

I am beginning to feel like I might drown in the poetry of it all, when Pasquette stops me in my tracks with a surprisingly profound idea of the Lived Life that every Timid Soul should consider. And it has nothing to do with vertigo.

'When one walks on the wire,' he says, quietly, 'it is a question of balance, of confidence in yourself. And at first this is not easy. It is really a question of mastering your fear and most people are frightened of walking on something so far from the ground. But the wire is like life. It is the line of life, if you stick on the right path, there is nothing to fear. For me, it is that fundamental, to have conviction, to stay true to oneself.'

On the RER train back to the airport, the sky above the tracks is criss-crossed with wires that pulse as we speed along. And for a moment the air is alive with possible pathways, a map of potential.

❧

Of course, the problem remains that choosing 'the right path' (and staying on it) can, under some circumstances, make tightrope walking look easy. Here is another 'nasty difficulty', and not of the 'lovely' variety:

You are a mountaineer and you are climbing Everest. Over several weeks, you have climbed more than eight thousand metres and, around two hours ago, in the middle of the night, you left the highest camp on the mountain to push for the summit. You have less than five hundred metres left to climb when you encounter another climber in trouble. He is sitting in a cave next to the main climbing route. He has frostbite and no remaining oxygen, but, unlike the other frozen bodies you have passed in the mountain's death zone, he is not dead, not quite. If you stop to help him, your chance to achieve the summit will be gone and, in conditions as extreme as these, your efforts may be in vain or even endanger your own life. If you do not stop, he will certainly die. What do you do?

To help answer this, you may cast yourself in one of two roles. You can be a keen amateur who has been training to climb Everest for years and now the day has come. The expedition alone has cost you the better part of your annual salary and to ascend the summit is the dream of a lifetime. Or you can be a mountain guide in which case it is your job to be here, paid as you are to 'facilitate' the summit ambitions of others. Your superior knowledge of the mountain may help a rescue attempt, but it also informs your understanding of how dire the situation is for the man in the cave. Your professional responsibility is to your clients, not to him. The quandary gets muddier still if you consider that, having chosen to pass the man on the way up, you and your clients achieve the summit and you encounter the man again on the way down. His chances of survival are now slimmer than ever, but dwindle to nothing without your help. On the other hand, your own safe descent (for this is when most fatalities on Everest occur) is by no means guaranteed.

Each of these individuals faces a distinct ethical dilemma. Does either, or each of them, have a moral responsibility to attempt to save the dying man, or not? And if so, to what lengths, in terms of risk, should such an attempt go? Is this a moment to be brave?

You may have guessed by now that this is no thought experiment. The man in the cave was a thirty-four-year-old English mathematics teacher called David Sharp, who died on Everest in May 2006. An experienced climber, this was his third attempt on Everest, his sixth climb above eight thousand metres and he had decided to climb alone. He too left before midnight, but progress was slow and he went for the summit later in the day than he should. In the afternoon of 14 May, he is thought to have achieved his long-held dream and stood alone on the top of the world. But as he descended he got into trouble. His oxygen ran out. He had frostbite and was exhausted. Sharp stopped in a cave by the climbing route next to the frozen body of a man who had sat down there ten years before. Night fell. In the small hours of the following morning, the next day's climbers began to come past. Some forty men and women passed David Sharp, both ascending and descending the summit. Some reported that he was conscious and capable of responding, others believed he was dead. Some yelled at him to get up, get going. Others say they did not see him in the dark. On the descent, the light revealed that Sharp, who had by then been in the cave for well over twelve hours, was in very bad shape indeed and one or two climbers tried to help by offering hot drinks or oxygen. The helmet-camera of one of them was later found to have recorded him murmuring 'My name is David Sharp', but, as he was too weak to stand, they left him. Others admitted that, believing the man was a lost cause, they had simply climbed around Sharp and carried on.

David Sharp's story lies in treacherous ethical terrain indeed. He was not the first climber left behind to die on Everest, but the fact that his was a lone expedition on a day when the mountain was crowded with others and that some of his last moments of life were filmed, all conspired to strike a particular nerve. Afterwards, much soul-searching ensued in the media and among the mountaineering community. Was this little more than a tragic accident? Or was it the dark underbelly of a sport that had got its priorities all wrong? Sir Edmund Hillary himself joined the debate, saying, 'On my expedition there was no way you would have left a man under a rock to die. A human life is far more important than just getting to the top of a mountain'. The dead man's parents said that they did not blame anyone, Sharp's mother telling journalists that, on Everest, 'your responsibility is to save yourself, not to try to save anybody else.' One of the climbing guides who had passed David Sharp was interviewed by *The Sunday Times* and equated 'the cold hard reality of that environment' to seeing someone 'mortally wounded on a battlefield ... a long way from the medic.'

I thought, reading this, of Martin Bell in the violent heat of Nahr-e Saraj, 'doing the right thing, even though it was the wrong thing to do', and it struck me that, while the Everest Death Zone was without doubt extreme, this was also no battlefield. I found myself wondering if the intense individualism necessary to pursue the goal of summiting Everest, the act of choosing this kind of Lived Life, somehow impaired the capacity for altruism. Just as the military story had been all about comradeship, the dominant Everest story, despite invoking similar values, seemed underpinned by an idea that Up There It Was Each Man For Himself. You might be brave enough to follow your dreams all the way up the highest mountain in the world but that was no guarantee you were brave enough, either individually or collectively, to take this one last risk.

I asked one of David Sharp's close friends what he thought, a climber called Richard Dougan, with whom Sharp first unsuccessfully attempted Everest in 2003 and who three years later spoke at his funeral. The image Richard Dougan seemed unable to shake was that of the climbers unclipping from the safety rope to climb around Sharp and then clipping back on, one by one.

'There's something inhuman about that,' he said. 'I don't want to be disrespectful to other people who have made their call. It's not black and white, but I just can't get my head round it. It still upsets me. It still angers me. All the experts say a rescue was not possible, but, oh boy, did anyone even try?'

❧

'Courage,' wrote G. K. Chesterton in 1909, more than a decade before the first (unsuccessful) attempt to climb Everest, 'is almost a contradiction in terms. It means a strong desire to live taking the form of a readiness to die.'

Who can say what 'a readiness to die' might look like, but a reasonable wager might be placed upon the men and women who – for fun – jump into the Cave of Swallows in Mexico. This is the largest cave shaft in the world, a gaping maw in the limestone rock, just forty-nine metres wide, and from its upper lip to the dark floor of the cave below, a three-hundred-and-seventy-metre free-fall drop. Hurling yourself into this hole in the ground is a must for serious BASE jumpers and the feat, as viewed from above, reads like one big, fat metaphor.

A ring of sunlight and lush foliage encircles the mouth of the pit. A human figure appears large and lively at one's shoulder and, at a cheerful half-run, he propels himself towards the chasm. This is when the sheer scale of The Cave of Swallows becomes apparent, for now you watch the falling body for several seconds, growing ever tinier, his splayed arms and legs like some Keith Haring figure, illuminated by the sunlight against the void beyond. At length, when he has dwindled to a speck and the sunlight can reach his back no longer, he is swallowed into the blackness. A few seconds later, like a breath of redemption, the tiny coloured canopy of a parachute can be seen puffing into the shadows and you know that the falling man or woman has defied the abyss.

It was here in the Cave of Swallows in 2004 that the

legendary climber and all-round daring aerialist Dean Potter was nearly killed when his parachute only partially opened, sending him towards one of the walls of the cavern as he fell. Turning to avoid the impact, Potter ran into the vertical line of 'some cameraman' and his chute collapsed altogether. Just three hundred feet off the cave floor, he grabbed the slim cord and slid painfully to safety. His hands were in shreds, but he was alive. 'That,' he told me, 'was the closest to death I have ever been.'

Not that this experience put Dean Potter off in any way. On the contrary, his fame has grown exponentially since, thanks to his exploits in some of the toughest vertical land-scapes in the natural world – ropeless ascents of austere rock faces, as well as 'slacklining' across canyons (tightrope walking on dynamic lines) and BASE jumping from unthink-able heights. (BASE stands for Building, Antenna, Span – or bridge – and Earth. These are the things from which you can jump, if you feel so inclined and you wish to qualify as a prac-titioner of the sport.) In 2008, Potter free-soloed the north face of the Eiger with only a parachute for safety. It was a new technique he called FreeBASE. The following year, he com-pleted the longest BASE jump ever achieved, leaping from the same mountain in a 'wing-suit' and 'flying' for nearly three minutes before he pulled his chute, covering around two thousand seven hundred vertical metres and almost six and a half kilometres.

Both feats secured global coverage, as did Potter's 'slack-line' walk in 2012 across the 1800-metre-deep Enshi Grand Canyon in China. And if Alain Robert is one side of the celebrity that comes with this kind of gravity-defying Lived Life, then Dean Potter is surely the other. As Alain's public image is self-consciously urban, so Dean's is self-consciously organic. Alain loves 'fancy' things, Dean 'simple' or 'beauti-ful' ones. Alain is pictured talking on his mobile halfway up the facade of a skyscraper, Dean in high-end photography of the natural world alongside interview clips that talk about 'harmony' and 'creativity'. Neither man seems to mind being pictured with his shirt off.

Curious as to what enlightenment the very act of taking risks might offer, I visited Dean Potter at his home in the Yosemite Valley, California. Here the landscape is a hymn to the vertical, great granite walls rising sheer out of the flat valley floor, where poker-straight pines point at the sky. The setting alone was enough to make a short Timid Soul feel even smaller than usual and then there was Dean, who is colossally tall and vaguely other-worldly. We walked to the base of El Capitan, the most famous rock formation in the valley, a three-thousand-foot monolith that is the Holiest of Holies for rock climbers. Scrambling up a slope and through the trees, we arrived at a broad rock platform that climbers call Pine Line Ledge at the foot of 'The Nose' of El Cap, one of the most famous and difficult climbs in the world.

First, Dean scaled the first twenty-five feet or so to show me how it was done and then he climbed back down and we sat on the ledge watching the valley and talking. He began by telling me that he often liked to come and sleep on this outcrop, or to meditate here; it was one of his special places. Having read the press beforehand – Dean was all over *National Geographic* that month – I was aware that this kind of little confidence, shared in an awesome natural setting, was classic Potter, as essential to the outsider's encounter with him as the glass of champagne was to a day spent with Alain Robert. Often reporters wrote of Potter's intensity, flattered to be invited into his extraordinary life. And I was too. Despite his fame and the evident formula to which these interviews seemed to conform, there were no agents or press officers. He signed his emails 'Ciao, Dean and Whisper', Whisper being his dog, and he described our day together simply as 'hanging out'. There were moments of apparent intimacy too, when for instance he turned to me and asked whether *I* believed in an afterlife or equated my presumed love of writing with his love of climbing.

In one sense, of course, all this 'openness' is a shtick like any other, but I believed he meant it when, in answer to a question about fame, Dean said this: 'It's funny because it all started out with a boy that didn't quite fit in and sometimes I now find myself in situations where people invite me to speak in front of thousands of people and I'm just like, I went to the cliff to be alone, not to come here and talk to thousands of people. That is like one of the hardest things for me, to deal with other people. For a while I couldn't pull it off, but what I've learned is just Complete-Truth-No-Filter and sincerity comes out easy.' He shrugged and looked down, smoothing one broad flat thumbnail with a gnarly finger.

Of course the chief legend about Dean Potter is less about what he says and more about what he does. There are many who argue that his high-altitude risk-taking must require some sort of death wish, or at least be the hallmark of a thrill-seeker whose adrenaline addiction borders on the suicidal. Certainly the stunts are both captivating and highly market-able, so it is not hard to find videos of Dean apparently in daredevil mode, all whoops and 'Bah-Boom's to the camera. However, when we met, this image was the very thing Dean spent the larger portion of our long conversation refuting in various ways.

'When you climb and you're going to die if you fall,' he said, in an echo of what sensible Kent Diebolt had said, 'you have one hundred per cent focus. I had trouble focusing as a child and I still sort of do, but you put me near the rock or I touch the rock and there it is, a hundred per cent. That's a rarity in life and a gift to have something that brings you that clarity, just with a touch of the stone.'

---

Moreover, Dean was at pains to point out that adrenaline does not give him a 'rush', so much as make him calm and 'hyper alert'. It is a feeling he described over and over again in the course of the day and he clearly regarded it as some kind of gateway to a higher state of mind that is meaningful in and of itself, like some kind of shamanic transformation.

'I can calm myself by an intense will and want and also by the simple ability to focus in the most dangerous situation on breath and nothing else. And then you're not scared any more. You perceive life in slow motion,' he said. 'That's the most beautiful part of it, your mind just goes "whoosh" at super high speed. That heightened awareness, I feel and hear and see and connect to more than I do in normal reality. It's a total meditative state.'

Well aware that such reflection on the actual moment of bravery was unusual, I asked Dean whether it was height alone that facilitated that state.

'No it's not,' he said, 'there are a few ways that I have found you can get that feeling, but the easiest way is to do something with death consequence. It's immediate.'

'Is the point,' I asked, 'that life is at its sweetest when it's in the balance?'

'No,' he said, 'I think that's a little too complicated. It's that if you mess up, you die – you focus. It's that simple.'

It is unsurprising perhaps to discover that Dean's mother is a yoga teacher, but it is also significant that his father was an army man. For that is the other side of the story here, all that 'heightened awareness' tempered by military levels of training and planning, years spent diagramming routes across the rock, each foothold and handhold rehearsed until he is sure he can make it.

'It's repetition,' he said. 'And that's a lot of what the life-style that I live, and others live that are similar to me, allows.' What Dean was referring to here was the climber-bum existence that alienated him from his parents for some years in his twenties and that is very much the Yosemite dream, the live-in-your-van-subsist-on-beans-and-rice-and-climb-every-day dream. 'This,' he added, gesturing across the valley to the other famous rock formations opposite, 'is like your living room, your house, and every day you're climbing and walking these lines across big gaps of thousands of feet, over and over, every day for years. You know it can kill you but you are so used to it that it doesn't take your breath away. I think that anybody could do that – it's just that few people choose to.'

This philosophy of Dean's is much focused of late upon a dream of flight that he has held since childhood. This was where it all began to get a bit kooky. Technically, what we were discussing was BASE jumping, whereby one leaps from a fixed and lofty object, using a parachute to break your fall. However 'BASE jumping' is a term that Dean says he 'hates', preferring to call it 'human body flying' or for short, er, '*flying*'. Conspicuously, there is no mention of 'falling'.

'Human flight,' he said, 'it's the most amazing – and I hate to even call it that but – extreme sport. The desire for human flight goes back forever. So for me it's such a metaphor for freedom.' Then he revealed that his 'biggest dream is to fly and land the human body.'

'Land?' I asked. 'Without a parachute?'

'Without a parachute. It's definitely achievable and there's a few of us that fly at speeds that are very landable.'

'To fly using gravity? Not to actually take off?'

'Not to take off. But to jump off a cliff and land on a slope is definitely possible.'

I paused for a moment, choosing my words, then asked, 'Is there part of you, do you think, that wants to challenge gravity?'

'No way.' Dean shook his head vigorously. 'You're not

going up to this rock and saying "I'm going to dominate you, I'm going to kick your ass, rock"! You're saying "please let me be a part of it, rock, and don't send me to my death – I want to be one with you". And the same with flying. You're definitely not going to say "I'm going to dominate you Mother Nature"! You're saying "Please let me join you"'.

It would be tempting to suggest at this point that perhaps Dean Potter had yet to comprehend the worst-case scenario, that his particular form of bravery, and the apparent enlightenment that went with it, was based upon naiveté. But then he told me about the death of his friend and fellow Yosemite climber, Dan Osman, in 1999. Osman had devised a free-fall system that relied on jumping from a cliff with a rope attached to a harness. However thrilling in principle, it was in practise, said Dean, 'a dangerous system,' and the only time he ever jumped with Osman, 'it felt like suicide.' Late one evening, a few months after they had jumped together, Dan Osman leapt from a rock formation in Yosemite called Leaning Tower. His ropes had been left for several days hanging in a storm and were compromised; they broke and he was killed.

A surreal account followed of 'the body recovery'.

'I was not going to go up there to find a dead body by myself,' said Dean, who had been asked by the park rangers to locate Osman and keep the animals off until dawn. 'So the only other guy around was this guy named Dave. His nickname was The Dangler, but he is a really timid guy'. So with Dave The (timid) Dangler reluctantly in tow, Dean at length found his friend's body and sat down with it to wait for morning. 'I stayed there all night long just staring at him and it totally warped me,' Dean said. 'At that time, Dano was invincible, I idolised the guy and there he was dead among the boulders. For me it was like, no matter how strong you are, you can die. What I realised with him was, he *needed* it.

He couldn't live without it. He knew the rope was a bad rope and he went up there anyways and jumped it. That's a big lesson to me.'

There was a pause.

'So that put a dampener on my ideas of flying,' he added.

But not, it seemed, forever. Lesson or no lesson, three years later, Dean began the reinvention of himself as a BASE jumper, or rather, The Man Who Can Fly (as National Geographic's 2012 documentary dubbed him). Notably, he never returned to jumping with ropes: that had killed Osman. Instead he opted for the flying squirrel suit and parachute that were then used for his famous leap or 'flight' from the Eiger in 2008.

Dean Potter conceded that this outlandish passion for height could be regarded as 'somewhat of an addiction and in lots of ways it is,' but he vowed that his was not the 'need' that had proved so fatal for Osman. Instead he told me he 'rations' his ropeless climbing, saving a free solo 'as a treat'. It is, he said, a way to play and win the odds, while continuing to lead this life of his choosing and to revel in the unique insights it affords him. I asked Dean if he thought it inevitable that something would eventually go wrong and he was adamant that a combination of a good system, meticulous preparation, combined with some intuitive ability to tune into the wilderness will preserve him.

'I've had some close calls but never a serious injury,' he said. 'I've done probably some of the most dangerous things ever, so I do think obviously there is some level of control there – I am thirty-nine-years old, I've been doing this since I was 15 – it's not just luck.'

Towards the end of the day, we wandered down to the meadow below El Capitan and sat side by side looking at 'the Wall', as one might regard a great painting in a gallery, Dean telling me how he dreamed of being the first climber to scale the whole face without ropes. 'This lifestyle that is on the edge,' he said, 'it makes me live well, all complicated ideas reduced down to that naked guy climbing the wall with nothing but his body and willpower.'

❧

In the letter 'On Daring' in his Treatise on the Passions, Thomas Aquinas argued that daring is born not of fear, but of hope. The cause of daring, he wrote, 'is the presence in the imagination of the hope that the means of safety is nigh, and that the things to be feared are either non-existent or far off.' However, the problem with daring, as Aquinas sees it (and, by implication, the Lived Life that relies upon daring), is that it does not quite have its head screwed on, which is why it cannot equate to (or rank with) fortitude, true courage. Whatever revelations it might offer up, however it might make a human temporarily *superhuman*, daring is, in the end, a little too passionate, too hot-blooded to be unequivocally good.

# Crime and Punishment

Our interest's on the dangerous edge of things.
The honest thief, the tender murderer,
The superstitious atheist, demirep
That loves and saves her soul in new French books –
We watch while these in equilibrium keep
The giddy line midway
                    'Bishop Blougram's Apology', Robert Browning

Some years after the end of the English Civil War, the great historian of the hostilities, Edward Hyde, Earl of Clarendon, wrote of the late Oliver Cromwell as 'a brave bad man'. A historical footnote it may be, but his observation raises a central moral conundrum for anyone serious about working out how to be brave. Is it, as Hyde suggested, possible to be both brave and bad? Is courage, of all the virtues, somehow morally neutral, the one where a Manichaean struggle of Good and Evil simply fails to satisfy?

A little over three centuries later, there were still no definitive answers. In 2012 came a storm in an English teacup, when a judge was reported to the Office for Judicial Complaints in the UK after telling a burglar in the dock that his crime had taken 'a huge amount of courage', adding, 'I wouldn't have the nerve.' As the official investigation began, the British press enjoyed a few days of editorial frenzy on the subject of courage and badness. Even the prime minister weighed in, declaring from a TV breakfast show sofa, 'I am very clear that burglary is not bravery. Burglary is cowardice.' This was about as nuanced as the debate ever became, but some months later, the judge duly received a formal reprimand. The whole affair reminded me of the strange furore over Xavier Alvarez's phoney Medal of Honor and how very exercised we become if the virgin purity of our favourite virtue is impugned. Yet is there something here of The Lady Doth Protest Too Much? And should there really be concrete, enforceable rules about who and what we can call brave?

In search of answers, I somewhat nervously took it upon myself to find a brave, bad man, one who might be prepared to share this dark side of courage with the Society of Timid Souls. And some weeks later I found Jimmy.

Now, Jimmy Norton had most certainly been bad. Not for some years, granted – he was now in his fifties and working for a prison charity – but in the past Jimmy had been, in his words, 'a nasty character'. By way of calling card, he ran me through his convictions. By the age of thirteen, he had 'been locked up three times'. By seventeen, he was in borstal for his second GBH. The next year, borstal again, this time 'for a petrol bombing'. Upon his release, at just nineteen, Jimmy toyed briefly with what he called 'the armed robbery thing'.

'Up to then,' he explained, 'most of my offences had been for violence. I wasn't really a thief. I'd done burglaries when I was a kid, but robbery, do you know what, I didn't really fancy it. But then I stabbed an off-duty policeman and I got five years. Am I boring you?'

'No,' I said, 'not at all.'

'OK, well, I stabbed a few people,' Jimmy continued, 'but I ended up getting five years, so I got that at twenty-one. And it was on that five-year sentence that I went in as a thug and came out with one goal in life and that was wanting to be a bank robber.'

So much of bank robbery, apart from the actual wrongness of course, seemed to map neatly onto other braveries: the broad-daylight effrontery of it, the premeditation, the moment of performance, the dynamic jeopardy, yes, even the whiff of Robin Hood glamour. I was, in truth, unprepared for the preamble about GBH and stabbing, but that was not the only unexpected part. I was also entirely taken aback when Jimmy said, during our first conversation, that if it was bravery I wanted to talk about, then in fact I would have to find another bank robber. There were brave ones, he said, of course – he would put me in touch with one – but the only insight that he would be able to share would be what Jimmy called 'my moment of cowardice'.

'Are you interested in that?' he asked.

This was the first interview in many months where anyone mentioned cowardice unprompted, much less offered to illuminate their own, so 'Yes, OK,' I said, 'let's talk about that.'

By way of warm-up to his 'Moment of Cowardice' – a phrase Jimmy Norton used so many times that I began to feel slightly embarrassed by it – he told me how he was in prison at a time before drug trafficking had taken over the criminal economy and how armed robbers were then, as Jimmy put it, 'the top of the tree' in the prison pecking order. The glamour of this particular crime and its perpetrators captured young Jimmy's imagination – 'it was immaturity to be honest with you, real immaturity,' he said and sighed as middle-aged men do. But a few months after his release, there was twenty-five-year-old Jimmy, doing an armed robbery of a security van delivering cash to a bank, which is when many bank robberies occur.

'It's a big test to jump out of a motor with a shotgun,' he said, 'to go across the pavement with a gun, knowing that if the police get onto you, you could be shot dead – especially in those days. That takes courage of some sort. And of course, you know it's wrong, but for you, the way you're living your life at the moment, it's the right thing to do.'

There was some curious echo here of that 'lived life' of climbing skyscrapers, or leaping from cliffs. So I asked Jimmy how it felt.

'I'll tell you what it's like,' he said. 'Your heart is going boom-boom, boom-boom and it gets quicker and quicker. It's a real build-up of pressure, because the security van's coming along, and you can see it coming and boom-boom, boom-boom, boom-boom but obviously you can't attack them until they get out of the van so you've still got another couple of minutes to judge it right. And then once you go into action all of that leaves you; all that fear. You just go calm. Everything is crystal-clear. I suppose it must be the same as soldiers maybe. I don't know. I've never had the guts to be a soldier.'

These words hung in the air for a moment, and then Jimmy said, jovially, 'So shall I tell you about my moment of cowardice? This is the moment of cowardice that I need to talk to someone about.' And he laughed.

The moment came on a hot summer's afternoon, during a hit on a security van delivering cash on a busy London high street. Jimmy and his two fellow robbers were waiting for the van on foot at a bus stop. They watched the van pull up and the bags of cash, five of them, crossed the pavement to the building, one by one.

'To our credit,' said Jimmy, 'we got on them and we got a

bag of money. And everything was fine, but what happened was there was a police car going by at that very moment. So now you've got police, the van's sirens going off, a shot's been fired by one of our group, so you've got smoke everywhere, people screaming. So then we get in the car and we drive away, but we've got this police car directly behind us.'

'We thought we'd lost them but we hadn't,' he continued, 'so when I looked, I saw them behind us again. And this is where it got scary, scary, scary for me, for me personally, right? My mate in the front was saying, "Fire at them! Fire at them!" and I didn't want to fire at them. When I say my arsehole was going' – Jimmy laughed a little too loudly – 'I was scared of being shot dead, because now we haven't only got a police car behind us, we've got three helicopters in the sky, one or two above us and we can hear more sirens in the distance. This is where I lost my bottle, because do you know why I didn't fire at them? Because I hadn't tested the gun. I thought somehow it was going to flash up at me, you know? So after that I always made sure I fired the gun so – it's just a learning curve isn't it?'

'Yes,' I said, 'it is.'

'The point is basically I froze. I didn't act in the way I should have acted. I felt like I should be doing more, that I should have jumped out or held them up at gunpoint or done something. I felt helpless – that's what I felt. I was more fearful than my mate. At least he was coming up with ideas and he bailed out while the police were still chasing us. I just froze and all of a sudden we smash into this estate. The police were seconds behind us. How I got out of it is an absolute miracle. An absolute miracle. It wasn't through any sort of resourcefulness at all on my part.'

Jimmy and the driver ducked out of the car in different directions into the estate and at that moment, a man opened his front door to see what was going on. Jimmy dived through it and got away out of the back of the building. He was never caught.

'Going back to that feeling that your nerve had failed you,' I asked, 'did it worry you at the time? That feeling that you'd bottled it?'

'Well,' said Jimmy, slowly, seemingly to be sure that I understood the fine line between bravery and folly here, 'I then went out and did another one. Of course. And I fired a shot, almost to prove something to myself. And I got ten years, didn't I?'

After less than a year out of prison, Jimmy now spent the next decade inside. 'So my reign as an armed robber was pretty disastrous,' said Jimmy. 'Maybe there was a little bit in my immature brain that was saying what-the-fuck-are-you-doing? But I wasn't listening to it. It's just a real period in my life that I regret.' Since his release in the 1990s, Jimmy Norton has had no further convictions and it seemed as though this almost cheerful assassination of his own character was one of the ways in which he had come to terms with his mistakes.

Having got these things off his chest, Jimmy drew proceedings to a close and said he knew who I should speak to about courage and crime, a serious bank robber, one of the bravest, a man who went by the name of Razor.

❧

It is curious that in modern English the words 'courage' and 'bravery' have largely converged in meaning. In fact, the word 'brave' shares little of the etymological nobility that trails like spindrift back from 'courage' to the heart, that ancient seat of the soul. The word 'brave' is instead rather like someone with a few deliciously murky ancestors. It is derived from the Italian 'bravo', which itself is thought to have roots in the Latin 'pravus', meaning crooked or distorted, as well as in 'barbarus', rough, and 'bravium', the prize typically handed out at the Roman public games. 'Bravery', as it then appeared in the first half of the sixteenth century, was more recognisable, now with a connotation of daring and boastful defiance, but it had yet to glow with moral probity. That would take until the end of that century, when the meaning of 'fine' or 'splendid', as in 'fine clothes', attached itself to 'brave', in turn paving the way for an idea that one might also be 'fine' or 'brave' on the inside too. Even today, inglorious ghosts haunt the word 'brave' in the pejorative undertones that accompany 'bravado' and even 'bravura'.

The point is that we all assume an unspoken but transparent hierarchy between words to describe this most mercurial quality of character and the degrees of virtue therein. 'Courage' will always rank a little above 'bravery', 'valour' above 'pluck', 'gallantry' above 'daring', 'fortitude' above 'boldness', 'grit' above 'derring-do', our language accessory to a thousand subtle, moral judgements.

You could devote many hours to quibbling the finer points of meaning here, but more pertinent is the far-reaching dominion of courage and its motley cousins, and how very elastic this would-be virtue can become in human hands. I had found this to be true over many encounters with the brave so far, and, whether the British press would like it or not – and I now guessed they would not – bravery seemed to be travelling with me into these shady regions too.

Intriguingly, writing at a time when the word 'brave' was undergoing its etymological facelift, William Shakespeare turns out to have been architect to many of our more nuanced ideas about what courage might look and sound like, especially when it goes bad. Hamlet vacillates over avenging his father's murder – 'conscience does make cowards of us all'; Lady Macbeth snaps at her husband to get on and murder

Duncan – 'But screw your courage to the sticking place / And we'll not fail'; Richard III twists logic to conclude, 'Conscience is but a word that cowards use, / Devised at first to keep the strong in awe'. Indeed, read the English national poet on the relationship between scruples and bravery and one finds some frankly rather subversive views. The overriding message seems to be that, while some quasi-moral rationale is essential in order to spark human bravery in the first place, once that justification has been ignited, it can then function to fuel brave, bad action in exactly the same way as an overtly good impetus to courage. As Jimmy had put it, 'for you, the way you're living your life at the moment, it's the right thing to do.'

Two millennia of Western philosophy have also wrestled with the relationship between courage and goodness and have generated an astonishing array of conclusions, but little consensus.

The Ancient Greeks were very clear that there was no such thing as a brave bad man. Plato, who insisted on the centrality of knowledge to all virtue, offered up a definition of courage as 'the knowledge of what one ought and ought not to fear'. Aristotle went one step further, insisting that this knowledge of good and evil was in fact the character of a good man, with an innate disposition towards virtue. Courage is a virtue that might then be cultivated and maintained by good habits, even among weaker characters. But, above all, if you wished to be brave then you had also to be good and being courageous was a step on the road toward that virtuous state, towards *eudaimonia*, or happiness.

With the Enlightenment came new questions about the relationship between the virtue of courage and those qualities of temperament that might, as it were, *go either way*. By the time Arthur Schopenhauer got to grips with it, he explicitly, if gloomily, declared courage to be a morally neutral trait with no particular tendency at all toward the good. 'It is,' he wrote, 'just as ready to serve the unworthiest ends', so delivering a boost to the brave, bad man.

Right into the twentieth century there were few ethicists who did not get stuck into the debate, either directly or by implication. Vigorous arguments have been made on both sides, amid many attempts to define ever more precisely the terms of the quarrel, but the point is that however many sages have grappled with the problem, no definitive answer has ever quite floated to the surface.

Timid Souls of a philosophical bent may continue the search if they wish, but I found myself curious as to how these ideas shook down on the mean streets of real life. I got to thinking about those whose institutions were set up expressly to uphold the good, as society had dictated it, and to fight wrongdoing, whether of the bold or the craven variety. Law enforcement was clearly a line of work that required real guts at moments, but to what extent was the average cop or police officer motivated by moral rather than professional duty, how different their mettle from that of their quarry?

⁂

So I hied me to find a brave, *good* man and was delighted to discover an Angel.

Angel Cruz is a detective with the New York City Police Department. The officers of the NYPD are nicknamed 'New York's Finest', in a pleasing echo of that old usage of the word 'brave', and their motto is *Fidelis ad Mortem*, 'Faithful Unto Death'. For Officer Angel Cruz, as he was in 2007, this motto came near-as-damn-it true, late one evening that spring. As it turned out, Cruz would elude the *Mortem* part, but what he did that night saw him decorated with the NYPD's highest award for bravery in the line of duty and at extreme risk to life – the New York City Police Department Medal of Honor. The odds are if you win this particular award, you are already dead – the NYPD Medal of Honor is that kind of medal – but Angel Cruz lived to tell the tale and I met him one Saturday morning at One Police Plaza in downtown Manhattan. There he was, on a swivel chair at the far end of a large, unstaffed office, the banks of desks divided by those scratchy partitions that move about on castors. Dressed not in uniform, but in the well-pressed, smart casual that is the livery of off-duty policemen the world over, Detective Cruz looked younger than his thirty-four years. He fidgeted back and forth on the chair, as though he were not quite used to sitting on one. I perched on another nearby and Cruz told me about the night he was nearly *Fidelis ad Mortem*.

On 13 March 2007, Officer Cruz was 'still a rookie', with less than a year on the job. That evening, he was posted with a partner on the 6 p.m. to 2 a.m. shift, patrolling the large Broadway Junction station in Brooklyn, where he had been born and raised.

A big part of those early months as a cop, as Cruz told it, was about getting to the point where you knew and trusted 'your authority'. This was a phrase Angel used over and over again, the point being that you had to learn to wear the uniform, not have the uniform wear you.

'Even though you might not feel like you're a boss or you might not be that type of person to give directions and orders,' he said, 'that uniform alone makes people look at you as if you're supposed to know what's going on, you're sup-posed to know what to do.'

This certain authority, put on like body armour when you got dressed for work, could of course become a menace in some hands, but, in most, it shores up the everyday nerve required to do the job. Like Jimmy had said, this was the way you were living your life. One should not, perhaps, confuse the authority with the rightness or the wrongness of what it upholds – that is the job of the legislature – but once established, it is his authority, and his gun of course, which serves to arm a cop who might find himself in a terrifying situation.

As proved to be the case that night at Broadway Junction. Sometime around half past ten Cruz's partner stepped away for her meal break and Cruz was now patrolling solo.

'I figured,' said Angel, "Let me keep myself busy. Let me go inspect one of the platforms where the trains come in". I wasn't actually looking for anything, it was something to do, something to kill time, just doing a random inspection, and that's, I guess, where my whole life situation changed.'

Down on the platform of the Queen's-bound J train, Cruz spotted two men smoking cigarettes. This was, as Cruz said, 'a minor violation' and he walked over and asked the men first to put the cigarettes out, which they did, and then to present some identification. One of them offered ID; the other said he had nothing on him. There was nothing particular about the atmosphere to suggest what would happen a few minutes later. The men followed Cruz to the upper level, as was standard procedure on transit patrol. There he asked them, as was usual, whether they had any weapons on them. One man handed over a Swiss Army knife. The second man was more argumentative. Cruz asked him to turn around so that he could frisk him.

'What's the reason that you want to search us?' said the man.

'You don't want to be having that one-on-one conversation' Angel told me, 'with somebody who has a loaded gun on his waistband and you don't know about it.'

Again Cruz insisted that the man turn around for the routine frisk. Angel told me, with a little shake of his head, that he had not even been planning to arrest the man, nor was the man himself 'aggressive at any point'. It was just late night Brooklyn business as usual.

Still complaining, the man turned and Cruz began the frisk. 'And,' said Angel, 'that's pretty much where everything went' – he shifted a little on the swivel chair – 'it changed. I guess it was in that two-second reaction of him first and then me second which pretty much changed everything. It went from a non-aggressive situation to a life-threatening situation in a matter of seconds.'

What happened was the man suddenly swung around and struck Cruz across the side of the head. Dazed for a second, Cruz did not know what it was that had hit him. There was a brief scuffle and Cruz fell backwards against a payphone.

'I'd seen him coming back towards me and I didn't see any weapons or anything in his hand, but the next thing that I remember is he has a knife in his hand. I was able to get away from him for a second and I remember seeing him coming back at me with this knife, and I'm guessing, by the way I felt, I'm sure he had already struck and stabbed me in my head because at that time I'm holding my head and all I remember is just him coming towards me a second time with the knife in hand, running towards me as if he was going to stab me again, so ...'. Angel trailed off and looked at me with two thick, black brows raised, as if he still could not quite get over why anyone would do a thing like that.

The knife penetrated Cruz's scalp at the left temple and travelled on, through his skull, a quarter of an inch into his brain. In that moment, all uniform and authority fell away and Angel Cruz simply became a man fighting to stay alive.

Unaware of how badly hurt he was, Cruz was beginning to feel light-headed. He half dropped down, half fell back and, drawing his pistol, fired at the man. Three rounds missed. There was more scuffling. Cruz fired again, a further two shots. These caught the man in the elbow and he hit the deck for a second, before leaping up and darting back down the stairs to the Manhattan-bound platform of the J train. This was where Angel Cruz's story took a turn towards some form of instinctive bravery. For now his sense of authority kicked right back in, both his moral authority as a victim and the good old-fashioned uniformed sort that came with the NYPD badge.

'I remember holding my head,' said Angel, 'and I chased after him, followed him down onto the platform. People tell me, you know, that a lot of officers wouldn't have reacted like that. I don't know what made me do it, what put it in me to even *think* that I still have to gain control of him and get him in custody. I guess it was an instinct, but I knew my obligations and knew my authority level and I knew what was right.'

By the time Cruz reached the platform, the man was lying on the ground, animated but with a broken ankle, the knife still at his side. Cruz dropped to one knee next to him, his gun pointing.

'At this point, I'm starting to lose consciousness,' Angel told me, 'I can feel myself getting dizzy, blacking out, everything is becoming blurry. I remember just picking up the radio and looking at it without being able to say anything, and then just putting it down and looking at him and holding him there until I get some backup.'

Within minutes, backup arrived. While two police arrested the man with the knife, the first one to reach Cruz, Officer Anthony Cairone, took the gun from his hand and began to rip at Cruz's vest and uniform searching for a gunshot wound to justify the quantity of blood around him on the concrete of the train platform. Cruz struggled to speak.

'He stabbed me in my head,' he said. 'He stabbed me in my head.'

---

'OK, just hold it,' said Cairone. '*Hold it*'.

Cairone picked Cruz up and ran with him out of Broad-way Junction station to their patrol car. They drove to Jamaica Hospital, with Cairone telling Cruz to 'just breathe, breathe, keep your eyes open, man'. Angel said the next thing he could recall was getting out of the car, but being unable to walk, so Cairone put Cruz over his shoulder and walked on into the emergency room. Cruz's next memory was days later.

At this point, Angel wheeled his chair closer to mine and bowed his head, pointing to a large scar under his close-cropped black hair. This, he told me, was not the stab wound but where the surgeons had removed a portion of his skull to relieve the swelling and extensive bleeding on the brain caused by the knife. He spent a week in intensive care and a further ten days in hospital. The doctors said Cruz was lucky to have survived at all, but his short-term memory was affected for many months. It was the names of people and things that got him. He told me about sitting with thera-pists, looking at pictures of squirrels, raccoons and elephants and trying to remember their names. 'I know what it is,' he said, 'I could tell you what it does. I could tell you what it eats, but what it is called?' Angel laughed, but this had clearly been a traumatic time, with little certainty that he would get his life and brain function back together, 'the way it was,' he said several times.

But he did, more or less, and, after eight months, Cruz returned to full duty, back on patrol in Brooklyn. This was to the dismay of his family and the bewilderment of many colleagues, who said he was crazy not to take retirement, but, as Angel said, 'I was still young' and besides he had wanted to be a cop all his life. In 2008, Cruz was promoted to detective, a plain-clothes role with the anti-crime unit, and he told me he expects to serve out his full twenty years with the NYPD.

And that is why one thing Angel Cruz said that morning surprised me more than any other. He had been midway through an explanation of how his religious faith had helped him to understand what had happened in March 2007 as part of God's Plan. But then he got sidetracked onto God's Plan for 'the individual' with the knife – an illegal immigrant with a violent criminal record who had already been deported once and who had open warrants within other jurisdictions – then onto his own feelings about this man, now serving twenty years, who had come so close to annihilating him.

'To this day I don't hold any grudges against him,' said Angel. 'You know, he had situations on his plate that he already knew of, that I didn't. And, I guess, he felt like he had to do what he had to do. He had to try and get himself out of it, but at the same time, I knew I had to take the action that was given to me to make things happen in a different way. Everything happened for a reason, is how I look at it.'

'You were brave, of course' I said, as he shrugged modestly, 'but are the bad guys ever brave?'

'Of course they are,' he said.

'Are they?'

'Of course they are,' said Angel again. 'They are brave to do a lot of the things they do. They're not *right*. I wouldn't say it's *right*. But you still have to put that fear behind you sometimes. So ...' Then Angel shrugged again, both smiling and frowning at the same time.

❧

It was the story of another knife attack in New York City, more than forty years earlier, which gave rise to one of the most important social experiments of the late twentieth century. And it reads like a kind of formula for How Not To

Be Brave, given the streak of collective cowardice it revealed. Most intriguingly, on this occasion, the focus fell neither on the perpetrator of the crime, nor on the victim, so much as on the people ranged around the periphery, the bystanders.

Published in 1968, the seminal paper was called 'Bystander Intervention in Emergencies: Diffusion of Responsibility' and in it, John Darley of New York University and Bibb Latané of Columbia set out to unravel a disturbing social phenomenon. The research was a response to an infamous murder that had taken place in 1964, in which a young woman called Kitty Genovese was stabbed to death in a street in Queens. The attack lasted over half an hour and it was reported that there were no fewer than thirty-eight witnesses in the surrounding apartments, but that not one of them attempted to intervene. No one, it was said, had even called the police. When an account of the murder and the apparent inertia of the witnesses came to light in a *New York Times* report some weeks later, there was an explosion of public soul-searching. It has more recently been asserted (Levine & Collins, 2007) that parts of the Kitty Genovese story, as it was disseminated, were exaggerated and became an urban myth of sorts. But what should interest us is how the story was read, first by the public and then by the psychologists.

The failure to intervene and save Miss Genovese, was, said some, a sign of 'moral decay', or the 'dehumanisation produced by the urban environment' said others; 'alienation' had to be at the heart of it, they opined, or 'TV violence', 'apathy' perhaps, or 'existential despair'. Of course, it was hardly news that fear of a dangerous situation might account for an individual's failure to act, or the familiar line cited in the paper, 'I didn't want to get involved', but these explanations did not account for the reported failure to call the police. Instead, posited Darley and Latané, there was another, darker factor in the perceived failure to avert the Kitty Genovese murder.

Each observer, they pointed out, saw the other figures in the lighted windows of surrounding apartments and must have known that they were not alone in witnessing, or at least hearing, the violence in the street outside. This fact alone, the psychologists argued, seemed to magnify each onlooker's inertia. Responsibility was diffused among them, possibly by an idea that someone else was doing something or had called the police. This led to an intuition that the blame – if the worst were to happen – would somehow be diluted by the sheer number of people who had also stood by. Darley and Latané went on to hypothesise that the greater the number of bystanders who witnessed any given emergency, the less likely or the more slowly any one of them was to intervene.

So they designed an experiment, closely mimicking the reported conditions of the Kitty Genovese murder, in order to test just that. And, for Timid Souls, it sheds a fascinating light upon the aptitude, or lack of it, to be brave within certain sorts of groups.

College students were invited to come and take part in what they were told was a group discussion of personal problems encountered in urban student life. Upon arrival, and without encountering their fellows, each student was led down a long corridor with doors opening off it into several small rooms. Each was asked to sit alone at a desk in one of the rooms, wearing a headset and awaiting further instructions. He or she was told that this was to 'avoid embarrassment' by making the discussion anonymous via intercom, rather than talking face to face. A voice soon came over the headset and said that the discussion would be unsupervised, but that the experimenter in charge would return later to gauge reactions. Each participant should speak strictly in turn for two minutes and, although they would be able to hear the other contributions, their microphones would be switched off except during their own turn, thus precluding all communication among participants. And then the experiment began.

A tentative voice duly piped up through the headset with a halting account of his early experiences on campus. He admitted that he suffered from seizures, particularly when studying hard or taking exams. Next another voice shared their experiences. Then another. And another. At length, it was the turn of the newly arrived student mentioned above and he or she also unburdened themselves of the trials of college life. Then the poor man prone to fits came back on the intercom to deliver the next portion of his testimony, but instead he began to have a seizure, his words becoming louder, more disjointed until he said:

> I-er-I-uh-I've got a-a one of the-er-sei-er-er-things coming on and-and-and I could really-er-use some help so if somebody would-er-give me a little h-help-uh-er-er-er-er-er c-could somebody-er-er-help-er-uh-uh-uh (choking sounds). . . . I'm gonna die-er-er-I'm . . . gonna die-er-help-er-er-seizure- er-[chokes, then quiet].

At this point, I should reveal that all the students' disembodied voices, including that of the man taken ill, were in fact recordings made by actors, all apart from one, that first 'naive' subject who had been led down the corridor into the small room. When the man suffered a seizure during his testimony, the naive subject believed that everyone in the 'group' was also able to hear his pleas, but the subject was, of course, unable to communicate with any of them. Recordings taken in that room (when subjects believed their microphone to be off) later revealed that each participant was entirely credulous of the deceit, and clearly moved by the plight of the man having the fit. They were not apathetic, or unconcerned. They gasped out loud, saying 'Oh!', or even exclaiming, 'Oh God! What should I do?'

But how many of them actually did *do* anything? How many of them demonstrated that essential ingredient of courage, the ability to act under pressure?

Fifty-nine female and thirteen male subjects went through this experiment, with Darley and Latané varying the perceived size of the 'group' by adjusting the number of recorded testimonies they played in those apparently round-robin discussions. What they then proceeded to analyse was both how long it took that naive subject to do anything about the man in trouble and what effect the perceived size of the 'group' had on the likelihood of their doing anything at all.

The results were both consistent and shocking. On the one hand, of those subjects who believed that they were in a two-sided discussion with the seizure man and that, when he got into trouble, that they alone could hear him, 85 per cent were quick to report the emergency, rushing down the corridor to get help before he fell quiet. However, as the perceived size of the group increased, that alacrity to act fell away steeply. In 'groups' of five, where one might imagine strength-in-numbers would embolden people to take action, *only 31 per cent* moved to help in any way at all. Every one of the subjects in the two-person groups reported the emergency at some stage, whereas in the six-person groups, an astonishing 38 per cent made no further mention of it. It was also discovered that if a subject had not reported the seizure within the first three minutes, they were then highly unlikely to do so thereafter.

What is most fascinating to me is how succumbing to the Bystander Effect, as it has famously come to be known, was not simply something that affected certain timid or apathetic personalities. Indeed psychological disposition turned out to be of little importance. The effect was present in both men and women with reasonable equity too. Indeed, Darley and Latané's subsequent questionnaires answered by those who had taken part, found strong evidence of indecision as the reason why people had failed to act, rather than any decision *not* to do so, and this was in some sense universal. Darley and Latané cited this indecision as being led by feelings of social etiquette (not wishing to look foolish by making a fuss) and of conformity (not wishing to spoil the experiment by leaving the room). Indeed, these strong social pressures have been proved over and over again in subsequent related experiments to dilute instincts of individual responsibility.

In other words – and this was my bleak revelation – what one might term the courage impulse, that drive to act *in extremis,* was undermined in many cases to the point of total paralysis. For these Timid Souls, it was the society of others that seemed to neuter the will to be brave, or even to be good. And the Bystander Effect has been borne out over and over again in real life. I found myself thinking of David Sharp on Everest, or the office workers who sat typing in the town hall across the street as the women and children of the Berisha family were killed. But there are many examples of people left to die on busy pavements the world over. Some commentators even cited the Bystander Effect as a possible factor in the most heinous failure of collective courage in the twentieth century: the Holocaust.

However, it was with a glimmer of redemption that Darley and Latané concluded their 1968 paper: 'Although this realisation,' they wrote, 'may force us to face the guilt-provoking possibility that we too might fail to intervene, it also suggests that individuals are not of necessity "non-interveners" because of their personalities. If people understand the situational forces that can make them hesitate to intervene, they may better overcome them.' Indeed, later studies (including Beaman et al, 1978) showed that learning about the Bystander Effect in fact made people significantly less likely to succumb to it. In realising their latent weakness, they in a sense learned, or recollected, how to be brave. And, with any luck, so now will we Timid Souls, too.

※

'At this point, I'm really quite clear. It's huge lucidity, you know,' says Gus, looking up from a diagram he has just drawn in my notebook. Moving his beer to one side, he slides the book across the pub table for me to look at. 'What happens now is training. As firemen, what we do is we deal with situations that everybody else is running away from and what we do is we walk towards them' – he makes a faint line on the diagram with the pencil – 'We don't run. *Never run*, because by the time you get there you won't have had time to think what to do. So we *walk* towards the problem and we confront it. That's what we do.'

Angus Campbell is a firefighter of more than twenty-five years with the London Fire Brigade, but he is not talking about fighting a fire. Nor is the story he is telling me – often with tears in his eyes – anything to do with his job, other than that he happened to be travelling to work when it occurred. For one day, during the long, hot summer of 2005, Angus Campbell spectacularly sidestepped the Bystander Effect, confronting a suicide bomber who had just attempted to detonate a device on the London Underground.

It was 21 July, just two weeks after fifty-two London commuters had been killed in the 7/7 suicide attacks. Given the previous fortnight of widespread paranoia, Angus Campbell's reaction on that Northern Line train was deemed to have been so outstanding that he was later awarded the Queen's Gallantry Medal.

Gus had got on the tube at Tooting Bec not long after midday, sitting down towards the back of one carriage. Four stations went by. He was deleting some old text messages from his mobile phone when the train stopped at Stockwell and Gus glanced up at a woman who had just got on opposite him with a toddler in a buggy.

'The doors shut,' he says, 'and the tube pulls away and we're travelling along and then there's a huge bang. I don't usually cower at things – but I flinched and cowered at that noise because it was so loud. It was like *fucking hell*.' Gus mimes the cowering for a second and then, taking a gulp of his pint, he leans forward and sketches the doors onto the layout of the tube carriage in my notebook.

The explosion came from a young man wearing a rucksack that was now apparently on fire. He was standing by the train door, more or less opposite Gus and immediately next to the woman with the baby. This was Ramzi Mohammed, a Somali national known around the North Kensington Muslim community for his increasingly militant views. The backpack was filled with home-made explosives, although at this stage only the detonator had fired. Three similar explosions occurred that lunchtime on two other tube trains and a London bus, part of a coordinated attempt to replicate the horror of two weeks before, although this time, all four devices failed. Not that Gus or the other passengers knew any of this at the moment of the blast. All they knew was that something had exploded and that the tube carriage was filled with smoke and commotion and fear.

'The smoke is white,' says Gus, 'and I'm good on smoke so I know white is a clean smoke and I realise actually it's probably a bomb.'

With the driver oblivious, the train rattled on towards Oval Station, a couple of minutes away. The carriage windows were open against the summer heat, the breeze from the tunnel quickly clearing the smoke to reveal the passengers on one side of Ramzi Mohammed running into the adjacent carriage, everyone on the other side of him struggling through the connecting door at the far end. Within seconds, only Gus, the woman and child and the bomber remained in the carriage. Gus too had started to run moments after the explosion, but the buggy was trapped between a vertical pole and Mohammed himself.

Gus now draws on the diagram in my notebook with arrows and crosses with circles around them to denote himself and the woman, with a capital 'B' for the buggy and then draws another cross in a circle to show the man who had just tried to blow himself and the rest of them to oblivion. This last symbol Gus redraws and redraws as he talks, until the paper goes shiny from the graphite of the pencil.

'What was really terrifying' – Gus draws around the circle again – 'was that I can clearly remember the smoke and flames coming out of his rucksack and him screaming, screaming like you wouldn't believe. He was obviously terrified. He thought he was meeting his maker, but he'd got it wrong and he was now confronting something different. I think he was being burnt up the back of his neck because he was doing this' – with the pencil in one of them, Gus flaps his hands behind the back of his neck – 'and he discarded the rucksack and threw it over here into this corner here.' Gus draws a little square on the paper with an arrow to show the trajectory of the smoking rucksack, which then lay there spewing and spitting bitter-smelling spongy stuff, flecked with black.

Gus went to the woman wrestling with the buggy and said, he told me, 'Look, I can help. Let me get the wheel' and she elbowed me and she pushed me and physically I had to get hold of her. All this is in a matter of seconds but, by this time, I know what Ramzi Mohammed is doing.' Gus pauses.

'Yeah, he's trying to kill us. In fact I should actually be part of the Northern Line right now. Oh, sorry, goose bumps.' His voice beginning to quaver, he adds, 'Yeah, I know exactly what he's doing and I know exactly what I'm going to do.'

The woman let Gus tug the buggy free and they were dragging it down the carriage, when Gus spotted the alarm lever and yanked it. The train slowed to a crawl and a peevish voice came over the tannoy saying, 'Someone's activated the alarm. Can you tell me what you're doing?'

'There's a bomb on the train,' yelled Gus into the speaker next to the alarm, 'There's a bomb on the train. Someone's trying to kill us down here. Help. *Help*.'

No answer.

Gus now yelled up the carriage to Ramzi Mohammed, 'What the fuck's that? *What the fuck is that?* What on earth are you doing?'

'This is wrong,' shrieked the reply. 'This is wrong. This is wrong. *You are wrong. You* are fuck. You are fuck. You are wrong. You are fuck.'

'And I swore back at him,' says Gus. 'There's a lot of swearing going on,' and he laughs apologetically.

Gus pushed the woman and the buggy through the door at the far end of the empty carriage and he found himself alone with Ramzi Mohammed. Where many might have just carried on through that door to relative safety, Angus Campbell now did something unthinkable. He walked back towards the would-be bomber.

'Now I did think he was trying to kill us, OK,' says Gus, 'but I don't want to hurt him. I want to help the idiot. What I was left with was a comical situation with a man who was literally smoking – there was smoke coming from the back of his neck or the hood of his top. There was smoke coming from the remnants of the dumped rucksack. He was clearly in pain.'

Like a good firefighter, Gus looked for the fire extinguisher, but it was not in its bracket. Ramzi Mohammed continued to flap his hands behind his burnt neck and made another gesture that Gus enacts for me, involving a flailing of fists like a frustrated child.

'What have you done? What have you done?' Gus shouted again. 'You're trying to kill us. You tell me what that is,' and he pointed to the spitting, smouldering rucksack.

A peal of incongruous laughter came back and Ramzi Mohammed said, 'No, no, this is bread. This is fucking bread.'

Flour had been used in the making of the bomb, but Gus did not know that; it made no sense to him.

'Lie down,' he said.

'You are fuck.'

'Look, lie down, LIE DOWN and I can come and help you, but I want you to lie down before I can come anywhere near you.'

'I wanted him to be submissive to me,' is how Gus puts it, but Ramzi Mohammed would not lie down.

'The police tell me that all this happened in a period of two minutes.' Gus pauses. 'It didn't feel like two minutes.' And he looks up from the pencil diagram on the table, his eyes wide.

The train now pulled into Oval station at a crawl and the driver came on the tannoy again.

'Whoever's pulled the emergency cord, can they please make themselves known to me.'

Gus ran back to the microphone by the alarm and said, 'Yes, it's me. Yes, it's me. Don't open the doors. Don't open the doors. We've got him. He's not going anywhere. Please don't open the doors. Just leave him here and get the police.'

But the doors opened and Ramzi Mohammed bolted through them into the commuter crowd.

---

'I could have got him,' Gus says and then he says it again, another three times, before adding, 'It doesn't matter because the police got him two days later in Ladbroke Grove, didn't they?' But the way he says it sounds like it does matter to him.

Still amazed by the decision to stay in the carriage at all, I ask Gus why he did not just head on through the door with the woman and the child.

Gus pauses for a long time, then he says 'I wanted to go back and help him,' his voice very quiet, 'It's funny isn't it?'

'Why did you want to help him when he'd just tried to kill you?'

'Oh,' says Gus, apparently overwhelmed by the recollection, 'he's only a child.' A brief internal struggle then seems to follow on the other side of the pub table, in which Gus murmurs, 'To help? What a fool. What a stupid ...'. He stops and shakes his head silently.

'So in a sense, do you not really hold him, as an individual, responsible for what he was doing?'

Gus shakes his head again, tears in his eyes. There is a gaggle of women at the table next to us and they scream with laughter at some joke or other.

'Don't you?' I say.

'No, no. He's just ... No, no, he's just a ... he's just a confused kid.' He whispers this last line, as the women next door fall about with mirth.

'Looking back, Angus,' I ask, 'do you think you were brave?'

'Everyone tells me I was brave. I didn't do very much. I rescued the woman and I rescued a child and I then went back and tried to deal with the situation that was causing the problem in the first place, but I didn't really do anything. I was there and I acted responsibly. Was it brave? People tell me it was very brave. I don't know. I don't know.'

Gus tells me that some people have asked him why he did not walk over and punch Ramzi Mohammed, 'but that would have been wrong in every sense of the word, wouldn't it?' he says. 'And I quite probably would have lost. I mean the adrenalin that was going on within this little man's body was immense. When he ran, there were an awful lot of people on that platform and he mowed through them like they were grass. So you imagine what he's feeling. Forget what I'm feeling, imagine what's going on in him, the fear, imagine the fear!'

I am beginning to work out by now that it is whenever Angus Campbell tries to envisage what Ramzi Mohammed went through that day that the emotion of it all overtakes him. The fact that he might have been blown to bits seems less affecting than the imagined thought processes of the man who would have done it, a man with whom Gus alone had shared this bizarre, intense moment. 'We'll never replicate that, either of us, will we?' Gus says.

I ask whether, in some twisted way, Ramzi Mohammed had also been brave.

'No, I think he was just misdirected,' he says, 'but *he* thinks he's right and that is hugely difficult to deal with. I've thought about him an awful lot, because we went to court and he was tried for attempted mass murder – quite rightly – because that's what he tried to do. But he never looked at me and the judge sent him down for forty years. I dwell on it a lot. He was only very young and it's such a waste. I always think everybody in the world has something to offer, *everyone*' – he pauses and looks up –'I worry about him, you know.' And for a moment, Angus Campbell, this brave good man sits there and he cries.

At length, Gus musters himself and says, 'actually, I didn't think talking about this would be so emotional,' and he necks the last two inches of his pint. Then, firmly closing my notebook with his diagram of the Northern Line tube carriage inside, he looks up and he smiles.

'It's nice talking to a picture, isn't it? But now shut that off, put it away and let it go. Otherwise you are living this every day, aren't you? You're not getting on a train. That's no way forward, is it? Or else he, or his ideology, wins, doesn't it?'

So I slip the notebook into my bag and we walk out into a warm, London evening.

❧

Years ago, I interviewed a man who had been part of the Red Brigades cell that kidnapped and murdered the former Italian prime minister, Aldo Moro, in 1978. This was the first time I had ever really talked to anyone who had done something so unequivocally bad, and I remember being surprised at the time by how alive he was to the horror of what he had done. I had been expecting a darker figure, more obviously amoral or unhinged, than this reasonable, if gruff, Italian man, who spoke of hopes and dreams and squabbles with his fellow *brigatisti*, who liked to go on holiday and felt guilt (or something like it) so crushing that as he stood with our film crew on the via Fani crossroads where he had shot Aldo Moro's two bodyguards dead, he seemed unable to bear it and begged us to leave. The other part that has stayed with me ever since was his description of the moment he looked down at the machine gun, seconds before the ambush, and noticing the barrel was rusty in places, was momentarily engulfed by doubt and fear.

In 2001, a week after the 9/11 attacks, Susan Sontag wrote in *The New Yorker*, 'In the matter of courage (a morally neutral virtue): whatever may be said of the perpetrators of Tuesday's slaughter, they were not cowards.' Her words broke every patriotic taboo in the book and Sontag was vilified from coast to coast. A few other public voices also questioned the rhetoric of cowardice that dominated those strange, scary days, but were forced by a deluge of outrage to recant or reframe their remarks. However, some years later, the forensic psychologist Professor Andrew Silke, expert on both terrorism and the radicalisation that leads to it, wrote a paper called 'Courage In Dark Places' (2004). In it, he argued that in fact many terrorist acts, whether we like it or not, satisfy the core conditions for courageous action (a perception of danger, a fear of that danger and the decision nevertheless to proceed). Moreover he argued that to ignore this fact was to undermine the efforts necessary to counter such acts. 'Amid the carnage and rubble of atrocity,' he wrote, 'we must not allow or encourage the luxury of a simple and demonized foe.'

OK, so I bought this idea that courage (or some simulacrum thereof) could be found in deeds as apparently repugnant as those of the al-Qaeda suicide attacker, but I found myself still intuitively resistant, as many people are, to the baldness of the notion that courage is 'morally neutral'. I did not quite want to believe that. I felt that there was a thread of hope in the various braveries I had met so far, even the slightly pointless ones. And this hope seemed tied to some complex idea of the good that was not necessarily always right, but *wanted* to be. I realised that in the search undertaken on behalf of Timid Souls everywhere, it was not simply a bravery quick fix that I was after, but some sense of how one might measure up to one's own life in a way that was meaningful and not blighted by the kind of 'non-living' with which timidity can so easily half-smother us. Yes, members of the Society, it is time to face the question of moral courage, but not before I pay a visit to one last brave, bad man.

Razor's real name is Noel Smith, although even his father, even the prison governors, used to call him 'Razor'. 'I did try to get away from it for a while, but it's like the tattoos,' he said, his forearms, hands and what you could see of his chest inside his shirt collar, covered with inky dots, names, initials and pictures. 'You know, you don't see it after a while.'

'I'm sure you don't,' I said.

It was a hot day and both of us had a pint of Diet Coke in front of us. The squat town-hall clock had not yet chimed noon, so we were the only people sitting in the garden of The Bugle, on the pretty red-bricked high street of a small Hampshire town, with its tea room and bridal shop, hanging baskets and Parish Council notice board. And yet here was one of the most feared bank robbers of his generation. Now fifty years old, Razor Smith had spent nearly thirty-four of those years behind bars and he looked every inch the jailbird. In his day, he told me, he had been involved in as many as two hundred armed robberies.

'Nine times out of ten,' he said, 'I was what they called "The Frightener". I was a gunman. I would have done all the shouting, and I think I was quite suited to that job because I'm quite controlled in those situations. The fear is a buzz to me, so it's not like I'm stuttering and stumbling. And people listen to what I say.'

'I'm sure they do,' I said.

In 1998, Smith was tried at the Old Bailey and, this being his fifty-eighth conviction in more than twenty years, was given a life sentence. In 2010, a little more than a year before he and I met, Smith was released on life licence. That means, as he put it, 'I can get recalled tomorrow if they think I'm a danger to the community.' And if he ends up in prison again, Razor Smith has had 'the gypsy's warning'. He will never get out; he will die in jail.

The key, so Razor said, to understanding why this life of

his had panned out the way it had was to recognise that he was 'an adrenaline junkie'. He was also, I quickly realised, a highly articulate adrenaline junkie, albeit of the brutal sort, and I guessed this collision of qualities was why the first robber I met, Jimmy, had suggested that Razor advise the Society of Timid Souls.

'I sussed it out a few years ago,' said Razor. 'I've done five years in therapy in my last prison sentence and they came to the conclusion that whereas most people walk up to the edge and look over, I want to throw things over and jump over. And I've always been like that, you know, I think it was just a mad streak in me that wasn't in other people that I knew.'

Then Razor talked about how as a kid he would balance on the edge of a high clock tower in South London, or run along the railway track inside the tunnel at Streatham Hill, sprinting toward the oncoming train as far as he dared before ducking into one of the tunnel recesses as it roared by.

'If I'd have been born into a better life with more money and status, I probably would have been skiing and jumping out of planes,' he said (and it briefly occurred to me that some forms of bravery might simply be a commodity of the affluent middle class). 'I just really wanted that feeling, you know,' he went on. 'It was like being afraid, but at the same time knowing that you're alright. I used to get the same feeling when I used to rob banks. As though you're in control. There's a feeling that you're in charge of your own life and whatever happens is down to you. So the only time I really felt alive was when I was doing stuff like that. It was the same for robberies. Don't get me wrong, the money was *handy*, but what kept me going back – because I could have earned the money working on a building site in the time I spent in jail – but what kept me going back was the rush. That is why I loved it so much.' And Razor shut his eyes for a moment and pulled on his cigarette.

---

Razor was an armed robber by the age of fifteen and boldness quickly became his hallmark.

'All the other criminals my age,' he said, 'were all doing burglaries and shoplifting. Burglary was never really my thing. Too much creeping about. To me that's just distasteful. I've always been the sort of person who would come up to the front door and knock on the door and go in the front door.'

This was not the only time Razor made clear the sorts of crime he had no truck with. He later mentioned with disgust a man he had met in Wandsworth Prison who had robbed sweet shops by squirting ammonia into the eyes of the person behind the counter and then emptying the cash register. 'If you've got to go and blind somebody to make two hundred quid out the till,' he said, 'you don't belong with us mate, fuck off. You're nothing but a thug.' He laughed, without quite smiling, at his own snobbery. 'No, we saw ourselves as noble criminals if you like.'

The point here is that, while the law-abiding majority might prefer their villains morally redundant or psychopathic in some neat, uniform way, actually the truth is more complicated than that.

'What you've got to remember,' said Razor, lighting another of the dozen or so cigarettes he smoked in the course of our meeting, 'is a lot of us have got our morals, my generation certainly, from Hollywood, from cowboy films and gangster films. We never had a war to fight, you see, no National Service, so I think there was something missing for us, and you see yourself as a kind of swashbuckling character like a pirate or Robin Hood. And the code itself was simple: you don't grass, you don't cooperate with the authorities, you never bully anyone weaker than yourself and you never cause anyone unnecessary violence while you're committing your robberies. That's not the game. When you're actually working – that's why we called it "work" – you have to be professional at all times. And that was the code we lived by.'

Armed robbers, Razor went on, were 'a different breed of people', their crime 'if you like, *pure*,' he said, not least because in their eyes there was no victim, just the penny in the pound on insurance. But it was in prison that Razor's image as the bravest and baddest of criminals seems to have been sealed. In search of that adrenaline hit on the inside, Razor became known for violence towards prison officers, despite the threat of solitary confinement and hits taken to parole.

'I knew the consequences,' said Razor, 'but I was addicted to that moment. There's a split second if I was arguing with a screw where I would decide to take control and say "right, I'm doing this", and I would punch them, BANG, and knock them on the floor and as soon as a screw went down, you would hear the rest of them running for you. And I enjoyed that moment when he went down and they were coming – before they reached me. I'd be very, very pleased with myself, but at the same time it was tinged with fear of the kicking that was coming. But to me, that moment was worth it, because you've got to remember, the worst thing about jail is the boredom.'

The other bad thing about prison, Razor told me, was that it could be 'absolutely terrifying'. He described the weekly routine at HMP Parkhurst, when the new prisoners arrived on a Thursday. As they walked in, two hundred-odd 'pug-uglies, all serving long sentences, all brutal, violent men' would come and lean over on the balconies above, looking down at the fresh meat. 'They don't say nothing, just look at you,' said Razor. 'Your bowels turn to water, believe me.'

This fear seemed to eclipse any experienced on the outside. 'So how do you get through it?' I asked.

'The thing is,' replied Razor, 'with me and with a lot of

people, it was about pride. So you have to force it. Whereas if you do a robbery it comes naturally, with those situations I would force that feeling in order to smother the fear. What you want to do is keep the fear down all the time because if it gets too much for you, you're fucked. And for me it was like an almost physical sensation. It was like having a box full of fear and it was all leaking out over the sides and you've got to push it back down and how you push it down is you put a heavier weight on it.' He looked up at me. 'And the heavier weight would be your own pride.'

Razor said it was his pride that gave him 'front', a kind of performance that relied upon initiating conflict before it found him – *Who you fucking looking at? What? You got something to say?* – thereby avoiding the 'painful' postponement and implied humiliation. Either you come out on top, or in his words, 'get what's coming to you'.

There is one last awful obstacle in prison, said Razor, almost as though he were some old samurai invoking bushido, and that is the constant pressure to renege on 'the code'. This, he added, is why 'the code' had to be 'uppermost in your life', that you neither turned bully nor grass. 'The courage is being able to live in that environment and uphold that code against the pressure that you're under. That's where you've got to have bottle.'

I asked Razor whether he thought there could be courage in a life that was so morally flawed. 'Yeah,' he said, 'I think so. The fact is courage doesn't have any morals. These are not things that you should be honoured for, that sort of courage, but it is courage nonetheless.' So I asked whether there was not an element of moral cowardice in failing to consider your victims and Razor nodded, 'Yeah, I think there is a bit of moral cowardice there, because even though you put your life in danger, you've no thought to whoever else is there, you don't give a shit, so yeah, there is a sort of moral cowardice in it. To a certain extent it's a brave thing to do, it's kind of a reckless courage, but you don't care about anybody else.' Clearly, in Razor's eyes, courage and moral courage are not necessarily the same thing.

Still, some glimmer of this different 'better' kind of courage came in what Razor did next. Against the 'absolute boredom' of year upon year in prison, Razor began to read a lot, and as he educated himself, he decided upon a change of strategy in his ongoing war on authority. 'So I looked for a way in which to fight the system where I could still get the satisfaction of doing something, but not keep taking the kicks to the head. And I discovered the complaints system, so I used to get my buzz out of that. In fact about 1994,' Razor said, 'I stopped physically assaulting prison officers, unless it was absolutely necessary, and I started working the pen.' He laughed. 'I've done hundreds of complaints, but I never complained about anything that wasn't a genuine complaint. I made up my mind that I wouldn't be one of them people who made petty complaints. You know, "the salad ain't crisp enough" or "my pillow's too hard" – I would look around for genuine grievances, I'd actually seek them out and complain about them. It's a long process, it's a dance, but I would have maybe twenty going on at the same time. And I very rarely lost. I remember the Principal Officer sidled up to me on the landing and he went "you know what, I preferred it when you were throwing punches!" I said "why's that?" and he said "I've got a pile of fucking paperwork in my office that I've got to do over you." He said, "In the old days we'd have just hit you over the head with a truncheon and thrown you in the block!" and I said "well, those days have gone now".'

Razor got out of prison in 1997, but his 'adrenaline addiction', as he called it, was still in rude health and he went straight back to robbery. The next year, he was serving life. Three years into that sentence came the moment when

everything changed. Razor's teenage son – 'he'd been following in my footsteps' – was found dead in suspicious circumstances, just days after getting out of Feltham Young Offend-
er's Institution. Razor could not get permission to leave the
prison and attend his funeral.

'I suddenly looked around', he said, 'and I started listening to people and you know when something just becomes
jaded for you? I thought "who the fuck are these people?"
All talking about the robberies they've done and why they're
in jail. I thought "well I'm not fucking interested in this no
more, there must be something else". I thought "Joe's death
can't have been for nothing," so I wanted to change my life
round as a sort of tribute to him. I was determined to make
his death be *about something*. So it was a personal decision to
look around to see if, after all these years in jail, there really
was any offer of rehabilitation.'

Razor found it eventually at HMP Grendon, the UK's
only therapeutic prison, where he was to spend nearly five
years in treatment and writing about his experiences. Now
I understood why his account up until this point, while
clearly nostalgic for the old thrills, had also been peppered
with moments where he had suddenly said 'we weren't noble
criminals, we were just fucking scumbag thieves,' or 'we were
greedy, lazy bastards that just nick everything'. I had over-
looked these remarks at first, but now realised that somewhere, somehow, regret had crept in and begun to rewrite
some of Razor's old scripts when he was not looking.

When Noel Smith left prison in 2010, he declared himself
'a Rusty Gun', underworld-speak for the convicted criminal
who has chosen honourable retirement from a life of crime.
But being a Rusty Gun in reality looked hard. When I asked,
'How's it been?', Razor answered, 'It's been terrible. Seriously.' He shook his head and suddenly looked a little smaller
than he had for the last couple of hours. 'I think when you

are going in and out of prison all your life and you're stuck in that life, it's easy. Life is just one big land of freedom when you're a criminal, believe it or not, even though they put you in jail for it. But now I'm in a different kind of world – this is a world that I have to engage in because I don't want to go back to prison, I've had enough of it. So to me, this is the hard work. It's testing my nerve. Still, even now, I walk down the street sometimes and I see a security van delivering and the old heart goes and I think, "oh, it would be so easy to do that" and of course I've got mates who phone me up and say "are you finished with all that straight life yet?"' – Razor laughed out loud – '"we've got a bit of work for you tomorrow", and that's why I say you need a lot of courage to stay out of crime, because it's like going into a warm, cosy place where you know everything, you know you're going to get some laughs, you're going to get some excitement and maybe this time you're going to get away with it. It becomes like a call in your head and you have to ignore it. You've just got to stop yourself. *Every single time.*'

And that, I now realised, was the sound of a brave, bad man, trying to be good.

# 9

# Tyrannies

*Sapere aude!*
Dare to be wise.

Horace/Immanuel Kant/Michel Foucault
(they all said it)

This was also a sound. It came etched into the surface of a series of blue, plastic loops, three and a half inches wide and twelve in circumference. They were called Dictabelts and they had been developed in the 1940s to replace the wax cylinder as a means of recording audio. Designed for office use, these Dictabelts were easy to fold up and post, and such sounds as were engraved into their surface by the slim stylus of the recording machine were, in theory at least, there forever. With the emphasis on practicality rather than posterity, it was impossible to erase, edit or reuse a Dictabelt, but over time folding made the creases permanent and the plastic itself became brittle; whatever sound was incised there long ago was, more often than not, lost to modern ears.

But the sound on *these* Dictabelts was deemed to be

unloseable. For what was here was the apotheosis of twentieth-century courage, the sound of a bravery that had not only become epic and ideal in the collective imagination, but that was also true and proven and *there* in those grooves on the plastic. If archivists were to be defeated by the poor state of preservation and nothing done to salvage some auditory fragments, it would be rather like saying, 'Oh well, can't be helped,' as paint flaked from Mona Lisa's cheek, or, 'Never mind,' having mislaid one or two of the Dead Sea Scrolls.

It took a British Library Sound Archive engineer more than a month to modify a Dictaphone machine in order to attempt a recovery of the audio on these venerable loops, seven of them in all. It was touch-and-go as to whether his efforts would work at all. The belts had been recorded at the wrong speed, which meant that the voice was shrill and gabbled, the needle jumping over large portions of the recording at every hardened crease. And so followed an operation of Heath Robinson complexity involving the addition of a variable speed motor and the use of an industrial hotplate that might warm the fragile plastic in order to render the folds more forgiving of the stylus. The sound could then be amplified, recorded and respliced on computer, before being played for the first time in thirty-seven years.

'*This then is what the ANC is fighting*,' says the voice. It is a voice we all know well, although the recording is crackly, and it sounds young and strong. '*During my lifetime*,' the voice continues, '*I have dedicated myself to this struggle of the African people. I have fought against white domination, and I have fought against black domination. I have cherished the ideal of a democratic and free society in which all persons will live together in harmony and with equal opportunities. It is an ideal for which I hope to live*' – the voice pauses, as one might at the edge of a precipice – '*and to see realised, but, my Lord*' – another pause yawns, terrifying – '*if it needs be, it is an ideal for which I am prepared to die.'* That last word, which a lesser man, or a lesser orator, might have swallowed, rings in the silent room.

I knew these words of course. The speech from which they came was famous by now, quoted many times over. You can buy a mouse mat with these words on it, or a T-shirt, but I was unprepared for the eerie power of hearing them spoken in that moment (20 April 1964), in that place (the dock of the Rivonia Trial, Pretoria Palace of Justice, South Africa), by that man ('Accused Number One', Nelson Rolihlahla Mandela). Two months later, of course, he was on Robben Island and he would remain imprisoned for the next quarter of a century, but not one moment of the celebrated courage that had preceded that April morning, nor followed it behind bars, had ever been captured in quite this way. And so it was that the restoration of the Mandela Dictabelts in 2001 became a global news story. Just as I had watched Mike Parsons surf his enormous wave or Dean Potter leap from the Eiger, just as I had looked on in the bullring as Rafaelillo was rammed by two Miuras in succession, or as I had sat with Hal Finney in his wheelchair as his computer voice talked of adaptation; just as I had pored over the CCTV from the tube carriage where Angus Campbell faced Ramzi Mohammed, or had observed Vjollca Berisha arranging some biscuits on a plate for the arrival home of her only surviving son, so I now listened to this recording of Nelson Mandela in 1964, over and over and over again. It was as if close study might yet yield the secret of the bravery therein.

Well, of course, it did not. I should have guessed by now that while courage in all its infinite variety makes compelling viewing – or in this case listening – that it was not really the mettle itself that you could see or hear; instead it was just the action (or the spoken word) held before you, like a mirror to your own timidity, all your own small failures to act or say or do.

It is indeed a final destination for the Timid Soul, this particular bravery that we have come to regard as the King of All Courages. I am speaking of course of *moral* courage, the decision to risk ridicule, disapproval, alienation, penury, even incarceration or violence, in order to do or say what you think is right. There is something about it that both compounds the mystery of its origins and heightens that nagging feeling that the rest of us may in fact be fundamentally second-rate.

Certainly much of the finest rhetoric surrounding moral courage redoubles this idea of inaccessibility. Some two years after Mandela made his speech to the Rivonia courtroom, Bobby Kennedy addressed students in Cape Town, calling upon them to challenge the old order of oppression and to build a better world, free from prejudice. He concluded by warning against the three key 'dangers' that stood in their way: futility, expediency and finally, he said, 'timidity'. 'Few men are willing,' Kennedy went on, 'to brave the disapproval of their fellows, the censure of their colleagues, the wrath of their society. Moral courage is a rarer commodity than bravery in battle or great intelligence. Yet it is the one essential, vital quality of those who seek to change a world which yields most painfully to change.'

Please, Timid Souls, take a moment to walk with me around a fine, imagined chamber. Here, in my mind's eye, our Society comes to congregate on the most important days of the (timid) calendar. Beneath a vaulted ceiling, the walls are hung with portraits of the brave, those Timid Souls who have completed their transformation, their eyes now filled with what they have seen and done and what they know. Among them, for there are many hundreds of faces in this chamber, are a few that are familiar. Look, there is Private Martin Bell; he taught us comradeship. And there, there is Sally-Ann Sutton; she taught us instinct. Cardiff Scott, he taught us how to rage; Greg Long, how fear can make you grow up; and Fleur Lombard too, although she also showed how high the price can be. Next to her is Eduardo Dávila Miura who trains young men first to look brave and then to be so. And on the other side, over there, is Renée Fleming, agleam with costume and make-up, although we now know what terror may lie beneath. Oh yes, and here is Lord Ashcroft, although no one quite knows how he got in here, which may yet be the lesson of his story. Ahead I can see David Alderson; he taught us the power of sober commitment. Opposite is a sun-bleached photo of a small crowd, the subjects of Darley and Latané's Bystander experiments; they, and we, learned about collective cowardice and in the process found ourselves a little braver than before. Nearby is the face of Hayley Ridgeway, young and lovely and the best friend you could ever have. Noel Razor Smith is a little unsightly next to her and yet somehow he proved the connection between the gravest disobedience and a certain strain of courage. High on one wall is Alain Robert, who taught us the power of believing your own story, even if you do cast yourself as Zorro. And below is Ruth Millington, who showed how action and application could save lives. Kent Diebolt is here too, although he did not expect to be, having urged us simply to focus on what was important; alongside him, equally surprised, is a group portrait of the Voice of Wales Speakers Club who taught us the rewards of being prepared to risk a little embarrassment.

Finally, there at the far end of the chamber, above a raised dais, are a handful of faces we all know well. These are the icons of courage, recast in modern minds as secular saints before whom the rank and file Timid Soul struggles to feel anything so strongly as awe. Mahatma Gandhi. Martin Luther King. Nelson Mandela. The 14th Dalai Lama. Aung San Suu Kyi. So transported are we in fact by what these people represent that it is tempting to overlook the curious contradiction that lies at the heart of their elevation. For the truth is that, while a certain blueprint for physical courage resides with soldiers and the fighting of wars – those portraits we viewed back near the entrance to the chamber – equally the blueprint for *moral* courage has been most significantly shaped in the last seventy-five years by those who have refused to fight and have instead embraced non-violence. That they have done so during a period of human history that has otherwise fetishised violence is key to their mettle. And there they are, each picked out in spotlight, each high above us.

The idea of moral courage, with its suggestion that there might be a form of bravery that did not necessarily require a physical girding of loins, was first formally articulated as recently as 1822, although, of course, the quality itself is as old as the hills. Besides, on closer examination, it is hard to conceive of a moral courage that would not, if need be, withstand some physical test of its commitment; we are, as Christopher Hitchens pointed out, *bodies* after all. So, then, to set moral courage apart and above all the heart, nerve, guts and balls of the other people I had met so far is, I suspect, to miss the point about how to be brave. For in those spotlit heroes, rare and extraordinary though they are, congregate many of the apparently more humble components of bravery that we can see in the other faces in this chamber – obedience, disobedience, anger, self-control, training, concentration, love, pride, denial, adaptation, antagonism, fear, the knack of pretending you have no fear, patience, impatience, calculation, spontaneity, independence of thought, a sense of community, the drive to make the most of one life, deference to a story larger than your own.

Is this moral courage then, in its sacrarium, out of reach to the Timid Soul, or might there yet be a way we can learn this part of being brave?

---

❦

'When I was seven years old, I was with my grandmother and I went to catch the streetcar' – Bernard Lafayette is telling me this sixty-three years later – 'and the practice was that if you were of Afro-American descent, you would go aboard the streetcar, deposit your fare in the receptacle there at the front next to the conductor, then you would dismount and go all the way to the back and you would enter the street-car at the back door. And there you had a segregated section where you would sit.'

Dr Lafayette and I are seated at one end of a large meeting room at a PBS TV station in Boston. He is here to take part in a celebration of the fiftieth anniversary of the Freedom Rides, in which he and other civil rights activists rode inter-state buses into the segregated American South. Already a veteran at just twenty of the Nashville lunch-counter sit-ins, Lafayette went to lead the campaign in a terrified Selma, Alabama and to work closely with Martin Luther King. One wall of the meeting room where we are sitting is glass with various posters stuck to it and, over the three hours that follow, I am periodically aware of the station staff stealing a glimpse, from behind the posters, of the man who had lived these things.

'Well the problem was,' he goes on, 'that sometimes you would pay your money and while you were en route to the back, the conductor would close the door and the steps would go up and it would take off with your money. You would try and run, you know, to catch it and' – Bernard smiles and shakes his head – 'no way. So it happened with my grandmother, we were both running to make sure we could get there and she fell. I could have made it onto the street-car but I couldn't leave my grandmother, so I was reaching for her and trying to hold the door and the tram took off. I remember, even at age seven, it felt like a sword splitting me in half. So I decided right then I didn't like it, I didn't like the way we were being treated and I said to myself, "when I get grown, I am going to do something about this".'

That moment, in Tampa, Florida, in 1948, was the instant of outrage that set in motion an extraordinary life. That was the impetus and a few months later came the first bold move.

Bernard grew up in the Latin quarter of Tampa, in an area called Ybor City built at the end of the nineteenth century by cigar manufacturers and populated by a multi-ethnic community from Cuba, Italy, Spain. Bernard's home was one of just two residential houses on 8th Avenue, one block over from the main business thoroughfare, and the house was flanked by two huge cigar factories. 'As a boy, that was my front yard,' he says. 'So I started smoking at five. *Cigars.*' He booms with throaty laughter. 'But I only smoked for forty-seven years. I stopped smoking after that.' Still chuckling, he tells me how as a small boy he used to get up early in the morning and go and take coffee orders from the factory workers before the day began. 'So I was like Mr Coffee. I would go to the café about three blocks away, which hadn't opened up for business yet. I'd get the coffee and bring it back to them. And I used to make ten cents a cup. So when I went to school I always had a pocket-full of money and I used to buy lunch for some of the kids who didn't have much money.'

The café, he tells me, had lunch stools at the counter, where, as was the norm at the time, anyone with a black face, man or child, was forbidden to sit. All the same, as the months passed, little Bernard got to know the man behind the counter. It was not his business, he just worked the morning shift there and they began to exchange a few words in Spanish. After many weeks, Bernard found himself chattering away about cigar smoking and other virile pursuits, as the man fixed the coffee. It was perfectly amicable, but one day, it occurred to seven-year-old Bernard that he would like to sit on one of those forbidden stools. And it was an idea that, over many mornings, refused to go away.

'I saw myself as a businessman,' he says, 'so I was doing business with him and before his store even opened he had sold ten cups of coffee. So he was not giving me something, I was not working for him, there was no favour and I began to feel a sense of equality. He was doing business and I was doing business. He was making money; I was making money. And the more coffee I bought from him the more money both of us made. So if I wanted to sit on the stool while I was waiting for him, then that is why. You cannot have moral courage until you feel your own sense of self-worth, because you can see that you *deserve*.'

Still it took many weeks to go through with it. To steel his nerve, the boy prattled on to the man behind the counter.

'So I kept talking and talking,' he says, '*and* talking and talking and then I finally leaned on the stool, like that' – Bernard crooks one elbow at the level of his shoulder and looks me in the eye. Suddenly you can see the little boy in the café.

Another three weeks passed of leaning casually on the stool that was almost as tall as he was.

'The real concern,' says Bernard, 'was how I was going to respond if he told me to get off the stool. In this particular situation, Polly, and it may be extrapolated to other situations, the fear was not the lack of courage. The fear was whether or not I would *lose* courage. The question is under what circumstances would you back away. Because I had to make a very strategic decision of whether or not it was worth the risk of losing my business, because you can't go back. And so you have to count up your potential loss, those other kids who needed my lunch money, whether or not the man and I were going to break friendship. What would happen to him if the boss came in and he was permitting me to sit there. So I had a lot of things to think about.'

He leaned and thought, thought and leaned, but then one day, little Bernard climbed up onto the stool.

'I eased up,' he says, 'and I sat there. And the guy was fixing the coffee and there was a huge mirror in front of him and our eyes met. I could see him looking at me and I was looking at him and there was a moment of truth. That's when the talking stopped and then he looked outside to make sure that nobody was watching. I didn't say anything and he didn't say anything. But from that point on I would go and sit on the stools while the coffee was being prepared.'

'Did it feel like a victory?' I ask.

'Oh, a big victory,' says Bernard. 'The victory was for me to respect myself. And as I think about it now, when I sat on that stool it was a form of protest. I haven't really thought about it as much before, but I realise now that it was not impulsive. And maybe real moral culture is contemplative rather than reactive? So' – Bernard pauses and smiles expansively – 'that was my first sit-in.'

❧

It was some months before I met Bernard Lafayette that I had started wondering about how moral courage might begin, and what it looked like when it was finding its way. That is why I had first typed the name 'Joe Glenton' into Google only to be shocked by what I found. For before I had got to the first 'n' of Glenton's surname, the search engine had predicted "Joe Glenton coward" as the phrase I was most likely to be typing.

I knew a certain amount of Glenton's controversial story from the newspapers, but the slur seemed outlandish in the modern age. Joe Glenton was a young British soldier who had gone AWOL rather than return with his unit to Afghanistan and who had been charged with desertion, a charge that was later reduced to absence without leave. In 2010 he had been found guilty at court martial and sent to a military prison, where he served out a little over half of his nine-month sentence. His failed defence, according to the press, had relied on a combination of deep ethical misgivings about the war in Afghanistan and the symptoms of post-traumatic stress disorder, left over from his previous and only Afghan tour.

Curious about how violence and non-violence parted company, I had that summer been reading Bertrand Russell's 'An Outline of Intellectual Rubbish' (1943), and – partly because it ran so counter to the military orthodoxy of the moment, partly because it offered a different path altogether for the Timid Soul – I had found myself homing in on one particular passage:

> Collective fear stimulates herd instinct ... Neither a man nor a crowd nor a nation can be trusted to act humanely or think sanely under the influence of a great fear. And for this reason poltroons [cowards] are more prone to cruelty than brave men ... When I say this, I am thinking of men who are brave in all respects, not only in facing death. Many a man will have the courage to die gallantly, but will not have the courage to say, or even to think, that the cause for which he is asked to die is an unworthy one.

And so I wrote to Joe Glenton via his lawyer, quoting this last line and hopeful that he might share his insights of the other side of military courage with the Society of Timid Souls. Uncommonly difficult to track down for several months, at length Glenton agreed to speak and one Sunday morning, about a year after his release from prison, we talked.

He told me how he had joined the Army Logistics Corps at twenty-two, how he had 'loved the lifestyle', 'the banter', but how 'brief moments of fear' began to prickle on the eve of his first Afghan deployment in the spring of 2006. Glenton's unit arrived in Kandahar in April and spent the next seven months 'slightly detached from the fighting' at the huge ammunition site at the airfield there. From time to time, mortars would be fired at the base, which undoubtedly rattled the nerves, but Joe said he did not see much death as such, other than 'the repats and stuff'. He talked about fork-lifting coffins about the site after a helicopter went down, adding, 'that stayed with me'.

When he returned from Kandahar, Joe's growing misgivings about the war began to cascade into what he described as 'all the classic symptoms' of post-traumatic stress – insomnia, nightmares, hyper-vigilance; what in days gone by might have been described as 'soldier's heart'. He resolved inwardly, so he said, to leave the army, but believed in the meantime that he would be protected from another deployment by the so-called Harmony Guidelines, designed to safeguard morale by discouraging the deployment of soldiers more than once every eighteen months. So when in spring 2007 Joe was called into his sergeant's office and told he would be going on tour that summer, he found himself replying, 'No I'm not.' The discussion that followed became heated and ended with the sergeant saying, so said Joe, 'You're a coward and a malingerer and you'll do what you're told.'

Several weeks later, not long before he was due to deploy, Joe did something that was very brave, or the very opposite of brave, depending on where you stand: he simply left camp and got on a plane to Bangkok. He passed the next six months in South East Asia, spending what he called his 'blood money' from the previous Afghan tour on 'cheap booze and cheap drugs'. 'Dark days,' he said, 'strange days.

From being a disciplined soldier to someone on the run, effectively'. Eighteen months in Australia followed. I asked whether it was a bit like 'a dark version of a backpacking holiday' and Joe said, 'more of a partially self-imposed kind of exile, drifting around, grew a big beard, very strange times.'

By the summer of 2009, Joe and his Australian girlfriend, Claire – an immigration lawyer whom he later married and was in the process of divorcing when he and I spoke – decided that together they would return to the UK and face the music. Upon landing on British soil, Joe handed himself in and was duly charged with desertion. The court case ensued through the autumn and winter, amid much publicity of what were by now Joe's clear anti-war arguments. He wrote an open letter to the then prime minister Gordon Brown, saying that Britain had 'no business' to be in Afghanistan. He addressed the large Stop The War rally in Trafalgar Square. Indeed, as he left Colchester Military Court after being sentenced in March 2010, there are photos of Joe Glenton, bound for detention, punching a clenched fist into the air, very much the political prisoner.

Joe Glenton's defiance struck a particular chord in certain quarters. There was a deluge of critical press, of course, as well as the Facebook "Joe Glenton Coward" group and another one pleasantly entitled "Hang Joe Glenton". Yet for the sizeable anti-war lobby, he became a poetic, even heroic figure. And you can hear this transformation in his own account, for when Joe reached the part in his story where the fight to defend his name began, I noticed his rhetoric shift, his phrasing at once more confident and more emotive, more certain of its ideological moorings. He would say things like, 'It's historically always been people like me at the bottom who are sent out to lubricate others' ambition with their blood'; or 'I think the "Hero or Coward" debate is a complete distraction.

The issue is Afghanistan – it's not whether Joe Glenton is a hero or a coward.'

Nevertheless, some notional personal courage clearly still mattered to Joe. Just a few minutes later, I asked him about the moments most testing of his nerve through all of this.

'Probably coming back to the UK, making that choice,' he said, 'that process of going "it's just little me but I'm going to fight you", knowing that you're facing some Leviathan. That was scary but I guess I still did it, so that could be argued to be a courageous moment.'

I wanted to be impressed by Joe Glenton, and at times I was, but his account was dotted with small inconsistencies like this and I could not help wondering about the extent to which his narrative of lucid moral outrage had been constructed after the fact. His timeline of the onset of his ethical misgivings was muddy; the assertions that his qualms were moral, not political – the grounds for conscientious objection – belied how he described his political position at other moments; I had to ask more than once for clarification of the extent to which either his PTSD symptoms or his ethical reservations had led the decision to go AWOL, without ever quite getting to the bottom of it. Nor was it clear why he had not looked into applying for conscientious objector status, other than that he said, perhaps accurately, that 'it would have been kicked out anyway'. All of which is not to imply that Joe Glenton had fudged the facts, nor that his now ardently held views were disingenuous. Only that the whole tale was a little bit messier when you got up close and, as is so often the case with the more conventional military courage too, the story of why people do what they do often seems to crystallise in retrospect.

Above all, Joe Glenton struck me as a young man who, ironically, had found his vocation not through *joining* the army, or *being in* the army, but through *leaving* it. And such moral courage as he had had to muster in the process had been improvised along the way, which is perhaps why he had not yet sloughed off the belligerence of its origins. At the end of our conversation, I asked Joe, who was just about to turn thirty, what the future held for him.

'Certainly I am an activist now,' he said, 'and it's some-thing which strangely the military lends itself very well to. It's another fight and we're trained to fight and now I have something to fight – bizarrely, it's the people and power that used to employ me. Whatever I do, at the core of me there will always be a soldier, and alongside him there will also be this antagonist with a sense of what's just and what's unjust.'

And who could say what these impulses would produce, or not, in years to come?

❦

William Ian Miller in his book, *The Mystery of Courage*, writes that 'Moral courage is a lonely courage'. This would certainly seem to be true if one were to consider the flight of young Lance Corporal Glenton to be brave, let alone the extraordinary actions at the coffee counter of the (far younger) Bernard Lafayette. Here are no platoon mates, no torero's *cuadrilla*, no police backup nor fellow Toastmasters to smile and clap. Of course, there is solitude in the moment of suspended animation that precedes decisive action (a soli-tude that I would hazard very few brave people escape), but to mistake that for an idea that moral courage is, of neces-sity, friendless in its hour of need, or that the person involved need be wolfishly independent to qualify, is, I believe, to miss the point about some of the very finest moral courage of the last few generations.

In her 2011 BBC Reith Lecture, Aung San Suu Kyi, the leader of the Burmese pro-democracy movement, described the subtle but communal project of her fellow dissidents in the face of the fear that has loomed large over their struggle. 'Fear is the first adversary we have to get past when we set out to battle for freedom,' she said, 'and often it is the one that remains until the very end. But freedom from fear does not have to be complete. It only has to be sufficient to enable us to carry on; and to carry on in spite of fear requires tremendous courage ... [This] is everyday fare for dissidents. They pretend to be unafraid as they go about their duties and pretend not to see that their comrades are also pretending. This is not hypocrisy. This is courage that has to be renewed consciously from day to day and moment to moment.'

The contemporary moral philosopher, Alasdair MacIntyre, has devoted much of his life's work to a revival of Aristotle's idea of the virtues, part of a wider and ongoing resurgence of so-called virtue ethics in modern thought. Placing great importance upon the role of community life in the cultivation of those virtues or good habits that will in turn yield 'the good life', MacIntyre writes of courage that it 'is important, not simply as a quality of individuals, but as the quality necessary to sustain a household and a community.' So I wondered what might be found if one were to look in some sense *past* the 'heroes' of moral courage, in search of those collective blueprints for morally courageous action. I fear Prof MacIntyre might despair of my terminology here, but I still wondered if it were possible to discover more of how *together* people might learn to be morally brave.

❧

I was nervous about my next encounter and not because it was some bristly bad guy or twitchy famous name. In truth, I find intellectual heavyweights scarier to interview than almost anyone else. And when I get nervous, what follows is a total collapse of my ability to read a map or follow simple, straightforward directions. That is why I found myself in run-down East Boston, doing laps of the street grid near Maverick station, searching for the unmarked door – I had been told it was green – of The Albert Einstein Institution. In the end, a man in the Brazilian corner store explained the arcane numbering system on the residential street I was looking for and at length, I climbed the three steep steps to the green door and rang the bell.

A woman answered and ushered me inside, across a narrow hall into the front room of the house, before disappearing wordlessly into another room at the back. The study, for that is what the room appeared to be, was lined on every wall with bookshelves from floor to ceiling and heavy curtains hung at the window, letting in only a dull glow from the grey street outside. Such light as there was came from a single bright angle-poise lamp on a large desk entirely covered with great piles of newspapers and books. Everywhere you looked there were more heaps of papers and precarious towers of paperbacks, hardbacks, bound and unbound manuscripts, and in the midst stood a stooped, white-haired gentleman with a long, wise, ancient face and two pens in the top pocket of his black shirt. He smiled a decorous smile, shook my hand and introduced me to the dog that was ambling past ('This is Sally'). He nodded to the corner of a lumpy velvet divan pushed back against one wall and also covered with books and paper. I sat down.

This was Dr Gene Sharp, the *éminence grise* of strategic non-violent struggle, whose writings on the subject were said to have influenced revolutionaries around the world. Long distinguished within his field for his seminal works on the ideas and methods of Gandhi, Sharp has been an academic at Oxford, Harvard and at the University of Massachusetts Dartmouth. In 1983, he set up the Albert Einstein

Institution, a non-profit organisation devoted to the study and promotion of non-violent resistance, and which took its name from the famous pacifist who had once written a fore-word to Sharp's great tome on Mahatma Gandhi.

However it was the work that Gene Sharp completed in 1993, when he was already sixty-five, that would turn out to have the greatest impact in the wider world. This was a slim handbook on practical methods of non-violent struggle, a distillation of decades of scholarship, penned at the request of a prominent Burmese pro-democracy exile. Knowing little of the specifics of the Burmese situation, Sharp had chosen to write the manual – or as he prefers to call it 'a conceptual framework' – generically. What emerged was ninety-three pages that read like a 'How To ...' of revolution. He called it *From Dictatorship To Democracy* and it was built around an idea that tyrannies were never as strong as they seemed to be; that if the subjects of those tyrannies were first to identify the sources of the tyrant's power and then to rescind their obedience to them, the regime would begin to crumble. The pages are then filled with practical advice on how one might be disobedient, dozens of methods from picketing and peti-tions, to symbolic colours and rude gestures, satires, vigils, mock funerals, strikes, boycotts and sit-ins, these and other techniques enumerated and precisely defined. Sharp writes:

> About two hundred specific methods of nonviolent action have been identified, and there are certainly scores more. These methods are classified under three broad categories: protest and persuasion, noncoopera-tion, and intervention. Methods of nonviolent protest and persuasion are largely symbolic demonstrations, including parades, marches, and vigils (54 methods). Noncooperation is divided into three sub-categories: (a) social noncooperation (16 methods), (b) economic

noncooperation, including boycotts (26 methods) and strikes (23 methods), and (c) political noncooperation (38 methods). Nonviolent intervention, by psychological, physical, social, economic, or political means, such as the fast, nonviolent occupation, and parallel government (41 methods), is the final group. A list of 198 of these methods is included as the Appendix to this publication.

First published in instalments, *From Dictatorship To Democracy* was also printed as a pamphlet and the Albert Einstein Institution made photocopies whenever anyone asked for one. One of these copies found its way to Serbia where it greatly influenced Otpor!, the youth resistance movement credited with bringing down Slobodan Milošević in 2000. Looking to the success of Otpor!, resistance movements in Georgia, the Ukraine, Kyrgyzstan, Lithuania, Latvia and Belarus also studied Sharp's taxonomy of non-violent resistance, each new struggle taking the pamphlet as though it had been written especially for them. In 2003, *From Dictatorship To Democracy* became available for free download online and, spreading like wildfire, has now been translated into more than thirty-four languages. In 2009, Sharp was nominated for the Nobel Peace Prize, although by then, the authorities in Iran, Venezuela and Burma had denounced this scholar as a dangerous man, part of some US conspiracy, even a CIA agent.

In spite of all this, few in the West beyond academia and diplomatic circles had heard of Gene Sharp before the Arab Spring, which was in full flood by the time I visited Dr Sharp in April 2011. In the early coverage of the unrest, assorted Egyptian dissidents had mentioned the use of Sharp's 198 methods and, overnight, this octogenarian intellectual became famous, despite mutterings from Tahrir Square that Egyptians needed no American to teach them revolt.

---

I, of course, was not here in East Boston to determine one way or the other what exactly had ignited the Arab Spring. What interested me was the way in which this strange little book, *From Dictatorship To Democracy*, might be read either as exhortation or a pathway to moral courage and how following it may have taught certain freedom fighters to be brave.

'First,' said Dr Sharp, before we began, 'the disclaimer: I never speculated on courage as such. So I don't have anything very useful for you on that.'

Instead, Sharp told me about his background, growing up as the son of a Protestant minister during World War II, and how these things had moulded his world view as a young man, even as his religious faith fell away. He described how in his twenties he had been a conscientious objector during the Korean War. Sharp was offered formal conscientious objector status, but turned it down and refused to report for the draft, favouring this actively disobedient approach. The stand earned him a two-year prison sentence of which he served nine months.

'My point was not just *how can I be a conscientious objector?*' he said, 'but *under what conditions could we get rid of war?* I wasn't objecting to the Korean War, as such. I was objecting to the whole development of the war system and the assumption that you have to have a military answer, which I didn't think was a very good answer.'

The old man's hands, which would occasionally sweep the air with some vague gesture, had cobbled knuckles and his voice was whispery and trembled. Yet there was nothing frail about the way that Gene Sharp looked you in the eye, or thought in silence, sometimes for many seconds, before answering each question with great precision. If he did not quite agree with the phrasing or premise of a question, he would courteously say so. If I asked anything that strayed into loose generality or beyond the realm of the scholar's discipline, he answered, simply, 'I don't know' and left it at that.

Dr Sharp told me that although he used to count himself as a pacifist, he no longer did, describing the position at which he arrived as 'a third position' of trying to change this status quo, for reasons that were pragmatic rather than moral.

'I was not thinking about how can man be *pure*,' he said, 'or holy or proud of one's halo. I have distaste for that. That's why,' he added, 'some people would call me the Machiavelli of non-violence. Machiavelli focused on understanding politics as it *is*, not as it should be.'

And, according to Sharp, it was the shunning of violence that, in the real world, most recently in the Arab Spring, had unlocked a whole armoury of new 'weapons' against tyranny.

'Because if you use violence you're helping to defeat yourself,' he said. 'It's as simple as that. If your opponent is a really ruthless regime, they always have the soldiers and the weapons of violence. You have very little in those terms. So why choose to fight with their weapons? You're almost certain to lose. Whereas without violence in Tunisia – and there is very little in Egypt – they won success very quickly. While in Libya, the faith in violence and its power, it's messed things up. It's an almost religious belief in the omnipotence of violence, but the reality is often as one of the Egyptians said: "We were wise to have left our guns at home". They had more power without the guns than they would have had *with* the guns.'

This is the heart of the Sharp doctrine and what is so fascinating is the extent to which it sidesteps morality and personality and wholesome virtues like loving thy neighbour.

'No,' he said, testily, 'you can *hate* your neighbour, he who has done all these terrible things; you can wish he was dead. Still you don't have to agree that you must kill him in order to win, because if you kill him, his whole family will come at you and you'll have no chance. So to assume you have to remake human personality to do this, that's nonsense. You can be the same stubborn so-and-so you've always been and still be non-violent.'

'And achieve a moral victory?'

'Yes. Yes,' he said, '*And* political victory.'

So I asked whether the key to the victory lay with the creation or strengthening of community among the oppressed. Sharp politely corrected my use of the word 'community', a little too cosy a terminology for him, but he said that yes, it was to do with a notion of 'working together' in institutions either pre-existing or specially created for the purpose. (And I secretly thought of our Society of Timid Souls.)

'People have to understand,' he said, 'that they have the potential for changing the situation. They don't have power at that time, but they have *power potential*,' he said, 'and yes, it is very learnable.' The only obstacle to that learning process was, said Sharp, obedience and the fear that went hand in hand with it.

'At times,' he said, 'there's a damned good reason to be frightened and you may think it's naive to believe that people can lose that, but did you notice, did you see the news reports of Egypt during the struggle? Where people were saying "We're not afraid any more"? This is what Gandhi was saying people had to do. Don't be afraid.'

We were getting to the heart of the matter, so I asked how that transition from fear to being unafraid might happen.

'It's sometimes terribly hard,' he said. 'But we know that it does happen. It can start off with something quite simple, people doing things that are relatively low risk and they realise there's potential here. And they are sometimes actually much *safer* than if they did nothing or certainly much safer than if they use violence, which always brings tremendous repression. And then they get a sense of empowerment, so what they can do next is they can tackle bigger issues. But sometimes it happens much more quickly than that and something almost magical happens, when people go from being obedient, submissive, fearful people to standing up, holding their shoulders back, raising their heads, they're not slaves any more' – for a split second, Sharp went from his crumpled posture to that he had just described, of emancipation, and then he sank back again against the side of the chair – 'But exactly how that happens I'm not sure. It's a very important question, but I haven't focused on it.'

Still, I had read *From Dictatorship To Democracy* and I knew that there were at least a dozen references to 'courageous' or 'brave' actions or people. So I said this and asked how Gene Sharp might then define that bravery.

'I've near completed a major dictionary' – this is *Sharp's Dictionary of Power and Struggle* (OUP, 2011) – 'and I don't have the entry for bravery in it. It may be a very serious gap in my thinking,' he said and he smiled. 'Certainly, if people aren't actually ready to act despite risks and dangers, they're not going to succeed. That's another way of saying *if they are brave*, I guess. But it's the *action* that's required and sometimes people never get that far. Or people can be brave and inspired and do something stupid. So this approach says they have to learn to be unafraid *wisely*, on the basis of studies of how this type of struggle operates. We can learn how to use those methods more skilfully than we have in the past. We can now see vulnerabilities in the strongest dictatorships in the world. And we are spreading this. So it's not dependent on one messianic leader, it's not dependent on imagination. You use your judgement and your wisdom to get the knowledge. And you can plan for your own liberation. *And succeed*.'

This certainly sounded like bravery to me, but I realised that Gene Sharp had no wish to become its new messiah.

———

At the end, I asked him whether the coverage claiming his inspirational role in the overthrow of Mubarak was uncomfortable for him and he nodded.

'Yeah,' he said and there was a silence, so I mentioned the clear links between his methods and other struggles, asking whether he was glad to have had that effect from a desk, to have stirred some people to change their world.

He shrugged and said, 'Well, all I did was write. Someone else took the action. Someone else took the risks. Someone else teased the change. It wasn't me.'

'Do you feel like you've shown any courage yourself?' I asked. 'Intellectual courage maybe?'

'There have been times when I wondered if some of my writings were brazen,' he said, 'but I didn't suffer anything for it. I didn't think I'd done anything too special. It was something that needed to be said. No big deal.'

Gene Sharp shuffled to the front door to see me out, waving and smiling as I left, as though I had just swung by for tea. And as I made my way back through the East Boston drizzle to the station, I realised how brave at least *I* thought it was to have no part of the discussion of this glamorous and all-too-often bastardised virtue, while so clearly playing a part in teaching many, many people one of the toughest forms of courage.

The following year, 2012, Gene Sharp was again nominated for the Nobel Peace Prize.

❧

Not everyone shares Dr Sharp's reticence, of course.

While writing or talking about bravery is not an inherently plucky activity – I can vouch for that, sitting here in the warm with the radio on – there is nevertheless a rule that often comes into play when people do. I like to call it The

Law of Reflected Virtue, or What Courage Can Do For You, although I suspect I am not the first to identify it. It goes like this:

*I recognise courage ∴ I am probably brave myself.*

In 1957, at the height of the Cold War, Norman Mailer identified in post-McCarthy America an anxiety among the populace at large. 'A stench of fear,' he wrote, 'has come out of every pore of American life, and we suffer from a collective failure of nerve.' A dose of courage was what was needed here and some months before Mailer's essay was written – and one wonders whether in response to the same climate of fear – along came a very good medicine. It appeared in the form of a book by the war hero and politician who would usher in the new era, Senator John F. Kennedy. It was called *Profiles in Courage.* In it, Kennedy wrote of long-forgotten US Senators who had stuck their necks out in one way or another for their beliefs. 'Without belittling the courage with which men have died,' the future president wrote, 'we should not forget those acts of courage with which men ... have lived.' The book, a tightly argued case for political and moral courage, became a bestseller, functioning as effectively as any campaign to promote the man himself to the American electorate, *his* political and moral courage, never mind those archaic senators. Small wonder, perhaps, that much of the book was rumoured to have been written not by Kennedy but by Ted Sorensen, a brilliant speech-writer who would go with JFK to the White House. At any rate, the Kennedy–Courage axis became fixed in the public imagination. 'Courage is in the air with bracing whiffs,' chirruped Robert Frost in a poem to mark Kennedy's inauguration as president in 1961, 'Better than all the stalemate an's and ifs.'

Nearly half a century later and an ocean away, at Number

11 Downing Street in London, the British Chancellor of the Exchequer, Gordon Brown, was finally poised to take the prime ministerial helm from Tony Blair. The year was 2007 and this had been one of the longest and least dignified waiting games in recent British political history. How then to take voters' minds off murky squabbles in Islington eateries and set out your political stall afresh? How to recalibrate that Moral Compass you have been mentioning in speeches lately? And how to deal with 'the stench of fear' that the post-9/11 years had brought to British life?

Simple. Less than a month before Tony Blair's announcement of his intention to stand down, Gordon Brown published a rather peculiar book called *Courage*. It consisted of eight bizarrely hagiographical portraits of historical and contemporary figures deemed by Brown or, one suspects, his Sorensens, to embody the virtue. Think Nelson Mandela. Think Aung San Suu Kyi. Think Martin Luther King. 'They are for us exemplars and icons,' the book intoned, 'at once daunting and cherished. Their stories live on and inspire us.' You get the idea – just as Brown was no Jack Kennedy, nor were his backroom boys any match for Ted Sorensen. Still, if someone in the Chancellor's retinue had not thumbed through *Profiles In Courage* and hoped to produce a similar glint of reflected steel upon the face of the future PM, well then, my name is William Wallace. That Brown's brief premiership was then said by some to be characterised by nothing so much as a *lack* of political courage should be read, perhaps, as the Public Health Warning that accompanies The Law of Reflected Virtue.

❦

Dr Bernard Lafayette, on the other hand, prefers in his words 'to stay under the radar.'

'How did you find me?' he asks conspiratorially, 'and *why*?'

The answer is easy. Like Gene Sharp, Lafayette also teaches non-violence and that means schooling people in some of the forms that moral courage can take. This has been his life's work since the death of Martin Luther King – which Bernard mentions only by whispering, 'You know I was with him at the Lorraine Motel in Memphis the night before'. King had said to him on the morning of his assassination, 'Now, Bernard, the next thing we're going to do is to internationalise and institutionalise non-violence' and this became Bernard's debt to his assassinated leader and friend. 'So I haven't had time to grieve, not even now,' says Bernard, in a strangely soldierly phrase, 'because I've been trained to fulfil his last wish and dream.'

Lafayette has spent the intervening years coaching people around the world in King's Six Principles of Non-Violence and his own ideas developed from them. These are different to Sharp's methods, less in technique than in the moral and redemptive framework in which they sit, with all its emphasis upon notions of righteousness and love. And notably there is no reserve on the subject of courage either; the first of the six tenets declares, 'non-violence is a way of life for courageous people'.

'Now, we don't go and tell people *what to do*,' he explains. 'We simply say that you are in charge of making decisions for yourself, so we're just going to show you what we did in the movement and how it came out and what made it successful. We explain that this is going to be much more difficult than learning how to shoot a gun, because in non-violence you don't go scrambling around looking for your weapon, because *you* are the weapon and you have all the ammunition. Everything you need is here' and he taps the fingertips of both hands on his chest.

___

Lafayette's faith in the teachability of these things comes from the fact that he himself was taught them, aged nineteen and after teenage years that were full of gang violence on the streets where he grew up. The teacher was James Lawson, who had studied Gandhi's *satyagraha* philosophy and brought it, with a Christian spin, to the American South at the behest of King in the late 1950s. There in Nashville, Lawson schooled students, including Bernard, in civil disobedience. Soon after, came the Nashville lunch-counter sit-ins, in which Bernard was to test both what he had learned about challenging segregation and about being brave.

He tells me about one particular all-night sit-in in the winter of 1960, at the twenty-four-hour cafeteria at the bus station in Nashville. As every customer left, the proprietor had taped up the refrigerator and the freezer, turned out the lights and shut up shop.

'So the eight of us sat there all night,' says Bernard. 'The next morning at about five o'clock, we decided that we'd made our point. So I went out of the restaurant and I went to the phone booth in the waiting room to make a call for someone to come with cars to pick us up. So while I was in there and the phone was ringing back at the college, a cab driver came and kicked the door in to the phone booth and hauled me out and put a headlock, like that, on my neck.' Bernard crooks and tenses his arm in front of him. 'And he pulled me outside and there were twelve other cab drivers and they started beating me. They knocked me down and I rolled over and got back up. They knocked me down again and they kicked me in the face. It was just knock-down, roll-over, knock-down, roll-over. I didn't resist. I went with the flow because you get less injuries when you go with the flow. Roll with the punch they call it. Somebody at the back said, "Get him! Catch him. Catch him. Catch him!" but I wasn't running. In the end I stood up and I looked at them. I said, "wait" and I brushed a shoe print off my face where they had kicked me' – Bernard draws his palm slowly across his cheek, pressing so hard that his face distorts for a moment – 'and I brushed off my coat and my pants and I stood there and I looked at them eye to eye.'

'Is that hard to do?' I ask.

'No, I'll tell you why, Polly,' says Bernard, leaning forward, 'because in non-violence we are taught to think about why people behave the way they do. I didn't choose to be born black and they didn't choose to be born white or American or poor, you know? Maybe some of their family members might belong to the Ku Klux Klan. Maybe they heard a lot of negative conversations about black people when they were growing up. So that's what was in my mind. And don't forget it was in November and it was cold but, because we were there sitting-in, the place was closed and they couldn't have coffee, so they were upset and they had had many hours to build up resentful behaviour.'

'So we were looking at each other,' he says, 'and the main thing is you always keep your eyes on their eyes, because one of the things they'll be doing when they attack you is reducing your humanity and causing you to become an object which gives them the licence to attack, because they don't see that you're human. So as long as you keep your eyes there, that is a form of resistance to them seeing you as an object. They are seeing *you*.'

Bernard and I share a moment of silence like the silence of that exchanged gaze at the Nashville bus station that dark early morning.

'And then I said to them, in this silence, "If you gentlemen are through, I need to finish making my phone call. Please excuse me."'

And that is where the attack stopped.

'So in spite of their behaviour,' says Bernard, 'I was

treating them with the utmost respect and congeniality. I did not condemn them, I did not scold them and I did not show any fear. And when were they last called "gentlemen"? That was the thing that was startling to them, but that had the potential of arresting their conscience because I wanted them to re-think what they were doing.'

'Not everyone would be capable of the kind of composure you came up with,' I say. 'Why do you think you were capable of that composure?'

'Because I'd been trained,' says Bernard and he picks up a plastic cup of water from the meeting room table and sips it, looking over it to me for my next question.

'*Literally*?' I ask.

He nods. 'We had scenarios. We had role play. We had social drama. We had acted out these situations so we could be emotionally educated' – I recall for a second the soldiers running around a fake Afghan village in Norfolk, the toreros caping a plastic bull's head on wheels, the tightrope walker pacing a wire less than a metre from the ground – 'You simply did not allow yourself to react,' Bernard continues. 'Some people would say "well it's normal to fight back, that's just part of your nature". Yeah, maybe so, but you also can *control* your nature. You have to believe in your training. You have to believe it will happen. And, you see, I did fight back. First, I fought back my urge to attack – '

'So you did have an urge to retaliate?' I say.

'Oh yeah,' says Bernard, 'That fellow who was in front of me, even right now I know what I could have done to him to stop it. I could have stopped him. Made an example out of him.'

'What could you have done to him to stop him?'

'I could have grabbed him and bitten his ear off,' says Bernard. 'You've heard of Mike Tyson?'

'I have.'

'You heard about the fight he had?'

I nod.

'The difference is that in my neighbourhood, you're supposed to chew the ear up. He only bit it off.'

There was a short silence.

'So,' says Bernard with a smile, 'in other words, I was thoroughly schooled in how to make an effective violent response, but I did not use that, but rather I used my new training and my new way of doing things. But I had to believe it would work.'

'So part of acting in a courageous way is to believe that you will succeed?' I ask, 'It's not purely turning the other cheek?'

'No, well, "turning the other cheek" has two meanings. One is a physical meaning. The other is the psychological "turning the other cheek" which means if someone shows you how ugly they can behave, you show them how beautiful they can be. And if they frown at you, you smile. If they call you a negative name, you try to find positive things – like 'gentlemen'. There's nothing gentle about them, but if you want them to be changed, you have to *be* that change that you want them to be.'

'And your point about training is that you can learn this?' I ask, 'You can learn how to be brave in that situation?'

'Yes,' says Bernard.

'Can anyone?'

Bernard nods. 'Because we have to also believe that in each individual, whether they're on the opposite side or whether they're on your side, they have the potential for bringing out the best that they have. So, yes, whether it's true or not, you have to believe it and you operate based on that.'

Bernard Lafayette's coming-of-age at the Nashville Bus Station happened when he was just twenty and the years that followed were built on that belief in redemptive change, in spite of many more dangerous and potentially lethal confrontations. As he rose to the forefront of the civil rights movement, there were numerous beatings, daily threats. The Ku Klux Klan nearly killed him on two occasions, once during the Freedom Rides in 1961 and again in Selma, Alabama in 1963, part of the conspiracy that saw the murder of Medgar Evers in Mississippi. After the death of Luther King, Lafayette swore to continue this work around the world and he did, taking the techniques of their struggle to the Miami police department in the wake of the Rodney King riots, to the Niger delta and the struggle over oil, to one of Colombia's most violent prisons, where, before Bernard trained them, there were frequently several murders a day. In 2002, Bernard Lafayette was even briefly kidnapped by the FARC, during a peace march through the mountains west of Medellín in Colombia.

Lafayette is an old man now, although his nerve, like Gene Sharp's, appears unclouded by his three score years and ten. Almost every big theme I had encountered along my journey – training, story, adaptation, rites of passage, the lived life, non-conformity, the collective experience – all seemed to meet in this one irrepressible figure. Yet, I came away from the morning we spent together struck by nothing so strongly as the single image of a very young man wiping a shoe print from his face, all that he had learned and could teach about how to be brave crystallising in that moment and setting the tone for a life to come.

❧

Something Bernard Lafayette said about courage, as we walked down to the street, has repeated on me. He said that people are more similar than they think they are, little threads of common humanity, common courage linking people who seem very different. What separates us, he said, is never as huge as what unites us, 'so I want to read this book of yours,' he said and boomed his big laugh.

Over the many months I have spent working in the service of the Society of Timid Souls, I have interviewed ninety-five people, many of them more than once. I have a hard drive containing recordings of more than a hundred and forty hours' of conversation and a stack of notebooks, pictures and mementoes, from the yellow and red striped cushion purchased at the door of the *Maestranza* bullring to the mug from Yosemite that warns 'Be Bear Aware'. That has been the formal process, if you can call it such, but alongside it has run another one, equally absorbing, equally persistent and hugely influential upon what is written in these pages. You see, you only need to mention courage over dinner or in the pub, and people will, I have found, tell you their own stories, long before they ask you for yours, tales of friends or family who have stepped outside of themselves and done or said something, small or large, that they think is amazing.

It is everywhere, this quality of courage, and people feel strong ownership of it, with clear rights to decide and to quarrel about what it is and what it is not. That it exists at all is testimony, of course, to our frailty. Yet the fact that each of us can, from childhood, recognise bravery and call it by its name, however it shape-shifts before us, offers all Timid Souls something to aspire to.

All of which makes it hard to stop this work – and it is a task impossible to complete – so I shall not even try before I have shared one last testimony that quietly embodies what the Society of Timid Souls is all about.

❧

Let me begin with a pocket-sized, true story. It is trifling in its way and there are no heroics, but it sheds light on one of the big struggles against injustice being waged in the world today.

The tale is of a young Indian man. We do not know his real name, but I shall call him Vikas. Now, Vikas had left the subcontinent in his late teens to study abroad and had met a nice girl, a foreigner, whom he married. He brought his new wife home to show her some of the wonders of Mother India and the Taj Mahal was one stop on their tour. The system here and at other major historical sites is that foreigners pay an elevated entrance fee in dollars and that Indians pay somewhat less in rupees. So Vikas's wife bought the foreigner ticket and Vikas an Indian one and they joined the queue to enter the Taj complex. Suddenly, a policeman pulled Vikas out of the line. He could see that Vikas was with a foreigner and he questioned his purchase of the lower price Indian ticket. 'But I am an Indian,' said Vikas, 'I am from – ' and he mentioned his home town. But the policeman began to search him and, finding the identity card of a foreign university, he threatened Vikas with jail. All the while his new wife looked on in dismay. Still protesting, Vikas showed the policeman his passport, which the officer took and pocketed. At length, the policeman suggested that there was of course a remedy to all this. A few thousand rupees later, Vikas had his passport and ID card back and the couple were enjoying the jewel of Mughal India. But Vikas was troubled at having paid the bribe. So, that evening, he sat down at his computer and logged on to a new website, set up to allow ordinary Indians a way of blowing the whistle on the corruption rife at all levels of Indian life. Vikas typed in his story, anonymously, and pressed 'submit'.

The website *ipaidabribe.com* was set up in August 2010, one of a number of initiatives of a non-profit organisation in Bangalore run by Swati and Ramesh Ramanathan and called Janaagraha. Its motto is a quote from Gandhi, 'Be The

Change You Want To See In The World' and the organisation is part of a great groundswell in India against the scale and reach of corruption within this, the world's largest democracy and ascendant would-be superpower. Stories like that of young 'Vikas' are entirely commonplace here and they run right up through society, from a few rupees to grease the buying of a train ticket to many more for securing a passport or a death certificate, right up and into the corridors of power where large-scale infrastructure, land or mining projects are facilitated with bribes worth millions of dollars. So rampant and large scale has corruption become since the liberalisation in the 1990s of the Indian economy that it is now worth many billions of dollars a year.

Furthermore, the rot has been very difficult to counter. Exposing corruption can be a dangerous business indeed, with many notable cases of whistle-blowers dying in murky or clearly murderous circumstances. Even lower-level whistle-blowing often has its price, with all kinds of practical and professional penalties being visited upon anyone bold enough to name and shame corrupt officials. Meanwhile a colossal judicial backlog hobbles many a prosecution and a bizarre loophole, that an investigating authority cannot pursue anyone in government without the permission of government, in turn lends the political class a form of immunity. In other words, however well intentioned, however honest, it is hard for ordinary citizens here to be anything other than Timid Souls in the face of a wrong so interwoven into their national life.

Recent years have seen prominent anti-corruption figures, of course. The most famous of these is Anna Hazare, who has clearly modelled himself on Gandhi. He conducts well-publicised hunger strikes and Team Anna, his organisation, rallies vast crowds. In 2011, Hazare lay dressed in white garb reminiscent of the father of Indian independence, beneath a vast picture of Gandhi himself, as crowds swarmed by chanting 'We Are All Anna Hazare!'

Team Anna's is one approach and many would say a courageous one. However, I was interested in this other approach, this online society of timid souls that, by inviting anonymous accounts of everyday experiences of bribery, took the sting of fear out of the act of whistle-blowing. Within it, a Timid Soul might not only be brave themselves, but might also help others to be so. At the time of writing, *ipaidabribe.com* has had nearly 1.3 million visitors and well over 21,000 timid souls in 488 cities across India have stepped up to tell their tales of corruption. There are sections for submitting testimony of bribes paid, bribes sought but not paid, of moments when an official did the honest thing and did not request a bribe, and of ways that people had discovered to dodge these rotten levies. Some told of proffering zero rupee notes printed off the internet, another of offering to pay double the amount requested made out in the name of the corrupt officer to the Prime Minister's Army Relief Fund. All the while, the site keeps tally of the market price of corruption. Moreover, through the anonymity that withholds the identities both of those who testify, and also of those who are testified *against*, the risk of becoming all noise and no fury, an arena in which claim and counterclaim can be traded, is removed in favour of a forensic analysis of the system of corruption as a whole. Such knowledge is a powerful political weapon. Similar sites have now been set up in Kenya, Greece, Zimbabwe and Pakistan. Philippine, Mongolian and Hindi language sites are under construction and more are on the way. Janaagraha had, by 2012, received up to twenty requests for use of the *ipaidabribe* framework. A Chinese version opened in 2011 and had hundreds of thousands of visits over just a couple of weeks, before abruptly being closed down.

The brainchild of the Ramanathans, *ipaidabribe.com*

was launched in the summer of 2010 when they brought on board an old friend, Thoniparambil Raghunanadan, although Raghu is what everyone calls him. A long-serving high-ranking civil servant, known for his challenges to corrupt officials, Raghu eventually left his job with the Indian Administrative Service that spring in order to devote himself to anti-corruption and devolution work and he spent the next year getting *ipaidabribe.com* up and running. I spoke with this mild-mannered and disarmingly astute man in the summer of 2011 when *ipaidabribe.com* had been live online for a year.

'Corruption may be rampant here,' he told me, 'but I don't believe that Indians are inherently corrupt. Our value systems are as good or as bad as anybody else's. No, it's born of systems failure. People are not born this way. Corruption is a crime of calculation, not of passion. Large numbers drift into it if risks are low, penalties are mild and rewards great, so the broad solution is to make the calculation risky for the corrupt and to stop looking at it from a moral perspective, but from an economic perspective.'

Surely, I said, systemic corruption is still the product of a moral failure, a thousand small instances of moral cowardice.

'That's a very tricky question,' he said. 'But let me put it this way. About 60 per cent of it is that we have created a system that makes people believe that moral cowardice is a practical, sensible state of mind to be in. We hear of youngsters that say they did not want to pay a bribe, but their parents told them to, saying, "Be practical. Grow-up. This is the real world." So we are passing on from one generation to another the submissive response. And the hardest part of combating corruption is to combat the scepticism of your immediate circle of friends and relatives who are trying to talk you into sailing with the flow.'

I knew that sailing against the flow here could sometimes

be dangerous, so I asked Raghu whether he had ever felt at risk himself.

'No, no I haven't,' he said, briskly, 'A couple of hate mails but nothing more than that,' but he said that in the end, 'I am sure we will annoy someone.'

'And does that worry you?' I asked.

'Oh no, I don't like to think of it,' he said, 'I've been in similar scrapes before, so – '.

With that he changed the subject, but Raghu was less reticent about courage than he had been about fear. Indeed, mustering courage among ordinary citizens is very much part of the *ipaidabribe.com* project. He listed the ways one might go about it, from doing your homework before confronting the officer, to managing your body language in order to be confident rather than submissive, maintaining eye contact, pulling up a chair and sitting down, using the officer's name and other small tricks that might mask your apprehension.

'And the best way to build up courage,' he concluded, 'is to go in as a collective. Collective action is very, very important. You see, generally if you take a cross-section of people who have a problem, you will find that there are always a few proactive people and there are always a few sceptics, but the large body of people are fence-sitters. They are waiting to see which side they can swing to and if the message is conveyed in a suitably inspirational manner then *those* people can get together. And it's been proven. It does happen.'

Raghu said that they had a dream for *ipaidabribe.com* – and this struck a chord with the Society of Timid Souls – which was to know that your fellows 'are there in flesh and blood,' said Raghu. 'Our dream is to create *ipaidabribe* chapters across cities where people can actually get together, face to face, for collective action.'

Generalisations can be trite, and are often wrong or sometimes actively dangerous. That is why I have tried, in the course of this book, to avoid extrapolating too strongly from one situation to another, one form of courage or fear to other forms. And yet there was, in this small Indian project, with all its modernity and collectivity, its modest apprehensions and overcomings, something that inspired me as much as had the greater acts of valour or daring or forbearance. It was about being ordinary and dignified and following your conscience, even if you did feel a little timid along the way. And there was a hint, just a hint, that if you can achieve that, then why can you not become remarkable too, capable of changing your world for the better?

I said this to Raghu and asked whether he thought an ordinary man or woman might follow some blueprint for moral courage and find themselves a braver man or woman than they were the day before.

'Most certainly,' he said. 'In fact if you read Mahatma Gandhi, he's actually laid down a remarkably simple set of rules. And I do this quite often – whenever I'm in doubt I go back and read Gandhi and you will always come back with clarity of thought. I mean the jargon has changed since then, but these attributes can be passed on very effectively and not necessarily only through broad inspirational messages, but by actually communicating individual techniques to individual people. I mean, we did not have any more extraordinary people in 1947 than we do now, did we?'

'No,' I said, 'I suppose not.'

'So,' he added, 'I think that courage, it can be learnt.'

And we both smiled.

# The Society of Timid Souls

I can see no reason why the shy and timid in any
community couldn't get together and help each other.

Bernard Gabriel, 1943

The day is cold for April. I can see steam rising from my lips as
I climb the steps from the 72nd Street subway on New York's
Upper West Side. I hear the trains rumble beneath as I stand
on the pavement getting my bearings. I put on my sunglasses
against the glare. Some of the other passengers from downtown have been reading newspapers full of the Arab Spring,
nuclear meltdown at Fukushima, the Royal Wedding. But I
have not been thinking about revolutions, or tsunamis, or
saying 'I do'. I have instead been thinking of a few nervous
pianists nearly seventy years ago. The thought gives me
just a hint of butterflies. I hesitate on the street corner for a
moment and check my map. Then I set off, crossing Broadway and cutting a diagonal across Verdi Square. I pass the
statue of Giuseppe Verdi, his coat slung nonchalantly over
one arm, and the Apple Bank Building where I glance up at
the clock above the door. Crossing Amsterdam Avenue onto
West 73rd Street, I stop for a moment to check the address

scrawled on a post-it and now folded – a little furtively – in my jeans pocket. Number One Hundred And Sixty. There it is – on the right. I pass beneath the portico and I step into the polished hallway.

There is a pair of older women in front of me and they are talking to the doorman. I wait and I look around. So this is Sherman Square Studios. I imagine the ghosts of Timid Souls Past making for the elevator to Bernard Gabriel's apartment and I wonder if they recognise me as one of their own.

When it is my turn, I approach the sliding glass hatch of the doorman's small office. I introduce myself and say that I am researching the Society of Timid Souls. He looks at me blankly. He has never heard of it, but when I mention the name Bernard Gabriel, he smiles.

'Yes,' he says, 'I remember him. I've worked here for seventeen years. He lived here for a long time. The pianist, right?'

I nod.

'But, ma'am,' he says, 'I'm sorry to say that he has passed away' – he pauses, mentally calculating the dates – 'must have been thirteen or fourteen years ago.'

He hands me a photocopied leaflet one of the residents has compiled with a history of the building – although there is no mention of the Timid Souls in here either – and then, as the phone is ringing, he bids me a good afternoon and turns away.

This visit comes just a few days before Bernard Gabriel would have celebrated his hundredth birthday. I guess it was too much to expect that he would be there and waiting with some 'strange and devious methods' to embolden me. But I am surprised to feel a stab of disappointment that I cannot tell him of my travels, of the remarkable people I have met and how his society has found a new life in a new century. I think the old man would have liked that. And it occurs to me that just as the bravest souls, those feted and decorated with our admiration, have each themselves been inspired by people whose names we may not know – mothers or lovers, teachers or friends – so then might Maestro Gabriel do that, from beyond the grave, for a few of us.

I walk back out onto West 73rd Street and over to Broadway, where I can see the bobbing heads of the Manhattan crowds stretching off into the distance. And I know that we are among them, timid souls and brave ones, and I watch as the crowd shifts and separates and gathers, like waves on the surface of the sea.

*Courtesy of Adamant Music School*

Bernard Gabriel, *c.* 1939

# Acknowledgements

First and foremost, I owe more to my interviewees than I can say, those Timid Souls who have learned to be brave; this is their book as much as it is mine. My agent, Patrick Walsh, helped to develop the idea from the first and spotted the potential of the original Society Of Timid Souls. Throughout, he has provided the most invaluable support.

I have been blessed with not one but two dream teams, at Profile Books in London and at Crown in New York. Huge thanks go to both my editors, Rebecca Gray and Vanessa Mobley; working with them has been a delight. Sarah Caro, Daniel Crewe (Profile) and Molly Stern (Crown) also played a vital role at the outset of the process, as did Penny Daniel, Anna-Marie Fitzgerald, Cecily Gayford, Susanne Hillen and Niamh Murray (Profile), and Miriam Chotiner-Gardner, Mary Coyne, Danielle Crabtree, Min Jung Lee and Shelly Perron (Crown) towards the conclusion. Much gratitude goes to the Royal Society of Literature and the Jerwood Charitable Foundation, whose 2011 Award for Non-Fiction threw me a timely lifeline.

Key sources are attributed within the book, but many additional interviewees also informed what is written here. Others helped to find people, stories or to set up, host and translate my interviews. Especial thanks for military matters go to Crispin Lockhart and Tim David at the MOD, Liam Bailey, Jim Bewley, Matthew Bridson, Petrus Delport, Jonny Kitson and Nick Nesbit, all of 1 Rifles, John Laverty of 1 Royal Irish, Anne Bevis and Steve Blundell in Wootton Bassett and to Didy Grahame at the VC and GC Association. Sue Clack showed great fortitude in sharing her son's story with me. Valon Dobruna and Violeta Hyseni in Pristina, Gezim Guri and staff at the former BBC Albanian Service, as well as Louise Norman in London, all made the Kosovo story possible, as did Harriet Fletcher, Emma Piesse and Laurent Pla-Taruella for the two gravity-defying tales that came from France. For bullfighting access and demystification, I am indebted first to Alexander Fiske-Harrison and later, in Seville, to Antonio Navarro Amuedo and Reza Hosseinpour, as well as to Sophie Payne, who provided additional translations. The writing of Blair Tindall first drew my attention to propranolol use by musicians and it was she who then kindly steered me towards other sources and several Inderal users. Medical access for *The Enemy Within* chapter would have be impossible without Stephanie Withers and her team at Southmead Hospital and without Nicola Rattray, Elaine Syrett, Jenny Taylor, and the patients of St Christopher's Hospice. Lauren Prestileo at WGBH hosted me in Boston, as did Maya Gabeira, Jim Kempton and Bill Sharp at Billabong XXL in California. Peter Elliott, Warren Faidley, Abram Heller, Lee Ivory, Jeff Marsh Margaret Purves and Roz Savage all helped to unravel the mysteries of the *Elemental*. Detective Cheryl Crispin at the NYPD, Erin Fisher at Beyer Blinder Belle, Dr Paul Greene and Dr Barry Lubetkin each opened up new vistas in New York City, as did Alistair Gellatly, Martha Holmes, Nick le Soueff and Jo Pope in the wild. Time and expertise also came from Alistair Gosling, Milton Justice, Jayashree Kumar, James Oliver, Leonie Roberts and Adrian Tuddenham.

Excellent additional research was supplied by Dr. Haran Sivapalan and Jane Slinn, as well as first-rate transcriptions by Sandra Down. I am grateful to the researchers at The Library of Congress, New York Public Library and especially so, to Mariam Touba at the New York Historical Society. Andrew Christiansen at the Adamant Music School helped to piece together evidence relating to the original society and its founder, Bernard Gabriel.

During my travels, several friends saw to it that I had somewhere

# Quotation Acknowledgments

# A note on sources

In the interests of readability, I have not used ellipses or brackets in certain quotations from the interviews that form the spine of this book, but, as with filmed interviews in a documentary, I have taken great care to remain true to the speaker's meaning. The names of a handful of interviewees have been changed to protect their privacy. I have also reported what each interviewee told me in good faith, relying chiefly upon their accounts of dates, times and facts.

---

# Further Reading

A comprehensive bibliography of courage, if such a thing were even possible, would certainly run to many volumes, so what follows here is both subjective and selective. Much of the material I draw upon is referenced within the body of the book, but I should make special mention of other works that may interest the Timid Soul keen to read further.

## General

There are many indispensable works that deal in whole or in part with courage, ethics, or with fear. Among the more recent are Alasdair MacIntyre's *After Virtue* (Bloomsbury, 2007), Geoffrey Scarre's *On Courage* (Routledge, 2010), Joanna Bourke's *Fear – A Cultural History* (Virago, 2005), Lars Svendsen's *A Philosophy of Fear* (Reaktion, 2008) and William Ian Miller's *The Mystery of Courage* (Harvard University Press, 2000). Philippa Foot's *Virtues and Vices and Other Essays in Moral Philosophy* (Clarendon Press, 2002) was vital reading. And I must confess an addiction both to the podcasts from *Philosophy Bites*, the brilliant brainchild of David Edmonds and Nigel Warburton, and to Mark Vernon's *Philosophy and Life* blog.

## Introduction

For me, the most vivid account of the original Society of Timid Souls is to be found under the headline 'Shy Soloists' in the Talk of the Town column of *The New Yorker* (May 23, 1942). Other contemporary articles include that by Morrow Davies, syndicated under assorted headlines across provincial America in July 1942 (*Prescott Evening Courier*, *The Toledo Blade* and others), also 'Mice Into Men' (*Time Magazine*, August 6, 1945), 'Down the Spillway' (*Baltimore Sun*, March 17, 1944) and J.P. McEvoy's article 'The Society of Timid Souls' (*The Reader's Digest*, April 1943). The JWT Anxiety

Index can also be found online at www.anxietyindex.com, as can the full text of Roosevelt's 'Citizenship in a Republic' speech at the Sorbonne in 1910 at www.theodore-roosevelt.com.

### Chapter 1

Plato's *Laches* I read in a translation by Rosamond K. Sprague (Hackett, 1992), *Beowulf* in Seamus Heaney's sublime rendering (Faber 1999) and Aristotle's *Nicomachean Ethics*, to which I return more than once, as translated by J. A. K. Thomson (Penguin, 2004).

### Chapter 2

For the academic papers mentioned in this chapter, here are the full citations: *The human amygdala and the induction and experience of fear,* Current Biology 21, 2011, by Justin Feinstein, Daniel Tranel, Ralph Adolphs and Antonio Damasio; *Fear thou not: activity of frontal and temporal circuits in moments of real-life courage,* Neuron 66, 2010, by Uri Nili, Hagar Goldberg, Abraham Weizman and Yadin Dudai; *Of snakes and faces: An evolutionary perspective on the psychology of fear,* Scandinavian Journal of Psychology 50, 2009, by Arne Öhman.

*What Neuroscience Cannot Tell Us About Ourselves* by Raymond Tallis (The New Atlantis, Fall 2010) struck a deep chord, while *Death in the Afternoon* (Ernest Hemingway, Arrow, 1994) and *On Bullfighting* (AL Kennedy, Yellow Jersey Press, 2000) were essential study on the *corrida*.

### Chapter 3

I read Hippocrates in a translation by I. M. Lonie (Penguin, 1978), guided as I was by Roy Porter's *The Greatest Benefit to Mankind* (Harper Collins, 1997) on the perception of the heart in antiquity. The *Discourses* of Epictetus came to me in a translation by P. E. Matheson (Dover, 2004) and Margaret Graver's essay on Epictetus, as well as that of Dirk Baltzly on the Stoics, from the Stanford Encyclopaedia of Philosophy (Spring 2009 and Winter 2010 respectively).

*Birth: A History* by Tina Cassidy (Chatto & Windus, 2007) was enlightening, as was the Associated Press's reporting of Ines Ramirez Perez's story (1.6.04) and *Self-inflicted cesarean section with maternal and fetal survival*, International Journal of Gynaecology and Obstetrics 84, 2004, by A. Molina-Sosa, H. Galvan-Espinosa, J. Gabriel-Guzman, R.F. Valle.

A small but significant epiphany I owe to Julian Barnes, whom I heard on the radio one day in 2011 pointing out the difference between death and *dying*. C.S. Lewis's *A Grief Observed* (Faber, 1966), Susan Sontag's *Illness as Metaphor* (Penguin, 1991) and Ernest Becker's *The Denial of Death* (Simon & Schuster, 1997) changed my thinking too, as did Christopher Hitchens' remarkable accounts of his final months, which I first read in *Vanity Fair*, (including the piece quoted, 'Miss Manners and The Big C', December 2010) and re-read when they were reprinted in *Mortality* (Alcourt Publishing, 2012).

Hal Finney's extraordinary *Dying Outside* post can be found on the Less Wrong blog (http://lesswrong.com/), Cicely Saunders's *Watch With Me*, in the Nursing Times 61 (48), 1965, and Andrea Dworkin's 'The Sexual Politics of Fear and Courage' reprinted as Chapter 5 of *Our Blood, Prophecies and Discourses on Sexual Politics* (Perigee, 1981).

## Chapter 4

Kurt Vonnegut's *Precautionary Letter to the Next Generation* originally appeared as an advertising spread in *Time Magazine* (Feb 8, 1988), part of a Volkswagen-sponsored open forum. Jack Zipes' translation of Grimm (*The Complete Fairytales*, Vintage, 2007) was my key source for The Boy Who Left Home to Learn Fear. *You Might Belong in Gryffindor: Children's Courage and Its Relationships to Anxiety Symptoms, Big Five Personality Traits and Sex Roles*, by Peter Muris, Birgit Mayer and Tinke Schubert appeared in Child Psychiatry & Human Development in 2010.

Studies relating to the Bam earthquake include: *Psychological distress among Bam earthquake survivors in Iran: a population-based study*, BMC Public Health 5 (4), 2005, by Ali Montazeri,

Hamid Baradaran, Sepideh Omidvari, Seyed A Azin, Mehdi Ebadi, Gholamreza Garmaroudi, Amir M Harirchi and Moham- mad Shariati, and *The prevalence of complicated grief among Bam earthquake survivors in Iran*, Arch Iran Med, 10 (4), 2007, by A. Ghaffari-Nejad, M. Ahmadi-Mousavi, M. Gandomkar, H. Reihani-Kermani.

### Chapter 5

Renée Fleming's *The Inner Voice* (Penguin, 2004) was a fascinat- ing window on her story. *Treating Individuals with Debilitating Performance Anxiety: an Introduction*, Journal of Clinical Psychol- ogy/In Session 60 (8), 2004, by Douglas H. Powell was a helpful starting point on the clinical realities of stage fright, while *The Psy- chology of Music Performance Anxiety*, by Dianna T. Kenny (OUP, 2011) offered a revealing synthesis of current research in the field. I visited *The Concept of Irony* by Soren Kierkegaard in a translation by Lee M. Capel (Harper, 1965).

### Chapter 6

Philippa Foot's *The Problem of Abortion and the Doctrine of the Double Effect* (from *Virtues and Vices* as mentioned above) is where the Trolley Problem was first laid out and Judith Jarvis Thomson's 1976 essay, *Killing, Letting Die and the Trolley Problem,* built upon it. Both are reproduced in *Ethical Theory: An Anthology*, edited by Russ Shafer-Landau (Wiley, 2012). David Edmonds' piece on the Trolley Problem in *Prospect* (*Matters of Life and Death*, 7.10.10) is also an excellent introduction to the ideas involved.

### Chapter 7

Some of G. K. Chesterton's musings on courage can be found in *Orthodoxy* (Doubleday, 2001) while Thomas Aquinas' mighty *Summa Theologica* can be read online at http://www.sacred- texts.com/chr/aquinas/summa/index.htm. Peter Gillman's and Richard Woods' *Sunday Times* articles (24.9.06 and 28.5.06 respectively) offer a brilliantly detailed investigation of the David Sharp story.

## Chapter 8

Reporting by the *Guardian* and the BBC (both 6.9.12) informed my account of the controversial courage of the Teeside burglar, while the original seminal study of the Bystander Effect is *Bystander Intervention in Emergencies: Diffusion of Responsibility*, Journal of Personal and Social Psychology 8 (4), 1968, by John Darley and Bibb Latané. *Opening Skinner's Box* by Lauren Slater (Bloomsbury, 2004) was a critical secondary source here. Susan Sontag's contentious *New Yorker* comment piece appeared in the magazine on 24 September 2011, while *Courage In Dark Places: Reflections on Terrorist Psychology*, Social Research 71 (1), 2004, by Andrew Silke, fleshed out some of her intuitions. Meanwhile, Noel 'Razor' Smith's *A Rusty Gun* (Viking, 2010) is simply the best crime memoir I have ever read.

## Chapter 9

Mandela's Rivonia speech can be read in full on the Nelson Mandela Centre of Memory's website (www.nelsonmandela.org); Robert Kennedy's Day of Affirmation speech at the JFK Library (www.jfklibrary.org); Aung San Sui Kyi's 2011 BBC Reith Lecture at www.bbc.co.uk. Matthew Pianalto's essay on moral courage in the International Journal of Philosophical Studies (*Moral Courage and Facing Others*, 2011) articulates a simple human idea with great precision. Norman Mailer's *The White Negro* (City Lights Books, 1967) got me thinking about collective timidity, as, in its way, did Bertrand Russell's 'An Outline of Intellectual Rubbish'. It is reprinted in *Unpopular Essays*, Bertrand Russell (Routledge, 2009). The magnificent *From Dictatorship to Democracy* by Gene Sharp can be downloaded at http://www.aeinstein.org/organizations/org/FDTD.pdf or found in book form (Serpent's Tail, 2012). Martin Luther King's Six Principles of Non-Violence are laid out in his *Stride Towards Freedom* (Beacon Press, 2010), while Bernard Lafayette's years in Nashville and Selma are among those explored in David Halberstam's epic, *The Children* (Random House, 1998).